SURFING'S GREATEST MISADVENTURES

(Photo, Sean Davey)

Surfing's Greatest Misadventures

Dropping In on the Unexpected

EDITED BY PAUL DIAMOND & TYLER McMAHON

Casagrande Press • Seattle

Published by Casagrande Press
3644 Albion Place N
Seattle WA 98103

www.casagrandepress.com

Copy Editors: Adem Tepedelen and Lisa Eilertson
Proofreader: John Ottey
Cover Design: Rob Johnson / Rob Johnson Design
Book Design: Steve Connell / Transgraphic Services
Map Illustrations: Paul Diamond and Jennifer Orr
Front cover: Bruce Irons goes over the falls at Pipeline
during the 1997-98 winter season. Photo by Sean Davey.

Library of Congress Cataloging-in-Publication Data

Surfing's greatest misadventures : dropping in on the unexpected /
    edited by Paul Diamond & Tyler McMahon.-- 1st ed.
        p. cm.
    Includes bibliographical references.
    ISBN 0-9769516-0-6 (pbk.)
    1. Surfing--Anecdotes. 2. Aquatic sports injuries--Anecdotes.
  I. Diamond, Paul, 1970- II. McMahon, Tyler, 1976- III. Title.

GV839.5.S87 2006
797.3'2--dc22

                              2005036511

Printed in Canada.

FIRST EDITION

Dedicated in loving memory to:

Carlos 'El Socio' Amador (1973-2001)
Laurie Cuoco (1975-2005)

Contents

The Old Days

Surf Safari Meltdown

Conspiring Coincidences

Characters and Character

Introduction

PAUL DIAMOND

One day two winters ago, the other editor of this book, Tyler McMahon, and I were riding up the chairlift at Snowbowl in Missoula, Montana. We were engaged in our usual chairlift discussion, a sort of competition of who could come up with the most cogent yet out-of-reach invention ideas.

I began with nitrous-carbonated soda—a creamier more delicious soda. He offered up octopus-flavored butter (hold your laughter until you're in Spain dipping your bread in the melted butter surrounding fresh octopus). I came back at him with Rent-a-Dog, for when you just want a dog for a few days. He countered with an inflatable surfboard bag that offers ultra protection on airplane trips and doubles as a sleeping bag and pad.

I hit back with the surfboard that plays your theme song as you take the drop. Then Tyler said, "*Surfing's Greatest Misadventures*, a book of surf stories for the people by the people."

"Well, we are qualified," I said, referring to the fact that we are both solidly mediocre surfers with hazardous tendencies. I seek too much from my waves, often riding myself into closeouts and then bouncing headfirst off my board in the throw down. Though a more cautious rider, Tyler has a larger set of problems: quick onset hypothermia, a blood sugar disorder, poor eyesight, and ribs that always break at the beginning of the summer. The rest of the summer he surfs in a Percocet daze. We both share a natural ability to distill from a wave its bruising, bone-breaking, fin-gouging elements.

"Well, we are qualified," Tyler said. "But we have no contacts, no connections."

"We both surfed with Sam George once," I reminded him as we unloaded from the chair. We strapped on our bindings and dropped silently through steep, waist-deep powder. I disappeared into the trees, into a conditional bliss of deep breathing and snow spraying turns. Rides like these are topped only by carving up and down the face of a sizeable, fast-breaking wave. After riding top to bottom in the trees without seeing anyone, I found Tyler at the bottom waiting by the chairlift. We loaded and began another ride up.

"I think we can put this book together," I said.

"Well, I've got a lot on my plate," said Tyler, employing the catch phrase he uses to duck anything that smells of responsibility.

"Okay. I'll call Sam George at *Surfer* magazine and tell him we need that story he told us in the lineup at Cardiff—the one about his brother winning the dance contest in Brazil."

Just then the chairlift jerked to a stop. It turned out to be a full-scale breakdown, not a regulation liftee stop. So we dangled up there and laid out the plans for the book. An hour later, a ski patrol came down and threw us a rope. He yelled up for us to toss the rope over the cable above us. That took me about ten tries with Tyler saying, "Dude, let me try," after each failed fling.

Tyler secured himself in the harness at the end of the rope, and then looked at me and said, "And another thing: there are two anthologies of surf stories already in the book stores, and they both mention rock climbing in their introductions. Promise me you won't mention rock climbing in the introduction."

"Why do you care?"

"Because climbers have enough of their own books, and they don't mention surfing in them."

"Fine," I said.

He eased off the chair and was lowered slowly to the snow. I followed.

And so the weeks went by and we did nothing, took no action. Tyler kept on with his job serving espresso drinks, and I continued with my job editing employee benefit directories. Winter ended and we had not managed to materialize one of our hundreds of collected invention ideas. The ideas, meant to catapult us out of low-income jobs, dissipated when they were spoken into the air. Perhaps all of our words floated upwards to become dim stars that might shine upon us another time. In late spring we parted ways and went off to teach at our respective surf camps, his in Southern California and mine in Northern Baja.

After surfing a thousand cold water, choice Baja waves, I moved to Seattle for the winter. I allotted myself plenty of time to go snowboarding, but the snow never fell. With nothing but rain, the ski areas never opened. (Thank our collective, obsessive use of petroleum, termed more pleasantly as "global warming," for birthing this book.) With my glut of time, I began finding and editing surf stories. After six months I've come up with thirty true stories with well-developed characters, gripping plots, and solidly paced action.

Some notes about the title of the book: The word "misadventure" is like the word "art." It is all-encompassing and much misunderstood. The word "greatest" is a superlative, and perhaps one could argue that this collection does not contain the greatest surf misadventure stories ever. But that is only because some people, like you and your friends, have not written your stories yet.

Looking over the final selection, I noticed three commonalities that link these stories. One, all the stories seem to arise from the surfers' sense of invincible possibility (for pleasure, passion, movement, escape, the perfect moment, or whatever lies out there). Two, surfers' indefatigable wanting and seeking eventually leads them a bit too deep on the surfer's continuum, which has at one end pure joy and at the other horror, with absurdity and mockery in the middle. And three, what we can say about ourselves as surfers, we can say about these stories: there is always a gap between our expectation and realization of reality, or to moralize: expectations can never be exchanged for reality.

We, like the subjects of these stories, are on a search which ends with the unsought. In this collection, the unsought is always right around the corner.

Red Water: Bethany Hamilton and the Teeth of the Tiger

MATT GEORGE

Ha'ena, Kauai, Hawaii—October 31, 2003.

She'd been leading a daredevil life for weeks now. And in the end, she had no idea of the trouble she was getting herself into. Swimming beneath the moon, swimming beneath the radar, but swimming. Always swimming. Hungry for life, for survival. Starving with need. Patrolling the reefs for opportunity, for flesh. Swinging her massive head with the regularity of a metronome, propelling her 14 feet of girth with the easy power and intent of a heavily armed she-warrior. With her ragged, 14-inch dorsal fin breaking the surface, she'd been bumping into surfers for weeks now. Testing them, feeling their fear, waiting for her time. They seemed such easy prey. Slow, awkward, lounging on the surface like something sick. And now it was in her path. It was time. Another was here, apart from the rest. Alone and weak, and this one looked so small and frail. She approached her prey from the side, taking her time, timing the strokes of the thin, pale arm that dipped off the surfboard in a slow rhythm of bubbles. Twenty feet . . . ten feet . . . five feet . . . and with one last savage kick of her great tail she opened her jaws in a ragged yawn. Taking the thin pale arm in her mouth, she clamped down with over sixteen tons of sawing pressure. As her teeth met, she effortlessly plucked the thing from the body that once owned it.

The bite was so clean and painless that Bethany Hamilton, 13, noticed that the sea had turned red before she realized that her arm was gone at the shoulder. A strange serenity came over her, a warmth, as her body began to scream its outrage. Spurting a deep, rich, burgundy-colored blood, she struggled over to her best friend, Alana Blanchard, also thirteen, and could only manage the words, *I think a shark just attacked me.* Alana told her to not even joke of such matters. Then Alana eyes saw something that her mind couldn't grasp. The bleeding stump where her best friend's left arm used to be. Alana's stomach revolted and purged twice before she called for her father and her brother who were paddling for a nearby wave.

Imagine the dilemma of Holt Blanchard, 45, who was now almost a half mile offshore with his son and his daughter and a profusely bleeding and gravely injured Bethany Hamilton and a large, dangerous shark somewhere below. After struggling to apply a tourniquet with his rash guard, he now had an impossible decision to make. Should he send his children on ahead, across the deep lagoon, to keep them away from a bleeding Bethany? And if so, how could he protect them? Should he keep them close? And if so, could he put himself between them and the shark if it returned? For one brief moment he even thought of slitting his own wrists on the ragged edge of Bethany's board and slipping into the sea to await his fate while the other three made for shore. He had no time to deliberate. He made his decision on instinct. Keep the family close, face the danger together. He instructed his daughter to keep talking to a quickly fading Bethany while he and his son rigged her leash and began dragging her to shore.

Cheri Hamilton, mother of Bethany, was driving so fast behind the ambulance that the cops pulled her over. She hadn't seen Bethany yet, and had no idea about her condition. Frantic, it wasn't until the ambulance driver called back to the cops with a walkie-talkie that they let Cheri go. As she mashed the accelerator to the floor, a call came in on her cell phone. It was Holt Blanchard. Cheri asked him how badly Bethany was hurt. The conversation went like this:

Holt: You mean you don't know?

Cheri: Know what?

Holt: Cheri . . . her arm is gone.

Cheri: (*long pause*) Gone where?

Tom Hamilton, Bethany's father, was just about to be put under for a knee operation at the small local hospital when he was informed that the doctors needed the table he was on for an emergency. There had been a shark attack on a young girl at Makua Beach. His heart sank. He knew he had only a fifty-fifty chance, since Bethany and Alana were the only little girls on the island with the guts enough to surf the place. He got up and stood in the hallway as the victim was wheeled into the hospital. He held his breath. He would know in a second. Alana had dark brown hair; Bethany's was almost white blonde. As the gurney turned the corner all the air went out of his chest. The hair was blonde.

It has been widely stated that the tiger shark's characteristic serrated tooth shape and grotesquely powerful jaws have evolved for specialized feeding on large sea turtles, whose shells cannot be split with an axe. Called the hyena of the sea, the tiger shark strikes with a sawing motion of its bottom jaw against the razor blades of the top jaw. Bethany's arm was removed so cleanly, with such precision and efficiency, that the operating doctor was confused when he first saw the wound. He wanted to know who the son-of-a-bitch was that had amputated without his permission.

The next day, after word had spread through the islands, Laird Hamilton called his father, the legendary surfer/fisherman Billy Hamilton and told him if he didn't go out and kill this fucking shark, he was going to do it himself. Fourteen days later, much to the outrage of the indigenous Hawaiian population, Billy Hamilton and Ralph Young hauled to the beach a 14-foot tiger shark with a ragged dorsal fin. It took a gutted 5-foot gray shark as bait and a barbed hook the size of dinner plate. Butchering it offshore away from prying eyes, they found no evidence of Bethany's arm or her watch or the 18-inch semi-circle of surfboard that the shark had taken with it. The shark would have long before regurgitated the irritating fiberglass and foam and probably the arm with it. However, removing the jaws and matching them to Bethany's board revealed a perfect forensic fit to within two micrometers. Aside from the jaws, the only other part of the shark that was saved was a section of its dusky, striped skin. This skin was presented to Boy Akana, a local Kahuna, who would fashion it into a ceremonial drum to call on the ancient spirits to calm the seas. Governor Lingle would decree in a public statement that the matter was now closed and that the tourist industry should "just get back to normal."

Seven days later, Bethany Hamilton pays a visit to Ralph Young's compound with Billy Hamilton and her father Tom. She is there to visit the jaws that took her arm. Crouching beside the bloody things in the middle of the lawn, they come up to her shoulder. For long moments the men stand around uncomfortably as she curiously pokes at the razor sharp teeth one by one. Then she looks up at Billy Hamilton and asks if she can have some of

Bethany Hamilton, 200 yards from the spot where the shark that attacked her was caught.
Hanalei Bay Pier, November 2004. (Photo, Matt George)

the teeth for a necklace she would like to make—an amulet to protect her in the future. The men are so stunned that nobody speaks.

Upon leaving the compound with her Father, Bethany is heard saying to herself, *I hope I don't have dreams.*

On the way home, with a sleeping Bethany next to him in the car, Tom Hamilton begins to hum a tune he hasn't heard or sung since he was in the U.S. Navy as a young gunner's mate. His lips move slightly as he recalls the words of the Navy hymn:

Eternal Father, strong to save,
Whose arm hath bound the restless wave,
Who bidd'st the mighty ocean deep
Its own appointed limits keep;
Oh, hear us when we cry to Thee,
For those in peril on the sea!

Driving on through the rain, the windshield wipers beating monotonously, these are the only words Tom Hamilton can remember. He reaches out to softly take his daughter's hand in his, but it is not there.

The Hazards of Recreational Lying

JOHN FORSE

"Bull makes the world go 'round."
—Arthur Fonzarelli

First Encounter: Age 12 (Aptos, California)

In the summer of 1960, a girl missing one leg from the knee down showed up at my family church in Aptos, California. She sat through the service in a wheelchair. She was sixteen years old and pretty. I was only twelve, but I kept thinking about all the sadness that would accompany such loss of mobility. I had to know what happened. The rumor was that she had been attacked by a shark and I needed details. I later found the newspaper article: Susan Theriot and some classmates were at the beach just south of Rio del Mar. Most of students were floating in inner tubes. She decided to swim away from them and no sooner had she done so than a 15-foot white shark circled her twice. It bit into her leg; she screamed; blood clouded the water, and pandemonium broke out with all the students screaming and kicking their legs frantically to keep the shark away. She was the first female to be attacked on the West Coast. My middle-class childhood had insulated me thus far from handicapped people. Her presence encouraged my twelve-year-old imagination, and the story of that day looped endlessly in my mind's eye.

Later that summer, my family was at Rio Del Mar—the beach adjacent to where Susan was attacked—having an outing with another family. David and Larry Guy, myself, and my brother were riding airmats in the two- to three-foot fun surf and having a great time. Someone pointed out past the breaking waves to two circling dorsal fins. We all came in quickly, but David and I piled some rocks on our mats and paddled back out. As hard as we could, we threw rocks at the fins. With the water cleared of people, David's dad spotted him easily, swam out, and dragged him in. David got a hard lesson right then and there, while I scored two direct hits on the fins and convinced myself that I had heroically driven these man-eaters away. My audacity would come back to haunt me years later.

The Lawnmower: Age 38 (Milwaukie, Oregon)

I wore sandals on the first sunny day of spring after a long, miserable, wet winter. I was mowing my lawn in a hurry, as I had planned to meet some friends down at the Willamette River in the afternoon. We were going to ride our surfboards using a tow rope behind a boat. We called it "skurfing." After finishing the front lawn, I pushed the power mower—motor still running—down the driveway to the back lawn. But the mower got hung up in the narrow gate, so I slammed my foot on the back of it to get it through. My sandal slipped off the case, and my foot went directly into the spinning blade. That's the last time I ever saw my toes: flying all over the yard like little Vienna sausages.

My first reaction was, *Man, that was stupid.* Then the blood gushed and pain and shock followed. The next day, in the hospital, when I was coming out of the anesthesia and surveying the damage, I saw that I'd lost all the toes on my right foot. *Bummer!* I thought. *How bad will it screw up my surfing, tennis, skiing, and all the other things I love?*

When the foot healed, my missing toes looked as though they'd been bitten off, and I wondered what outlandish B.S. people would believe if I spun some yarn about how the accident happened. I remembered calling out this liar in high school for telling an outlandish, but entertaining lie. Later, my friend Patt Burr reprimanded me with this mantra: "It doesn't matter if a story is true or not. It just has to be entertaining and have the little odd details that make it believable." Limping around in the hospital I considered the possibilities.

The Oregon coast is known for its population of white sharks, and shark attacks are common here—at least once a year. A white shark hit my surfing buddy, Randy Weldon, back in 1983. He was launched off his board into the air by a powerful eighteen-footer that came straight up from the depths. He wasn't injured, but people still wanted to hear the story and see the arc of tooth marks in his board. I suppose it was only natural for me to start telling people that a shark took my toes off.

My stories changed depending on the audience. To another surfer, a tourist, a prospective date, I would stretch the limits of credulity, reading expressions and body language to see how much weight I could load on to the story. In this way, I reeled in or pulled back when it looked like they'd take or shake the hook.

Once, I was a guest on a local television program featuring surfing. The crew interviewed my buddies and me on the beach after a surf session. The reporter raised the inevitable questions about the danger of sharks. I couldn't help myself. I pulled off my bootie and showed him a foot with no toes, and launched into a heroic tale about using martial arts in defending myself from a white shark. My buddies were bent over, receding from the camera frame, trying to contain themselves, barely keeping straight faces. This, apparently, was better material than the reporter expected, and I became the centerpiece of the program. Not even professional doubters doubt dismemberment.

I soon discovered that there is a certain kind of person who asks about dismemberment. I think they are intrigued with terror, separation and reintegration in all its forms. They seek a connection over the truth. So I indulge myself and them. Yes, I could tell them with little embarrassment that I stuck my foot in a lawnmower at age thirty-eight. I could do that. But it's not what they crave. They want to hear about inextricable forces at play, hungry forces that can sever you. They crave shark stories.

Another time, I was a guest on a local cable show about surfing in Oregon. I had already covered all the usual hazards, cold water, strong currents, and powerful waves when the subject of shark attacks came up. (Television is a great opportunity for the recreational liar.) I related how I had been waiting for waves in the lineup, alone one day, when suddenly a shark clamped my thigh. I threw some hard fists at its nose and eyes, and luckily, it loosened its bite on my leg. But then it took a parting chomp on my foot, taking my toes with it. Being stoic and undaunted, I paddled in, walked to the hospital, got stitched up, and walked home. Some surfing buddies saw the broadcast and thought it was hilarious—we were all in on the joke, and the public soaked it up as gospel. I basked in the glory of this B.S. for days. All the while, I was unaware that my lies were unforeseen rehearsals, foreshadowing an attack that would have eerie similarities to my prevarication.

Man in the Gray Suit: Age 50 (Gleneden Beach, Oregon)

April 21, 1998, I was up at 7:00 A.M. It was a beautiful spring day. I headed south of town looking for the promising swell I'd seen getting blown out the evening before. Going over the crest of a local lookout, I spotted corduroy lines stacking up and with just a breath of wind. I was stoked! Normally, I would pull out the video camera and film the boys on a few sets—I am always after a decent segment to add to my next surf video. But today the call was strong; I had to get in quick. I waxed my new Russo longboard, which I'd only ridden once in crappy teaser waves. Only four guys were in the water, including Randy Weldon of legitimate shark-attack fame. The waves were bitchin'—a couple of feet overhead on the sets with long outside sandbar rights and a few lefts too. You learn to treasure days like this in Oregon as the norm is big and blown out or closed out, or both.

I couldn't get into my wetsuit fast enough. I ran across the park and paddled out in the channel to the peak, all the while watching almond-eye barrels pitching into the slight offshore wind. These were the best waves in three or four months. I got a few set waves that were unreal—long, fast, and perfect. I was tucking in the tight sections and driving hard down the long walls. Everyone was getting choice waves and having a great time.

Looking back, I should have realized that you don't cut it short in conditions like this unless you are truly, truly spooked. And Randy Weldon suddenly got spooked. He told me that he saw something which gave him a bad feeling, and then he paddled in. I reasoned that since his attack, he probably gets spooked easily, and maybe one of the many seals swimming around us had broken the surface and startled him. The rest of us surfed for another hour or so, then the early crew started going in. Soon, I had the waves all to myself and I surfed in blissful gratitude. Then, while relishing my good fortune between sets, I caught some movement out of the corner of my eye. I didn't think it was anything but a seal. So I continued to sit on my board, waiting for a set and soaking up the sun.

Suddenly I felt a hot, vise-like grip on my right thigh, not pain, but pressure. I reacted by hitting whatever it was with my fist, and then my board and I got pulled six feet under water. I couldn't see anything but boiling water and bubbles. In the confusion, my first thought was, "Why is a seal going after me?" Upon reflection I'm sure it was just my mind trying to protect me from the obvious. Then it released me, and I floated to the surface, where I saw a two-foot dorsal fin attached to a monstrous mountain of gray flesh hovering right at my side.

I started pounding on the shark's back, at a spot just in front of its dorsal fin. I got in three or four punches, which felt as useless as hitting an elephant, then the shark dove under. I felt relief for a fraction of a second, and then I got pulled under again—my leash was in the shark's mouth. I opened my eyes to get my bearings, but all I could see was a gray mass pulling me down and bubbles going by. I tried to unstrap the leash attached at my ankle, but with the force of being pulled down rapidly and with my torn-up thigh, I couldn't reach the release. At that point, about fifteen feet deep, I reconciled myself to the fact that I was going to die and there was nothing that I, or anyone else, could do about it. My board, my lies, my toeless foot, and I were all headed for Davey Jones' Locker with that shark. The feeling I had wasn't panic, just a calm resignation that this was the end of the road.

As I accepted this fate, the tension released from my leg. The shark's teeth had cut through the cord. The board and I surfaced separately and my resignation turned to serious worry. I was bleeding badly from my thigh; I was floating, dangling a bloody open wound in the water; I didn't know where the shark was; my board was about twenty feet away; and the beach was three hundred feet away. I sprint-swam to my board, and almost got on

John Forse's leg just after the shark bite. (Photo, Ali Ben Hammou, courtesy of John Forse)

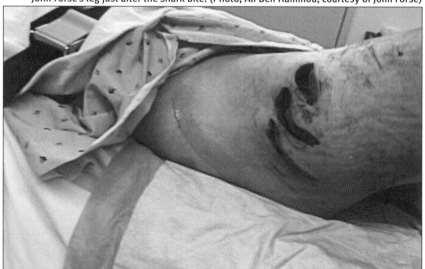

it and paddled it in upside down as I didn't want to stay in the water a second longer than I had to. But I took the extra second, righted my board, and stroked for the beach hoping I wasn't going to get hit again.

Of course, when you need a wave the most, it never comes. I was stuck in the longest lull of the day, maybe the year. I left a widening trail of red behind me. I didn't want to look at the damage to my leg. I just paddled hard to get to the beach. When I got to shallow water, I was able to support myself with the bad leg, so I figured it wasn't life threatening and that I'd probably suffered no irreversible damage. My friends Parrish Olsen and Ali Ben Hammou had seen the commotion and waited for me at water's edge. They wanted to call 911, but I insisted that they drive me to the hospital. We got stopped for speeding a few minutes later. After running our plates, and looking at my leg, the cop let us continue on our way.

We screeched into the hospital parking lot at the same time and pace as hospital surgeon, and fellow surfing buddy, Bruce Watanabe. He'd heard the news that someone got attacked, and he wanted this operation. "John!" he said surprised, "I figured it was somebody I knew, but not you!" He cleared the trauma room of the other doctors, while an orderly wheeled me in. He got out the safety scissors, but I made him wait until Ali got out the video camera to film. Doc Watanabe gave me a shot of morphine, then cut off my wetsuit. Soon I was blissfully zoned. Somewhere before stitch number fifty Randy Weldon came in. He said, "Hey John, didn't mean to bring the shark on you. I could feel it out there. Thought it wanted me, not you. Wow! Eight tooth marks. Look at that."

A media circus appeared outside of the hospital—news trucks from almost every television station in Oregon. They would have liked the video we'd just made. But I was saving that for my second surf movie, *Another Endless Winter.*

After I left the hospital, I found myself with a gallery of interested parties: more news stations, documentary crews, the BBC, *Extra, Evening Magazine, Hard Copy,* and Zoeller (a German cable concern) all began doing stories on me. David Letterman, Maury Povich, and Jerry Springer's people called to suss me out as a possible guest. Nike even included me in a commercial that showed one famous Olympian, two famous professional athletes, and one unknown liar showing their scars. Then the piece showed us pressing on in our respective sports. With all the media inquires and attention, I ended up telling the true story of the attack more than a hundred times. I actually got a little bored of telling it—there was no challenge, no sell, and no spin. In a

First Assault: After ten years of trying to surf the 35-foot wave that occasionally shows up at Nelscott Reef in front of his house, John Forse gets towed in for the first time. Another lie or the truth? Lincoln City, Oregon. (Photo, Nate Lawrence)

month the stitches were out and I was surfing again, grateful to be back in the lineup. Pulling my booties off after this first recovery session, a beach-goer asked about my missing toes. "My toes," I said, "oh, a tiger took them off while I was on safari in Africa."

Four Circles to Meaning: Diary of a Shark Attack

BUTCH CONNOR

It was Friday of Memorial Day weekend, 2004. I arrived at North Salmon Creek Beach around ten in the morning. If it were any later, the beautiful California weather would bring big crowds. Parking would be miserable or impossible by noon. The sky was clear and blue—the sun, bright and warm. The winds that howled onshore for weeks had stopped the day before, leaving the ocean with small ripples of surface texture. A south swell was winding down from the previous couple of days, leaving us with waist-high, and occasional head-high swells rising up in the calm, murky water.

The main parking lot was already filling up, but the space right next to the handicapped spot was open. Knowing that crowds of beachgoers were not far behind me, I got out of my truck and into my wetsuit. With my 6' 10" under my arm, I headed down the trail to a relatively secluded spot on the beach. After warming up and stretching, I donned my gloves and hood and went into the water.

I paddled in where the main pack of surfers sat atop their boards in the water. Generally, I try to find a less crowded wave to ride, but today there was really only one rideable peak. We were all sitting where Salmon Creek empties into the ocean, taking turns on the waist-high, slow, mush burgers. I had ridden about three waves by now, but wasn't getting any of the bigger sets;

the longboarders were picking those up on the outside. Thirsty for something bigger, I looked up the beach a bit toward the big rock that juts out of the water. It's called Tide Rock because it sits at the water line and makes it easy to judge tide height. At certain tides a wave peels on either side of the rock. I had seen a good wave almost breaking and decided to go and catch a couple before anyone noticed, before half of the crowd came over to share it. I paddled north about forty yards or so to the spot and waited for a set to come my way. One other surfer had the same idea but he kept on going to the north side of Tide Rock.

I sat there looking out at the ocean, thinking what a great start to a three-day weekend this was turning out to be. After three or four minutes, I saw my wave and turned my board around. I was now facing the beach and in the process of lying down to paddle when something caught my attention. It must have been a splash but no sound registered in my brain. In ten years of surfing, I've always looked quickly when I hear things splashing near me. Most surfers do, and perhaps this is an expression of our latent fear of sharks. I sat up quickly and turned my head over my right shoulder. I saw fourteen inches of light-gray dorsal fin sticking up out of the water moving slowly behind me. I inhaled with a gasp, and then started repeating, "Oh shit! Oh shit! Oh shit!" in a whisper. I froze with fear and became hyper-aware of things: my feet dangling in the water, my hands squeezing the rails hard enough to leave pressure dings, my heart pounding so loud I could hear it, and the sun reflecting off the rim of water disturbed by the fin. I could not move. Maybe it was fear, maybe it was fascination, but I was frozen.

The wave that I had been waiting for lifted and revealed the shark like a magnifying glass passing over it head to tail. I should have caught this wave, but it didn't occur to me at the moment. The shark, not in a rush, not acting aggressive, took a slight turn and arced around my right side, keeping a distance of about six feet. Now in front of me, it turned again and headed straight down my left side where my leg dangled in the water. Like the cameras in the shark movies, my attention was focused on the tip of the dorsal fin, which was four or five inches out of the water. The submarine attached to the fin had the same girth as a Volkswagen bug I once owned. I had this urge to reach out and touch it, as though feeling the gritty skin would make it less surreal and qualify the level of fear welling up inside me. I knew I was going to die very soon. Why should I not touch it?

Transfixed by this fin and the massive body under it, I did not see the shark's head and eyes, as it briefly came out of the water to hit my left thigh.

Empty A-frames at Salmon Creek Beach, Bodega Bay, California. (Photo, Butch Connor)

Not a particularly hard impact, just like a friend might give you a shove on the shoulder when playing around. I was shocked that it had hit me. It tilted me to the left, so I counter-shifted to the right and into the water I went, into that "what if" horror that had crossed my mind many a time. I believe I actually whimpered a bit as I fell in. As soon as I broke the surface, the shark went crazy: the water exploded and boiled around me. Beneath the surface, the shark was whipping its head and tail back and forth, snapping its jaws open and shut as I had seen in so many films. My terror became absolute. Water flew in the air all around me. I was suddenly in a spinning vortex of water. I knew where those teeth were and thought: I have to stay near the middle of its body.

The shark made one turbulent circle around my body, but it hadn't touched me. My feeling of helplessness passed and survival mode took over. I moved my board sideways and in front, hoping it would provide some kind of a barrier between us, and if there was a surface strike, I could push it into the animal's mouth. It certainly would fit between its jaws. Holding my board like this allowed me to float my feet a bit, which had been dangling straight down. The shark stopped thrashing and continued in a second circle. It came around again, and this time we were face to face six feet apart. I knew what was going to happen this time; it was coming straight at me to take a bite. I got pissed off. I had to do whatever I could to fight back. I pointed the nose of the board where I thought it would surface, and just as it came up I jabbed as hard as I could just above its gills. (The nose guard I usually had on my board had fallen off about two weeks before, and I hadn't replaced it yet.) The shark reacted instantly by thrashing back and forth. I climbed on my board, and while it was still thrashing, I yelled "shark!" as loud as I could toward the others in the water. The two people closest to me looked at me with their heads tilted as if they didn't understand, so I yelled it again. This time the whole group bolted toward shore.

I remember talking to a friend once about the spook factor of surfing alone. He said, "Butch, you're always out there alone." The totality of his statement struck me as I saw the pack stroking in as one in the distance. The shark began its third circle. I felt desperate. I needed to get out of there. I lay down on the board. The shark came slowly around to my right side. I took a couple of swift strokes, and the shark exploded the water all around me with its thrashing. Immediately, I pulled my hands out of the water. My board and I spun 360s in the troubled water, giving me various glimpses of horizon, shark whipping its head and tail, beachcombers peacefully walking the beach, and water flying everywhere.

When a 14-foot shark, weighing as much as a luxury car, decides to have its way with you, it will have its way with you. There was nothing I could do but watch as the situation grew worse. Lying on my board, I was spinning in circles, but I couldn't use it for a barrier or a weapon, nor could I paddle myself away. My thoughts went from pure denial (this can't be happening; I will not actually be eaten by this beast), to sorrow (what are my three kids going to do without me; how many tears will my girlfriend cry before getting on with her life?), to intense fear (the hit is coming; the bite is coming; my entire chest can fit in its mouth). My whole body from neck to feet was shaking. I told myself that I had to calm down. Otherwise, the shark will feel my fear in the form of vibrations or electrical impulses and strike. I calmed enough to stop the shaking. My body did as my mind told it to do—that surprised me. The shark stopped thrashing and swam its fourth circle around me—this one at about three feet away all the way around. It began a fifth rotation at the same proximity but then straightened out a bit, increasing its distance.

This was my chance to escape. I started paddling with only cupped hands—no arm in the water at all. I paddled quietly like this for at least a full minute, maybe more, and I made no forward progress. I had to get out of the water, so I dug in with both arms and set my sights on the beach. Everyone who had been in the ocean was now gathered at the waterline. They were watching to make sure that I was going to make it in, or perhaps to make sure they didn't miss anything should I not make it. I was paddling and not going anywhere, like in a dream about being chased by a shark. I was a bit too far back on my board, so instead of gliding efficiently, I was inefficiently pushing a lot of water. But I was too scared to stop paddling and adjust myself.

Intense fear came over me. The shark had gone, but where—under my board, perhaps, to attack from below? I just kept paddling as hard as I could. My strokes were getting weaker, but it didn't matter. I was moving. I made it to the shallows, stood up in knee-deep water and walked the rest of the way up to the beach. Out of breath, my arms dead from exhaustion, I pulled off my hood. Everyone was there waiting. Some had smiles on their faces, some had looks of concern, but what really caught my attention were the people with their jaws agape, mouths wide open. To step on land never felt so good!

Now, the surfers who had been out in the water and up on the cliff, surrounded me, and one by one, gave me a pat on the back, or a handshake, or a word of support. I wish I could thank each one of them personally for being there. I generally tend to be a bit of a loner, but I'm not sure how I would have fared if I had been out there truly alone and had returned to an empty shore.

After talking to people on the beach for some minutes, I walked back up the trail leading to the parking lot. A park ranger intercepted me, pulled out a pocket sized spiral notepad, and took my report on a scrap of paper that had plenty of other notes on it. He took down my name and number, and not many details. I went to my truck, took off my wetsuit, and put on my clothes. A few more people wished me well and shook my hand. I climbed in and realized I was still in shock, so I sat for a few minutes and took some deep breaths to calm myself. I looked back down at the beach. The surfers were now gone, the water empty of people playing. Only groups of sunbathers and holiday vacationers were down on the sandy beach, probably oblivious to what had just happened.

As my mind cleared, I thought that if that shark had wanted to eat me it would have. It could have chomped me from any angle it chose. Perhaps the shark had not been trying to eat me. Was this supposed to mean something and, if so, what? When I got home and told my kids, they didn't believe me. That was interesting.

Later we watched the newscasters, reporting from the information that the ranger wrote on his paper scrap. Eyewitnesses on the news said the interaction with this animal lasted thirty seconds or so. I would put that figure closer to twenty minutes. So it seemed to me. However, it did take me almost five minutes to paddle in to shore. I was stuck in a rip current and wasn't aware of it. As I was paddling in, I felt the presence of another person still in the water, and I wondered why it took this other guy so long to paddle in. Why did he keep looking at me instead of paddling like hell for the beach?

I took a two-day break from surfing to think about my life. And I thought, sharks or no sharks, good waves or bad waves, life or death, I need to surf more than I need to make excuses.

A week later, I was talking about the attack with a friend when he mentioned that his neighbor, Sean, had paddled over to me to see if I needed help. Shortly thereafter, I surfed Salmon Creek and ran into Sean on the beach. He told me his story of paddling over to help me out. Twelve to fifteen surfers in the water and as soon as someone yelled, "shark," they couldn't get out fast enough. No hard feelings. They couldn't have stopped the shark from doing anything, and I don't honestly know what I'd do in the same situation. But one guy, a slim 160-pounder, paddled straight at a pissed-off, extra-large shark to help a stranger get to safety. On the beach that day, I said it to him, "Sean, you're my hero for life, bro. You've got more guts and courage than anyone I've ever met." Thanks, Sean.

Editor's Note: *According to shark researchers, attacks usually last one to two seconds; this thirty-second attack was unusually long. Butch Connor's attack is the seventh in a series of shark attacks in the Bodega Bay area of California. None so far has been fatal. The first five attacks listed below are reported in detail in Ralph S. Collier's* Shark Attacks of the Twentieth Century, *published in 2003 by Scientia Publishing.*

Oct. 4, 1959—Freediver James Hay is struck on his diving fin, escaping with only a twisted ankle.

Aug. 20, 1961—David Vingenson, out on a Sunday swim, is circled twice, and then both his thighs are clamped. At the time he feels pressure but not pain. He makes it to the beach where he collapses.

July 27, 1968—Freediver Frank Logan suddenly finds his chest between the jaws of a violently shaking shark. The shark carries him fifteen feet and then releases him. Surgeons use two hundred stitches to close eighteen puncture holes.

Oct. 3, 1996—Surfer Kennon Cahill notices a 15-foot white shark next to him; he reaches out and touches its fin. The shark thrashes wildly, and Cahill catches and rides an incoming wave. He is unhurt.

Nov. 29, 1996—Surfer Greg Ferry, feels a strike at his shin, which he dis-

misses as odd, until a 12-foot white shark brushes his thigh and begins to thrash violently. He escapes to shore and examines a two-inch gash shaped like a Nike Swoosh.

Nov. 28, 2002—*Bodyboarder Mike Casey, while lying on his board, is struck from behind by a 16-foot white shark. Casey spends eleven days recovering in the hospital from bites to both of his calves and thighs and his right foot. X-rays show tooth marks on his bones.*

May 28, 2004—*Surfer Bernard Connor Jr. escapes uninjured after being attacked by a 14-foot white shark.*

Oct. 19, 2005—*Surfer Megan Halavais, while paddling in the lineup, is struck from behind and pulled underwater by a 14- to 18-foot white shark. She wrestles herself free of the shark. While paddling to shore with the help of two surfers, she notices that she has been bitten on her right leg. Halavais is taken by helicopter to a local hospital where doctors close lacerations stretching from her upper thigh to her lower calf.*

The Place Where Anything Wrong Comes to Death

CARLOS BURLE

The producer of the Brazilian documentary *Surf Adventures* approached Eraldo Gueiros and me about being in his movie. He spoke in Portuguese, our native language, but the direct translation was funny. He said, "We need bigger than what is considered normal waves for the movie. I want to film at the place where anything wrong comes to death."

We accepted his invitation to film at Dungeons in Hout Bay, Cape Town, South Africa. I shivered when I imagined the big waves, freezing water, and cold air. We'd been lucky surfing big waves at this spot in the past, but I have never left it without feeling immense respect for the ocean's power.

At Hout Bay the film crew was ready, but our WaveRunner® wasn't working well. Reliability in big waves is crucial, so we towed it to the house where Shawn Alladio was staying. She helped us fine-tune some repairs, and we were ready to go. But then she said: "Before you go out, I'll scout the break on my WaveRunner.®"

"Scout for what?" I asked her.

"You know, shark patrol. I'm going to remove the half-eaten seal carcasses floating out there. Sometimes they bite the seal's rear fins off to immobilize them; sometimes they chomp the seals in half; either way, the sharks come back sooner or later."

Eraldo Gueiros, Shawn Alladio and Carlos Burle regroup twenty minutes after the incident at a small cafe (complete with fireplace and Rooibos tea) at the Hout Bay launch, Cape Town, South Africa. (Photo courtesy of Shawn Alladio)

Eraldo and I looked at each other with wide eyes. I like to pretend there are no sharks; it's easier that way. Shawn's remark pulled my nerves tight. As she launched her WaveRunner®, I said to Eraldo, "Friend, you surf first today."

When we first got out past the lineup, we were paying attention to every single thing that was moving in the water. We couldn't relax. We were totally paranoid about sharks. After an hour surfing, we lost the paranoia and focused on the waves. Apart from one South African tow-in team, Gigs Celliers and Jason Ribbink from Durban, we were alone out there in perfect waves. The lineup at this spot is so wide that we only crossed paths with them twice the whole day. They were just small people on the far end of the break.

Suddenly, we saw them coming in our direction, and they were waving at us. They must have surfed a good one, we thought, the best of the day. They flew towards us at full throttle. Weird. Maybe that wave was really special. Then they passed us at full speed, and we thought we heard the words "white shark" as they headed toward the channel. This was not what I expected. We were at a low speed, going away from the channel. I was driving, and Eraldo was standing on his board holding the rope thirty feet behind the WaveRunner®.

Eraldo glimpsed behind him and saw a figure in the water. A shark was swimming calmly, part in and part out of the water. That's not a white shark following us, I thought, it's a white van! An impressive, extremely threatening van. I got so scared I couldn't move for an instant. Then I turned toward the channel, and the shark turned with us. Eraldo was holding the rope, standing on the board, yelling, "Let's get out of here!"

I throttled up to go faster, but not too fast, or Eraldo might wreck. The shark, without any trouble, was also going faster, keeping right by Eraldo's side. They looked into each other's eyes. Then Eraldo started pulling the rope hand over hand until he got to the WaveRunner®, which, by now, was going almost full speed. Eraldo got on the back seat. I looked down, and the shark was now right next to us.

In the channel we met the relatives: two other white sharks. We got back to the crew boat and our hearts were almost jumping out of our chest. Back on land somebody told us that this species is both violent and clever ... that you are done being attacked before you realize it started. I looked at Eraldo and said, "This is the most frightening experience I've ever had in the ocean."

"Well," he said, "here they live, here they eat."

I told him I was changing the name of the place from Dungeons to "The White Shark's Crib" (*Berço dos tubaroes broncos*).

In a Place Called Transkei

TERRY GIBSON

Who trusted God was love indeed
And love Creation's final law—
Tho' nature, red in tooth and claw
With ravine, shriek'd against his creed.
—**Alfred Lord Tennyson**

In June of 1997, I went on a ten-week solo surfari in South Africa. I was twenty-three, and had just finished my first year of teaching high-school English in Belle Glade, Florida. I played club rugby at home in Palm Beach County with a South African expat who'd given me a list of surfing and rugby contacts throughout the country. I hoped a sojourn on the mother continent would improve my frontside cutback and clarify perspectives on racism, environmental degradation, and religious conflicts that confronted me as a young southern teacher and aspiring writer working in the heart of Florida's Everglades Agricultural Area. The sojourn would lead me right through the valley of the shadow of death.

The rooms in the hostel at Mosselbaai were painted in the colors of South Africa's new flag. Red for bloodshed. Blue for open blue skies. Green for the land. Black for the African people. White for the European people. And yellow for the natural resources, i.e., gold.

The hostel had been dead-empty for a week, during which time I made daily forays into the remarkable and empty surf. Nearby Outer Pool, usually a big and shifty right pointbreak, was orderly and predictable.

It was so good one morning, I spent four hours in the fifty-degree water in my flimsy 3/2 wetsuit. Shivering and hell-bent for a hot shower, I hardly noticed the slight Aussie strumming a guitar sitting by the brick fireplace. A familiar string of chords finally made me stop and take note of him. He wore baggy brown corduroys, a gray shirt that fit like a sheet, and Ugg boots. His curly russet hair spilled over a pale, delicate face, while tiny hands strummed the Cult's "Sweet Soul Sister."

"That's a good tune," I said when he finished.

He looked up so briefly and almost malevolently that I felt I'd interrupted him. Then he started in on a Nirvana song. Mark Penches had arrived and somehow made the hostel seem even emptier.

After thawing, I came back to the fireplace with two Castles in hand. Mark hadn't moved, but the guitar was quiet, and he stared pensively into the fire.

"Terry Gibson," I said, feeling apologetic without knowing why.

Again, he seemed startled and annoyed. He took the beer and introduced himself as "Mark." I asked where he was from.

"Dee Why, and you?" he asked, as if forcing himself to be polite.

"Southeast Florida," I said. Suddenly, he was paying rapt attention to me.

"Know a guy named Mike Tabeling?"

"He's from Sebastian Inlet, about two hours north of me. Depending on who you ask, he's either the biggest bully or one of the most influential surfers to emerge from the East Coast of America. I heard he bought a big house in J-Bay, after finding a pile of Spanish bullion."

"The cunt dropped in on me three set waves in a row a couple of days ago at Super's, then he sucker punched me in the mouth when I said something. He must weigh fifteen stone."

The cheap shot is the lowest form of disrespect. It leaves you angry and outcast. For that reason, I thought, Mark camped out on the hostel's lawn. He must've had a long, shivering time that night, as the land breezes picked up and blew so hard that the roses climbing the hostel's Dutch colonial exterior were bare of petals in the morning. At daybreak, his tent was a flapping patchwork of canvas and duct tape. The zipper slid down and Mark peeked out, wrapped in a shawl of stolen airline blankets.

"Where's your sleeping bag?"

Emerging with a battered board, he pointed to the four taped-up slashes on the side of the tent and said, "Moroccan thieves."

That morning he surfed eight-foot Outer Pool so well you would have thought he slept in a feather bed. Tight snaps in the curl, pelicanesque floaters, and tight-radius cutbacks characterized his surfing. He was the standout everywhere we surfed together over the next month.

I quickly learned to get on with Mark by saluting his solitude. When he wanted to share, he would, and I soon pieced together parts of his story. After graduating from university with a degree in marine sciences, he'd delivered pizzas and read electricity meters to save up for a year-long surf trip. He flew with his girlfriend to the UK, and they made their way through Europe. They split up along the way. Mark headed to Morocco and on to South Africa. He didn't provide any details about her departure and didn't seem happy about it. More than once, he said something about "working things out." He spent heaps of time on pay phones.

After a few more days at the hostel, we scored a ride to the Eastern Cape with a couple of English rugby fanatics. We strapped our board bags on the roof with our leashes and some twine. The coffins soon became a point of contention because they slowed us down and made the gas needle drop precipitously. Still, the Brits offered to split the fuel bills evenly, though they had hired the car. I was a little taken aback when Mark tried to negotiate the price. But because money was a concern for me, too, I didn't really mind. Then we saw a sign for Port Alfred. The turn-off for the road to Port Alfred was just ahead, but the town itself was a few hundred kilometers down that road—a few hundred kilometers away from where we were going. Mark insisted that they take him there.

"But there's a Kirra-like right there, and I'm not coming back this way," he pleaded unsuccessfully as the turnoff receded in the rearview.

That was the first thing he'd said in hours, and he didn't say anything else. When we got to the port city of East London, he got out and said, "Thank God! The ocean." The Brits thought him rude, but I understood. Though unrealistic at times, Mark was determined to surf through as much of Africa as possible while his money held out.

We checked into the Sugar Shack hostel. Even though it was late and freezing cold, Mark chose the cheapest accommodations and pitched his tent on the lawn. Boiling ramen noodles for dinner, he let a little homesickness slip and said, "Fuck all, I miss Mum's peas and carrots." Mark ate the whole package and was the first surfer in the water at daylight.

The Sugar Shack is a delightfully eccentric backpackers' hub across the street from a fun beach break and a short hike away from Nahoon Reef. Mark and I hiked up to Nahoon late morning and were puzzled that no one was out. Thick but slightly bumpy rights reeled in and the current was an absolute bitch, so we chalked it up to laziness. We surfed alone for two hours. Later, we found out a fisherman had seen two giant great whites patrolling the lineup the day before and warned off the locals. Mark didn't bat an eye, and because I come from Southern Florida, a place where everyone has a shark story—if not scars—I liked my odds.

Two of the surfers who ran the hostel, Craig and Brad Cuff, clued us in to the numerous breaks in the area. A diverse, friendly cast of well-traveled surfers made the hostel a lively place. Mark and I got on well with a mild-mannered physical therapist from Sydney, Australia, named Clyde Crawford. The three of us surfed some fairly remote breaks: Igoda Mouth, Yellow's Point, Gonubie Point, Queensbury Bay, and others.

The empty East Cape breaks afford a sense of surfing on the edge of civilization. And still I wanted to go beyond the edge and deep into the heart of the Wild Coast, to Transkei province, a rugged, unpopulated stretch of shoreline full of crystal-clear lagoons, sea cliffs, plunging waterfalls, dense forests, deep gorges, and world-class right pointbreaks.

You need your own wheels to explore the Transkei and hiring one was out of the question for me. One morning, while I watched the north wind whipping spindrift into the Indian Ocean and pondered with dread the upcoming school year, Mark and Clyde came striding up the forecastle stairs together. Clyde stood well over Mark, with thick shoulders and long limbs.

"Look, mate," he began, "Mark and me, we were thinking of heading into the Transkei . . . an' three's a good number."

Clyde's buzz cut made his cheekbones and the reef scar on his cheek (courtesy of Padang) protrude. With a soft voice and a gentle manner, he almost belonged in monk's robes. At twenty-six, Clyde had already found his vocation as physical therapist which gave him the time and money to surf and rock climb around the world.

We bought provisions at an East London grocery store. Mark carefully sought out the cheapest brands. He shot me a glare when I insisted that we buy coffee as well as the tea he wanted. We wouldn't find out how broke he was until we searched through his wallet to find his parents' phone number.

I bought a newspaper off the grocery rack and the headlines ran: "Car-jackings in Epidemic Numbers," "Demonstrations Brewing to a Riot," and "Third-level Warfare in the Transkei." Back at the hostel, I showed the paper to Brad Cuff, who waved it off and said he was bummed he couldn't tag along due to work.

"*Lekker*," Brad said about the Transkei, meaning it was nice. "Just don't drive at night."

"And pay local kids to guard the vehicle," Craig added.

That night in the bar we announced our plans. The old seamen voiced out, "fucking *kaffirs* (pejorative for black African) will cut off your hand for your watch," and, "you can take the *kaffir* out of the bush but not the bush out of the *kaffir*," and, "it's an awful risk just for some waves."

Riding up the coastal highway, the N-2, we watched the veldt's winter-brown foothills, anthills, and huts through the square side window of Clyde's gray '73 Volkswagen pickup. The sky was so blue the cab felt like a submersible passing through a strange and beautiful underwater world. The Drakensberg Mountains loomed like snow-capped seamounts.

We pulled into a Pottsville gas station to fill the water jugs. The station was busy. Ours were the only white faces, but the stares were polite and curious. I asked a man, the driver of a farm lorry, if the water was okay to drink, and in the most punctilious English the man replied, "Why, yes, it is potable." I felt a surge of goodwill.

Clyde turned off onto a grade made of crushed white shell, and we headed east on an improvised short cut. Hours into it, we discovered the road ahead had been washed out. We retraced our tracks and didn't get back on the N-2 until late afternoon.

Sunset meant resignation to our growing fear, which set in like the cold with the sinking sun. A full moon rose as if counterbalanced by the sun, and fewer and fewer people walked along the road as the night offered a light show of cattle eyes and fireflies.

Over the engine's din we heard strange sounds, rising, sinking, swelling in pitch carrying choral across the veldt. The road wound around a hut where a few people stood outside conversing. A woman spun around a walking stick, ululating—her voice shrill and dazzling as the moon. Down the way were crowds of people drinking, cavorting, and gesticulating wildly—all of which stopped as we approached and waved.

We passed through a gauntlet of expressionless stares. When the last dark face glowed red in the taillights we burst off through the night.

We came upon another village gathering. There was no discussion among us, only the silent agreement that we needed to find a safe place to camp for the night. Clyde stopped the truck and left it running while he went to ask for help. I slid over to the driver's seat, wondering if I could drive a stick well enough with my left hand to make a getaway. Clyde looked like a giant next to the Xhosas that surrounded him, and a few minutes later he returned to the car, grabbed two beers, and went back to the party. Eventually, a battered white sedan emerged from behind a hut, and we followed it.

"He'll show us to some kind of massive, all-inclusive resort—the Haven. He said we'd be safe there for the night and to ask directions in the morning."

We followed the man for what seemed like an hour. When we arrived we gave him a beer for the road. He thanked us profusely. Then the night became much less charitable. With its ring of concertina wire, AK-47-toting guard, and gate, the Haven gave more the impression of a compound than a resort. The guard was a black man, and I wondered if his Kalashnikov had been smuggled in from Russia, Angola, or Cuba, and if it had once been used against the class of people the guard was now using it to protect.

"We're closed," he said matter of factly. "You can camp by the sea."

That we were close to the ocean was a revelation, but the road had not been maintained beyond the Haven. We got as far as we could, but not as far as the campsites. Around 2 A.M., we washed down granola bars with beer. Mark pitched his tent. With only a few hours until daylight, Clyde and I racked out in the truck's bed.

I searched the sky for the Southern Cross, wondering whether it is best to understand those stars as guiding principles or arbitrary arrangements. The former seemed decadent, the latter bleak. Best to be content with the mystery.

In the morning we realized it was Sunday. A church service was underway at the Haven, attended only by blacks. Hymns came from the same throats that'd made those unfathomable incantations the night before.

"Wrap your brain around that one, mate," Clyde said.

We found the turnoff to Dwesa Preserve easily enough, and arrived by noon at Breezy Point. The surf was flat, but the wilderness was just as gorgeous and pristine as the guidebooks described. Two young boys swam along the rocks searching for lobsters.

Six armed, uniformed natives halted our camp setup.

"Good morning, sirs," said the oldest. "I am sorry to inform you of this, but you may not camp here. Preserve rules."

Mark took louder umbrage than was appropriate. "We won't make a mess, sir." Clyde quickly intervened and walked off with one of the officers to check out the huts. I told Mark to go suss out the breaks, that I'd stay with the vehicle. Using Australian slang helped placate him. I guess he took it as a sign of deference.

A group of kids came by and offered their services as guides and guards. Clyde returned, having struck a deal of eight rand for a *rondavel* with a large glass window overlooking the break. Eight rand wouldn't break anyone, so we agreed. When Mark returned five hours later from sussing out the waves, he accepted the arrangement with an insincere, "Cheers, mates."

As we boiled pasta, a storm rolled through that felt similar to the low-pressure systems at home that explode with rain when they reach the warm Gulf Stream. The wind went sideshore from the south and a band of clouds marched out over the warm Agulhas Current. Static electricity pulsed like silver capillaries in the black sky. Weather such as that means one thing to me: waves.

We drank a bit of wine while it stormed, and we traded maps to favorite breaks around the globe. When thunder cracked, I said I was glad we weren't camping. That comment apparently rubbed Mark wrong, and he went back to his Nelson Mandela biography. Soon Clyde was snoring, but I couldn't sleep. Occasionally, the moon broke through the clouds but mostly the light through the windows came from the lightning. The air was dank, and there was a chill in the hut that I couldn't escape even in my down sleeping bag.

Dawn broke bright, clear, and cold. We saw through the window that the surf was cracking. Six-foot sets groomed by land breezes raced in and across the bay. A volley of bigger channel-boomers followed.

Clyde and I suited up quickly, but Mark didn't budge.

"Me insides," he said, holding his belly. "I'll be along."

We walked along the narrow strip of beach between the headland and the rocky shore. The sunlight was bright on the rocks and caught the white plumes off the waves from behind like a lamp behind a billowing curtain. We found a little channel and paddled out dry-headed directly into the overhead rights.

The sets were so consistent I hardly saw Clyde during that whole session, except for a set where he took the first one and I took the second. I saw him crashing the lip while I trimmed across a speed section. Occasionally, I heard someone hoot at us, but didn't realize that a white family from Johannesburg had also arrived. Two hours later, Clyde and I wound up outside together, and he said he'd go in and cook "brekkie."

Clyde caught a bomb all the way through, but I was too deep for the wide-swinging set. Then came a long lull, which I didn't mind because the sun was warm, terns and gulls were diving gracefully, and pods of dolphin frolicked all around me. Waiting, I gazed at the most sublime coast I've ever seen, and by the time a set came, I'd drifted off the peak.

The next set swung wider, and I rode one halfway to the beach. I caught the second half of another screamer and road it into the shorebreak, right under Clyde, where he waited with piping hot porridge.

While we ate, Mark emerged in his tattered wetsuit. He'd lost the zipper string and asked for a zip, never taking his eyes off the waves.

He found a flat rock on the end of the point and did his ritual sun salutes. He said it made his sessions better. Every time I saw him stretch like that, I wondered if, for him, it was just stretching, or if it was prayerful stretch, an athletic supplication. I never felt right about asking him.

We watched him surf as I washed dishes and Clyde fixed a ding in his board. The tide pushed in and the swell was rising. Mark, as usual, was surfing with wings. As soon as the chore was done, I zipped back up and ran down the point watching Mark ride a bomb. He took off under the curl, and came flying out of a deep barrel. He executed a perfect roundhouse and stood again in a high-pocket tube. He flew past me, but Clyde later told me he got bar-reled again.

That was the last wave Mark ever rode.

Walking toward the point, I stopped to study the tide pools and thought about their diversity of organisms and the interdependence of the communities. Then a voice, muffled by the din of the surf, called out to me. I looked up on the headland and a white woman had her hand cupped over her mouth. She looked hysterical, but I couldn't hear her over the surf. I set my board down on a rock and climbed up to find out what was wrong.

She was wild-eyed and speaking Afrikaans.

"English," I said.

"Your friend," she stammered, "your friend's been taken . . . by a shark."

Later, she told me the great white had knocked him five meters in the air then taken him down. I had been musing over snow-globish, microcos-mic pools, thinking about how harmonious these communities seem, even though they are arenas of predation, while my friend's lifeblood had dissi-pated into the sea.

Turning, I saw nothing. I told her to get Clyde. I ran down to the rocks and sought out the tallest ones for vantage. About half way to the shorebreak I saw his head lolling about as if struggling for a breath. But there was no way to get to him—big surf broke right on the rocks.

I ran northwest toward the beach until I saw a channel through the rocks. I waited for a wave, lay flat on the white wash, and let it carry me out headfirst over the shallow rocks into the chaotic eddy along the headland where I had last seen Mark. Clyde had gone to the far end of the crescent beach, where you wind up after taking a wide one. But I had last seen Mark in the eddy. I surfaced from under a wave and a wall of white water smacked Mark into me like a rugby center back. I caught his leg as the wave pushed him past me. I put my forearm under his chin and back-peddled to the beach. The waves kept rolling me over and his long hair kept falling down my gasping throat. I lost him once and had to dive to retrieve him.

The waves washed us inside. I stood and tried to lift Mark, but the rocks were sharp under my feet and he was too heavy. Clyde waded over with Mark's board under his arm. It had drifted north, away from its owner. With Mark in the hands of someone with medical experience, I had hope that he would live. Clyde threw Mark over his shoulder, leaving me in the shorebreak with the board now impressed by the shark's jaws. Mark's leash trailed and got caught on a rock. I gave it a jerk to free it and Mark's right leg slid onto the beach, ankle still in the cuff. Hysterical, I gave him CPR until Clyde pulled me off him.

"He's gone, mate," Clyde said, in the softest voice.

I looked down and saw sheer horror frozen in Mark's blue eyes. His forearms were in ribbons from fighting the shark. His wetsuit was ripped off at the waist. His genitals lay against a bloodless, cavernous hole where the leg had been torn from the hip. It was the first dead body I'd ever seen outside of a casket. I turned and puked seawater. My eyes watered, and I thought I was crying, but I was too numb and disorientated to feel anything. Clyde patted me on the back, asked if I was all right, and bent to close Mark's eyes.

By then, the villagers were on the beach or looking down from the headland. Two Xhosa men helped us place the body on the board, head on the tail, and Clyde shoved the leg into place. We bound the body to the board with the leash and lifted it, me in front, Clyde in the back, and the two black men across from us. We walked up the beach, sinking to our shins in sand, rails pressing into our shoulders, one black foot, one white foot, forced into unison by the weight of death.

After a hundred yards or so a young man my age insisted on taking my place. Following in their footsteps, a strange clarity and a profound serenity replaced my nausea and disorientation. I still don't know what to make of it, and it didn't last.

We carried the body back to the *rondaval* and placed it in Mark's board bag. Peter Barrable, the father of the Joberg family that witnessed the attack, had gone for the police, and Elizabeth, the mother of the family, helped us pack Mark's things. She hugged us before we left, and as she pulled me to her breast I smelled the cook fire in the rough cloth of her dress. I knew then I was in the arms of Africa.

As we loaded Mark into the truck bed, we met Alan Shaw, a white baker who lives in the Transkeian capital, Umtata. Alan's family had bought property on Breezy Point, and he had come down to check on a house he had under construction. The death did not seem so much of a shock to him. Perhaps he'd seen enough of it living in the Transkei. Realizing that we were in a bad way, he invited us to his home in Umtata.

What a procession we made back across the veldt. The locals turned out of their *rondavals* solemn and respectful as we approached. The news clearly preceded us. A herd of reporters awaited us at the Shaws'—black, white, and colored (mulatto). The reporters were pushy and rude, and one tried to physically prevent me from entering the compound. I shoved him aside.

The Shaws' phone rang 24-7 while we stayed there. I felt bad for their kids, who were in school. The Shaw family shielded us from the media. They fielded the calls and helped us navigate South African bureaucracy. But they could not shield us from racial politics.

We'd arrived late in Umtata and had to put the body in a meat packing plant overnight. In the morning, we met the coroner, an Asian Indian one shade lighter than the Xhosas. He berated the black police for "mistreating" the body and "botching" the investigation. He wanted to know why no one was hunting down that shark. His attitude pushed us past shock and denial and into the next stage after a loss—anger. I unloaded on the coroner in front of the cops, telling him to do his job and that if he said another word, I'd kick his ass.

He stopped talking then. I pray he didn't send anyone after the shark.

The coroner took Mark's body, while Captain Nonzuzo Nkqayi, mother of many children, treated us like one of her own and expressed sympathy for Mark's parents.

I felt guilty when I called them, just for having the rest of my life to live. Clyde and I each spoke with Mr. and Mrs. Penches. They were sincere in their thanks. We said we knew that Mark would've done as much for us.

I don't know what I'd say if I ever met them, but I'd like to.

The coroner refused to release Mark's body for repatriation until we identified the corpse. In revenge for my outburst, he made us identify the body four days in a row.

After a week, Mark was shipped home. He was cremated and his mates spread his ashes at his home break.

The Shaw house, a single-story building with many rooms, sits inside a perimeter of concertina wire. Clyde and I often played with their dogs. They were a source of solace. One of them, the bulldog, was acting sick and would not eat. Raised in a house full of bird dogs, I'm more comfortable with strange dogs than strange people. Clyde held the animal. I searched its throat with the hand I'd cut on the rocks while dragging Mark's body through the shorebreak. Clyde took a turn and couldn't find anything lodged in the dog's throat either. The next morning, the vet diagnosed it with rabies and put the pup down.

"We can't skip the vaccine, mate," Clyde said.

I shook my head in denial.

"There's no cure once you come down with it," he said firmly.

We had three days from exposure to find the vaccine and someone to inject it. South Africa's socialized medical system has rules against treating foreigners, and we were initially denied help in Umtata. But then a doctor at the hospital where Mark's body was autopsied rounded up some vials of the vaccine and gave them to us with written instructions on how and when to inject it.

We went back to stay with the Cuffs and the Scheepers in East London. The public hospitals wouldn't give us the injections. They suggested we try the nuns at the Catholic clinic in the bowels of the city.

The clinic was the only non-dilapidated building in the slum. Outside, orange bougainvillea climbed freshly whitewashed cement walls. It stood amid clusters of tin-roofed shanties and labyrinths of alleys.

Inside, we were the only white faces in the spotless clinic. The black nuns were stoic, determined, and convinced that suffering is a form of redemption. Black, white, or purple, we were just naughty free spirits to whom God was teaching a painful lesson. Moreover, to them our suffering was clearly relatively minor, compared to what lay down those alleys.

A short black sister in a white habit treated us. She removed a clean needle from a sterile package, cracked a smile, then jabbed me hard in the shoulder, as though she was giving a philandering teenager a shot for the clap.

"Heeey," I said, shocked at myself for looking at a nun so malevolently.

"You should offer it up, sir," she said, jabbing Clyde.

That night, and the nights to follow, I dreamed that Clyde came down with rabies and descended into vicious madness—the essence of nature. I followed him into the darkness soon after he died. After a few days of watching us mope like zombies, Pete Cuff made us get back into the water. Mustering the nerve to paddle out with Clyde and him at Queensbury Bay seemed like working myself up to jumping off a sea cliff for the first time. We paddled across the bay. Watching double-overhead sets grind across the shelf, we edged over toward the peak. For the first time in my life, I was afraid of falling off a surfboard. Clyde led the charge adroitly. I followed and fell twice, then rode a wave most conservatively.

"You gotta have a go, mate," Clyde said, as a big set approached. I made the drop. Presence, confidence, and the slight stirrings of the lust for life returned as I felt the rail and inside fin engage exquisitely in a bottom turn.

Clyde decided to go to Zimbabwe and we parted ways. I had a few days left before my flight, so I went to J-Bay. There, I scored good waves and fell in with another lot of good-humored rippers. I tried to surf and hang like nothing had happened, but still had to deal with the rabies.

The woman who owned the hostel was married to a colored doctor who injected me. A diabetic friend of my rugby buddy's family gave me another one. Back in Cape Town, I couldn't get to the Catholic clinic and still catch my flight. Finally, while my plane boarded, I worked up the nerve and jabbed the needle deep into my shoulder.

It seemed symbolic, an affirmation of life and of the coming school year. I bled badly through my T-shirt and put on a fleece so as not to worry the flight attendants.

As we lifted off, I couldn't help looking back at the insane ocean beating against the mother continent, where I had made a friend casually and lost him in the most horrific way a surfer can imagine. Thirteen hours later my parents would greet me with shocked but relieved looks that made me understand a breath of the grief Mark's parents felt.

Heavy Water

SHAWN ALLADIO

When I have seen the hungry ocean gain
Advantage on the kingdom of the shore,
And the firm soil win of the watery main,
Increasing store with loss, and loss with store.
—William Shakespeare, *Sonnet LXIV*

Hout Bay, Cape Town, South Africa—June 18, 2001

The sun rose, red and orange like a peach, as I stood on the Sentinel, the land-mark bluff that is to Cape Town what Diamond Head is to Waikiki. Below me the edge of the continent met the merging Atlantic and Indian oceans. The sea rarely wakes up and shows the full range of its personality. But now, here in the Roaring Forties, the ocean was awake with forty-foot faces: cold, thick waves with hard sideshore winds. The morning was a crisp fifty degrees and the water temperature was about the same. The waves thundered in like connected train cars—twelve to a series.

The reef below the bluff is named Dungeons because it's cold, sharky, powerful, and lined with jagged rocks. There are thick kelp beds and steep cliff walls on the inside. A wave here does not peak and fade; it jacks straight up, instantly, as the swell hits an underwater rock shelf. There is no shoulder-hopping on this massive, walling pointbreak. You're committed to a long ride or a long underwater thrashing.

Red Bull hired me to manage the water safety for the surfers, photo boats, and spectators of its second Big Wave Africa Surfing Contest. Alongside the elite international men's club of big-wave surfing, I watched the swell models for three weeks as the surfers watched me. I can read eyes, and for this time period, I read from some: "I don't trust a 40-year-old mom with my safety in the hungry ocean." But that's okay. Gender initiation, like trust, is earned, not gifted, in this league.

At Todos Santos in 1998, during the inaugural Reef Big Wave World Championships, I earned it, charging the pit twenty-four times, pulling out one worked-over surfer after another. I pulled a beaten-up, half-drowned Carlos Burle out of two back-to-back death situations. I saw a deep respect, gratitude, and relief in his eyes. I've never paid dues like that, and maybe there will always be this degree of separation in our bond. He gave me a kiss after the rescue and the nickname *Menina* (girl). He now insists that I watch him whenever we're at the same spot.

The waiting period for the Red Bull contest came and went with no contestable swell. A lot of these guys had traveled a long way, at their expense, and went home disappointed. Brad Gerlach headed to Jeffrey's Bay to console himself, while Mike Parsons and Grant Washburn returned to California. I decided to stay in hopes that a predicted swell would materialize. Four days after the waiting period ended, a swell came. Only the Cape Town crew and Hawaiian Jamie Sterling were still there.

I'd spent six winters hunting elusive monster-sized waves around the world. And here it was rattling the ground underneath me and cracking and booming in the air. With sponsorship from Red Bull, Droomers Yamaha, Gath Headgear, and K38 Water Safety, I volunteered my rescue boat services for the crew.

Outside the lineup, a dozen men jumped out of the 66-foot *Nauticat* boat and paddled to the peak. Two lifeguards piloting Gemini inflatable boats spotted from the channel. I sat in the channel on my WaveRunner® going through my usual routine of timing the interval between waves, calculating wave speed, eyeing the currents, and watching the men as they bobbed on their 10-foot boards, waiting to see who was next. I shadowed the repeat offenders. My livelihood and reputation is built on their troubles.

From the channel I watched the show: brothers Conn and Cris Bertish simultaneously dropped into a monster. Conn, unaware that Cris was behind him, stalled deep into a cavernous tube. Cris yelled, "Nooooo, I'm coming through," then plowed into his brother. They both got pitched onto the reef and I went after them. Next, Justin Strong bombed through a barrel, escaping with the wave spit. Cass Collier took the following wave, dropping wide-eyed down a huge face. Later, I saw what looked like a swatted gnat rushing on the wind of a giant's backhand. It was Sterling, driving with insane speed on a late takeoff. He clutched both his rails as he skipped and bounced over the troublesome texture. By 11 A.M., I'd made thirty-five rescues. The boys were still charging even though the waves were hard to read and acting freak-ish—doubling up and going lopsided with the bottoms dropping out below sea level.

Then it was Ian Armstrong's turn. Armstrong, the 1999 ISA Team World Champion big-wave surfer from South Africa, positioned himself deep in-side—a risky spot, as only kelp and craggy rocks separated him from the cliffs. He looked back at a train of eleven waves and eyed the third and larg-est one. I was watching him, but I had a different vantage of the wave, which raised the hair on my skin. The waves were coming in at twenty-six mph. They were explosive, violent, and deafening, with sixteen-second intervals between them. If Ian wrecked, he would have less than sixteen seconds to find his way to the surface, and I'd have the remainder of those seconds to find him, get him on my sledless WaveRunner®, and get back to the channel.

A week prior, I'd had dinner with Ian, his wife, and their three children. When Ian was out of the room, his wife said, "These waves are serious and dangerous. Shawn, we're glad you're here. We'll be on the cliff watching." I told her that I would do my best. I have another line for the contest surfers: Rescuers on WaveRunners® are fallible resources, especially in big condi-tions.

"Fallible" is an easier word than "death." One wave can retire these ath-letes, but nobody uses the D-word. It carries pressure and doesn't feel right. When Ian is out there, his thoughts are on death's obverse—survival and gratitude for the ocean's gifts. And when he's inland, his thoughts are on gar-dening, painting, raising his kids, and teaching at his surf school. At dinner, Ian was mostly a listener. He receded and became introspective a few times, and he spoke only from the heart. Now here he was scrabbling vertical over the top of a forty-foot face, and then another—placing me on total red alert. Even with my experience pulling people out of trouble at Maverick's, Killers, and Teahupoo, even with all my training at cold and nasty Cape Disappoint-ment, I felt entirely inconsequential watching these waves march forward. They're heavy like liquid concrete and nothing can stop them. When you sit in the channel at a spot like this, you're terrified of your engine stalling out. When you sit in the lineup, you are seeking life with a blazing indifference to it. One must go with definite intention.

Ian spun his board around, and I protested in prayer: "Not this one. Please, God, not this one." I guess God answered that prayer with a "No." Ian paddled hard and stood up at the crest, but the wave held its breath, then released him into a massive buckle. He fell straight off the ledge. Dungeons cracked on his head, and sent him twenty-five feet below. His orange board tombstoned upright at the surface for one second, and then it went under.

I saw all of this before it happened; instinctively, I pulled throttle and positioned myself on the backside of that spilling wave. The gallery screamed. That was the last human sound I heard before entering the roar. I held my breath along with Ian and rode deep inside by Seal Island, near a kelp bed where I thought he would surface. The boiling water lent a syrupy slow motion to time. "Stay here. Stay here," I told myself as a twenty-foot wall of water cascaded from the break zone. Then, five feet to my left, Ian's nose poked out of the white soup. He blinked with a look of sheer terror, then screamed, "I can't feel my feet." Then he was gone. I'd stayed too long. The next wave loomed, and I had to take it head-on or I'd lose Ian.

I positioned bow first into the wave; it was the second most frightening experience in twenty years of professional riding. Backing off the throttle, I relaxed to let the craft take the transfer of speed. As I crested the lip, I separated from the WaveRunner®. In the air I saw the gallery of boats. They were so far away. Were they watching? On my wrist I wear a lanyard that kills the engine if I become separated from the machine. It popped, and the red coil flung and wrapped around my thigh. I landed femur first on the gunwale, and then spilled into the water. Stung, I climbed back on. Ian was paralyzed. I had one chance to get him before he drowned.

I used my emergency lanyard, betting the house in all the ways I train to avoid. I calculated where Ian would come up. I could feel him underneath me. I moved a few feet ahead and turned myself around on the seat so that I faced the back of the craft. He cleared the surface for the second time, no arms above water, just a face screaming at me: "I can't feel my legs or my arms. My children! My children!"

I grabbed his wetsuit with both hands and pulled until his face was pressed into the back seat. He was slumped, motionless, but yelling about his children, his legs, and his wife in an indelible, complete moment. The next wave was bearing on us, eliminating valuable terrain. I wrapped my thighs

Shawn Alladio rescues Ian Armstrong after a paralyzing wipeout at Dungeons, Cape Town, South Africa. (Photo, Brenton Geach)

around his upper torso to secure him. With my left hand I grabbed his wet-suit; with my right I found the throttle. We accelerated facing backwards, watching a huge wall of white water surge and gobble at Ian's limp feet. We sped through the pit and the inside section to the channel where Dungeons' voice groaned and tragic possibilities loomed as we got him to our Gemini inflatable boat. I put him back into the water, to relax and breathe, then we packaged him for transport onto the *Nauticat*.

Soon after seeing Ian, the boys decided it was time to call it a day. I had made sixty-four rescues and was getting cold and hungry. Back in Hout Bay, we all jumped on the *Nauticat* where Ian was lying on his back. Under a doctor's supervision, he was moving his fingers and feet, slowly recovering from temporary paralysis. The crew exchanged stories like excited groms, bouncing up and down, gesturing wildly in the replays of their rides. Soon an impromptu awards ceremony began. Ian took first prize in the hold-down and wipeout categories, as the boys, in full stoke, shouted, "Ian! Ian! Ian!"

"Any words about the wipeout?" I asked him.

"It was bad," he said laconically.

The Cape Town papers published photos of the rescue with headlines that called me an "Angel of Mercy" and "Guardian Angel." This sensationalism was disquieting, slightly off the mark—I'd prefer Hellwoman.

Lesson Six

RAN ELFASSY

It was Christmas Day. My wife, Delian, and I were learning how to surf. We'd just completed the fifth of our six introductory lessons at the Easy Beach surfing guesthouse in Ahangama, Sri Lanka. We ordered pre-dinner drinks and enjoyed the sunset from the porch. The waves crashed and lapped against the shore.

Two traveling surfers, Ollie and Matt, joined us. They ordered pints of Lion lager and welcomed our surf-related questions. After a few tales of their wave exploits, Matt held up his glass and looked right at me.

He warned, "Don't forget that every surfer's got a story. We all have a story about the wave that was almost too big, the rip that was almost too fierce, the call that was almost too close." I laughed and reminded him that mine was the story of a thirty-two-year-old man vacationing in Sri Lanka, a beginner. I wasn't about to go chase big waves. The head-high peelers greeting us each day were all I wanted.

Easy Beach was owned by a Norwegian hippie named Oystein. Three years ago, he'd sold his auto body shop in Norway and permanently moved to southern Sri Lanka. With the cold behind him and his beautiful lodge built, he was now living his surf dream. Early, on the morning of our final lesson, Oystein was already in his board shorts and rash vest. His blond mane blew faintly in the breeze as he sipped at a glass of Sri Lankan milk tea. He wished Delian and me a great sixth lesson, finished his milk, then jumped on his bike and pedaled off to his favorite break, his board held under his arm and the sun on his back.

Yannick, our laid-back French surf teacher, showed up in his van. My wife and I climbed over the boards to our seats. Already inside was Akalan, Yannick's Sri Lankan assistant, and Sophia, a Swedish beginner along for the day. Everyone was beaming, talking about yesterday's perfect Christmas waves and bright full moon. Yannick reviewed the day's lesson. He spoke about popping up and taking the drop, while Delian and I coated our calves with sun block. The van grumbled down the coastal road, which seethed with bikes, people, cows, *tuk-tuks* and *Tata* trucks.

We parked in the sparse grasses in front of Weligama Beach, and Yannick turned from the front seat to hand out our rash vests. Red for me and Yannick, white for Delian and Sophia. Akalan gave us a smile, pulled out a newspaper, and told us he would wait in the van.

We each grabbed a longboard. The path to the sand led through coconut palms and morning glories. I skipped across the hot, bright, sand fly-infested beach right into the knee-deep water. I put on my leash. Delian and I stretched out in the water. The sun was bright and the sea was calm. Leaning in close, Delian gave me a squeeze and kissed my neck. Biting gently at her earlobe, I said, "Don't forget to put on your leash."

Yannick walked into the water and called out, "Who's got more quarters? Looks like the wave machine's shut down." I tugged my board back to me and paddled out over the morning's tiny surf. The four of us lined up and scanned the flat ocean. I splashed some water onto Delian.

We spoke of yesterday's perfect green head-high faces. We had learned to read the horizon, prepare for sets, anticipate a good wave, paddle and launch. I wondered how this whole world, this unbelievable fun, had eluded me for so long. Now, as we bobbed through the last surfing lesson of our trip, Delian and I stared out at the waveless sea and felt let down.

"No matter," said Yannick, "just take a small wave when it comes and practice your launch. Remember, quick and smooth."

I sat up on my board and looked around. The sky was cloudless, open and wide. Two boys were playing on the beach, screaming taunts in Sinhalese. A school of small fish skipped through the ocean's surface, flashing silver just over twenty feet away. Four white egrets sailed low over the water past us toward the small island in the middle of the bay.

"Hey, you see that?" I called to the others and nodded to the shore. When we had entered there was a bright sand beach. Now, the water covered the

Stilt fisher at Weligama Beach before the tsunami. (Photo, Colin Brenchley)

sand and seemed to be slowly creeping toward the morning glories. Soon, the water stretched into the trees on the side of the road. The two young boys were now splashing loudly in and out of the rising shallows. "You think it could be a full-moon tide?"

"I don't know," Delian said. "It's pretty crazy, though."

"Sophia, you see that? The water's reaching the road!" I said.

"Stay away from the shore," warned Yannick in an uncharacteristically serious tone. "Make sure you stay away from the shore. As long as you're on your board, you'll be okay. I'm going to see about Akalan and the van. I'll be back. Don't come ashore."

The current quickly took Yannick right into the trees and out of our sight. Sophia, Delian, and I paddled as hard as we could out into the bay. Looking over my shoulder, to where the road should have been, I saw the van. It was drifting and bobbing, panning onto the opposite side of the road and into the jungle trees. Yannick had disappeared. "What's going on?" I demanded as I paddled harder and harder, keeping pace with Delian and

Sophia. We'd made it deep into the bay. The water kept rising behind us. It pushed into beach houses, smashing out the windows. Resting fishing boats were set adrift. "Delian," I yelled, "what's going on?"

Our frantic gazes darted from shore to horizon as we paddled hard to put distance between us and the chaos on shore. A few hundred feet into the bay, we stopped and looked back but saw nothing. A woman wailed, wood cracked, and men yelled out from the trees.

"What should we do?" I demanded.

"I don't know, but Yannick said stay away from shore!" cried Delian.

Just then the current switched directions. Brown silty water drained off the land. We spun around and paddled against the murky flow to keep from getting swept out to sea.

"Come on, Ran! Keep up," Delian yelled. My shoulders were sore from the past few days. I fell back in the streaking current as we struggled toward shore. Palm trees, doors, wood planks, beach chairs, branches, leaves, Coke bottles, plastic bags, dung, foam, and other muck from shore streaked by. I paddled and pushed against the garbage as the deep green ocean gave way to the chocolate silt scooped from the coast. I saw Delian stumble to her feet. I stepped into the current and found that I'd been paddling in less than a foot of fast flowing water. Beside and around us, the ocean floor was exposed, veined with rivulets of water still draining off the land.

Covered in grit, I lifted my board and trotted toward Delian. A red rash vest came running out of the trees, carrying two halves of a snapped board. Yannick, pale and shaken, yelled, "But you must—you must stay away from the shore! It's too dangerous. Stay in the water! Another surge will come."

He eyed us and the horizon. About two miles behind, at the mouth of the bay, a line of foaming green water was swelling. "Quickly, make it to higher ground," he pointed to the island a couple of hundred yards out in the bay. Minutes ago that island had jutted from the water, now it was bare to the elements on the exposed sea-floor; hardly an island at all. Yannick hurried back to Akalan and the van, which had been smashed into the trees.

The distant swell approached us. Our panic rose. Delian and I joined Sophia in the run across the slippery seabed back toward the water. The rivulets were a foot deep when we began. As we got closer to the exposed island, the rivulets grew deeper and their currents sucked harder. Sophia somehow managed to plow ahead through the mud. Delian and I were caught in a section of surging currents. A little upstream, the flood waters caught Delian's surfboard and pulled her down. "Lift it!" I yelled, "You have to keep it out of the water!"

"I'm trying! I'm getting tired!" Her words were raw and cutting.

In a moment of unbridled fear, I undid my leash, tossed my board, and screamed for Delian to do the same. I thought that without our boards we could better continue walking through the currents. She stumbled again and was pulled into the raging silt. My heart raced. She was carried fifteen feet before she found her footing and staggered up covered in mud. As quickly as she stood up, she was pulled in again by her board. This time I jumped in after her. The current was nonnegotiable; it sucked me into deeper water, away from the direction in which it had pulled Delian. I fought to keep my head above the surface, to keep my eyes on the place where I thought she should come up.

Thirty yards away, I saw her board surface in the incoming swell, fins skyward. A splash of blonde hair flashed in the sun. I felt relief as her arm reached over and grabbed a rail. She was okay, I told myself.

A palm tree floated by me, gangly fronds hung from its solid trunk. I grabbed on and screamed for Delian to paddle to shore, not knowing if she could hear me or not. Then a miracle happened. My surfboard drifted by twenty feet away. Two fins pointed up. There was a small nub of hard plastic where the third fin had been sheared off. I let go of the tree trunk and swam hard to my board. I reached the leash, pulled in the line, and then fastened the Velcro strap around my wrist. I climbed onto my board and clutched the rails tight. The choppy current led me out to sea.

I was pushed right past the rocky shore of the island that we'd originally attempted to reach. I turned into the current and paddled for the rocks as hard as I could. Chop came at me from every direction. I had a hard time staying on my board. I let my legs drag for better balance, but they only slammed into floating trees and other debris. I paddled frantically. The island slipped out of my reach. Exhausted and terrified, I gave up hope of reaching land.

I turned back to the open ocean and tried to think. Far off, an empty fishing boat spun 360s in the current. The current pulled me in that direction. I paddled hard until the nose of my board slammed into the boat. A thick piece of rope hung off the rear, and I used it to pull myself aboard. The boat pitched and yawed in the huge waves as I reeled my board in and lashed it to a wooden post. I felt a bit safer in the 25-footer.

Another surge of water came, this one bigger and moving more swiftly than the last. The boat spun and leaned deep in the white-capped current.

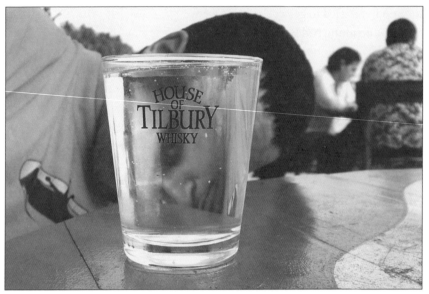

Portrait of the author in Weligama, Sri Lanka, the evening before the tsunami devastated the region. December 25, 2004. (Photo, Delian Gaskell)

I gripped a guide rail and pressed myself into the deck. A triggerfish, huge and dead, spun in an eddy and gently bumped into the boat's hull. Watching the carcass float in the current, I tried to imagine what was going on by the beach and how I would find my way back.

I stood up to take an inventory of my situation: a locked engine room, old wooden poles with nets and hooks at the end, but nothing I could use to pick, smash or pry the small brass padlock keeping me from the engine. I paced the boat, holding on and trying to find the solution to my desperate riddle. Thinking that one of the poles would make a good flagging signal, I lifted it and noticed a small key held fast to a peg with a length of fishing tackle.

The key fit the padlock. A smile crossed my face as the door opened. I peered into the old, greased-up machinery. I had no idea, not a clue, as to how to start the motor. There was no switch, no pull cord, no throttle, nothing but an old, grease-bathed hunk of metal. I screamed and slammed my palm against the doorframe, holding on as the ship leaned deep. After the pitching calmed, I howled again and kicked at the doorframe.

I scrambled back up to the deck and found a rusty trident anchor in the bow. I dropped anchor and tried to sense if it hit the bottom. I tied the nylon rope to a post on deck. The shore was now more than a half-mile away. I squinted and tried to get a glimpse of what was going on. I sat down and held on to the creaking rudder. I told myself that Delian was safe. I talked it out: *of course she made it, she's the strongest woman I know, she made it, she must be onshore.* Looking to the far-off shoreline, I repeated: *Delian is safe.* In reality, I had no idea if she made it to shore or drowned trying. Regardless, *Delian is safe* remained my mantra.

For more than two hours, I rose to scream at far away dots only to sit down again in despair. There were other boats like mine in the bay, little black mites on the horizon, too far away to reveal signs of life. Every once in a while, I would take a breath and start screaming again in futility. I was still unsure whether or not the anchor had set or was just dragging along below. The sea was alternately rising and falling. Every once in a while I would angle the rudder to coax the boat away from waves that were suddenly slamming against shallow reefs. I saw a far-off boat moving along the turbulent ocean. I waved my surfboard to get its attention and howled as the little boat puttered away and out to sea. I sat down again and replayed the image of my wife being pulled into the silt.

In my shock, a fracture developed between my hopeful thoughts and my desperate actions. There is no video, but if there were, it would show two hours of a man hopping in and out of the shade, muttering, taking off his rash vest and waving it at the shore, pulling and pushing the rudder, staring at the engine, toying with fishing gear strewn over the deck, tying and untying the anchor rope, staring out to sea, staring toward shore, and yelling himself hoarse.

The water eventually calmed. I stood up again to scan the horizon. The boat that recently passed was headed straight toward me. As it neared, I screamed "*Hundai!* Thank you!" and "Help!" to the driver. He yelled back in Sinhalese when he saw that I was going to leap from my boat into his. He confirmed that my anchor was secure then let me board.

In this small boat packed tight with bodies, we motored through the flotsam and garbage, floating trees, broken boat hulls, and other refuse to investigate intact ships. These were the ships I had screamed to as I spun in the current. In one boat, we picked up two bewildered fishermen, two guys in their twenties. Their teeth flashed white as yells erupted between them and the man driving our boat. We were a mile into the wide bay. After securing their boat as best as we could, we finally turned back to shore. Everyone aboard stared at my bright rash guard and shorts. My surfboard knocked erratically at my feet.

As we neared the shoreline, the sea reeled and threatened to toss us on the rocks like a lidless crate of live crabs. The driver backed in slowly. The sea inhaled and we bottomed out. The ocean surged back and crashed us into a standing palm tree. I jumped out, ecstatic to feel solid ground beneath my feet. I thanked the men who rescued me, grabbed my surfboard and ran.

I sprinted up the paved slope and onto the coastal road that led to Weligama Beach. The reality of what had happened on shore came to me sharp and swift, like waking from one nightmare to another; this one more horrific than the first. My restless two hours on the boat were a violent see-saw of flooding and death for those on shore. *Delian is safe* remained my desperate assumption as I ran past the hundreds of Sri Lankan faces. We stared at each other, shocked and dazed. I later learned that half of the coastal people were drowned or sucked out to sea never to be seen again. Half.

I ran on the hot pavement. The buildings looked like they'd been bombed then wiped clean. Unlike images of a war zone that feature fire, soot, and ash, everything on this coastal road was flattened and washed. No dirt, no dust, just slabs of shattered walls and strewn things with wiped faces. Everything was flattened, except for the buses and cars, which were either heaved onto their sides or folded around tree trunks.

I jogged past families wailing at the foundations of their lost homes. Everything these people called their own was strewn like splintered props across the landscape. Two men my age, brothers perhaps, stood silently over a drowned woman, a woman old enough to be their mother. A mongrel stood where a house used to be. He howled for all who were left living.

I knew that I still had a long way to run to get to Weligama Beach. I repeated to myself that Delian was okay. But the pit in my gut deepened as I looked at the destruction. I ran over shattered plates, bent cutlery, and picture frames; past smashed cars and half-ton boulders strewn on the road; and by corpses—still wet, but with gray skin and bulging veins. I ran my way through groups, people crying over the dead, people staring at the dead— hushed voices all around. I kept running, running back to where we had entered the sea, each step bringing me closer to the possibility of a life without Delian. Life without her, the looming thought I tried to deny with each step but which crept ever nearer, was a nightmare that would always end with Delian slipping, falling into a cruel current that I was powerless to save her from. What would I do without her, if I survived and she didn't?

Then my breath was cut, cut to the quick. I saw her familiar step and the flag of her white rash vest approaching down the road. She began running to me, both of us doing the same tip-toe dance between shards of glass, wood, and rocks. There was nothing to say, nothing we could say. We rushed into an embrace. For the second time that day, language failed. The first time was when we were separated, the second was this moment when we held each other, shocked and disbelieving. Delian and I cried and were quickly held tighter by Yannick, Akalan and Sophia. Our little group, each with their own trauma and slice of the whole, looked at each other in awe, crying, incoherent and uncertain. In the calamity of our surroundings, one thing was clear: we were the lucky ones.

We made our way through the grotesque panoply and carnage, creeping along the ravaged miles back to the guesthouse, past giant boulders strewn like marbles across the road and tragic, silent train carriages swept off their tracks into the jungle below. We kept a wary, weary eye on the sea, as everyone feared another deadly surge.

Easy Beach guesthouse was structurally intact, though listing. Delian and I braved the upper floors to gather our things. The building pitched and rolled with the wind. It gave us vertigo. We descended the stairs and found ourselves next to Oystein, owner of a now broken guesthouse. Only a few hours ago, the elegant courtyard had been furnished with tables, chairs, counters, refrigerators, three motorcycles, and display cases filled with wax and gear. Now it was hollow. Nothing. Not a chair, not a shard of glass, not a torn scrap from the stacks of surfing magazines. The motorcycle Delian and I had rented to ride down to southern Sri Lanka was gone. It was either drifting at the bottom of the sea or had been carried high and far into the jungle.

"I'm so sorry. Oystein, what are you going to do?" I asked.

His bright eyes, now forlorn and almost washed out, looked past me. "I'm finished," he sighed, his beautiful dream collapsed.

"Have Matt and Ollie turned up?" I asked.

"Yes," he said. "They moved into the village temple, high in the jungle."

Shaking his hand and feeling helpless, I told him that if he rebuilt surfer's paradise, I would spread the word about his establishment. Shouldering our packs, Delian and I left Oystein to his fate and headed for higher ground. We spent a sleepless night in a jungle villa, hidden by trees and safe from the waves. We held each other tight as we heard the distant surf crash against the beach.

Turning her face to mine, Delian said, "Up on the roof of that house, I kept waiting and waiting, looking for your red shirt, hoping to see you paddling back. I felt like I'd been waiting so long, so long that I couldn't possibly wait any longer. But then I thought that if you died, if you never came back, I would be waiting forever."

That we would return to Sri Lanka was a promise we did not need to make; it was a given. Staring at a midnight ceiling, waves calling from beyond the trees, I remembered the cold beers of the previous evening and Matt's promise that every surfer has a story.

Baptism with Bradshaw

JOE DOGGETT

The rent-a-car clock read 10 P.M. and Ken Bradshaw was not home. This was a disconcerting revelation for a Texan standing against the black roar of heavy surf on the North Shore.

Sea mist hung in the night air as I stared at the note pinned to the door: "Doggett, I had to go to Honolulu. Big surf tomorrow! Make yourself at home."

Bradshaw, who lives at Sunset Beach, is one of the most respected big-wave riders and surfboard shapers in the islands. He was born in Houston and learned to surf in Texas, and I was relying on his Lone Star roots for counsel and support.

The North Shore of Oahu is no place for amateurs, regardless of origin. Winter storms originating in the Aleutians drive thick swell across the Pacific. These bands of energy focus on the reefs and produce the waves by which all others are measured. The North Shore is intimidating but compelling, terrifying but beautiful, and stands ready for any surfer with conviction.

Some, such as Bradshaw, arrive young, fit, and restless in 1972 and claim a lifestyle. Others arrive old, late, and nervous in 1990 and wonder where the hell everybody went.

"Hello! Anybody here?"

I pushed open the unlocked door and carried my duffel and board bag inside. A single lamp illuminated the room. In the empty corner, below a wall rack for surfboards, was a mattress and a heap of fresh linen. Surfers do not stand on ceremony. I was lucky to have a pillow.

I pulled my board from the travel bag, an 8' 6" Bradshaw Hawaii, a thick semi-gun. I had tested the board twice in slow, small Galveston waves, and it felt stiff and frustrated.

The silent board seemed to glow with a core energy in the low light. I gripped the rail and felt the positive weight, hoping to leach confidence from the clean foil.

Sleep under the shadow of the waiting board came fitfully. The muffled boom and pound of the rolling surf beckoned. The North Shore is the outpost of renegades and one-eyed jacks—the hard-core surfers. You do not go to the North Shore as a tourist. You go to ride the largest waves of your life.

"Get up! We've got a swell!" Bradshaw kicked the mattress. He had arrived from town during the early morning.

Bright sun creased the window and illuminated the tall palms. The fronds were already being tossed by the gusting trades which funnel from the mountains. We walked the narrow, shrouded trail, stepping around the sharp cones of Australian pines to "check it out." The surf check had been Bradshaw's ritual for fifteen years.

Bradshaw's house backs the beach at the reef known as Kammieland, a name given by vanguard surfers in honor of Kammie's Market, a sagging general store located across the two-lane Kamehameha Highway.

You stand on the beach and look to the left, down the high, white berm of crushed shell and check Monster Mush. Beyond, framed under a morning rainbow, are Rocky Point, Gas Chamber, and Pipeline. Far in the distance, reaching gray into the ocean, is the foreboding headland of Kaena Point.

Look to the right, across the sparkle of a green and blue channel, and you face the wind-blown peaks of Sunset Beach. The mountain breeze carries the scent of plumeria across the panorama of rich wave fields. This is Bradshaw's real estate, the wild and raw Hawaii that the tourists have not trampled and the Japanese have not purchased.

A neighbor, Roger Erickson, sipped a cup of coffee under a palm and viewed the ocean. He wore only a pair of faded board shorts. You could have bounced an ax from his chest. The forty-something Erickson, like the thirty-something Bradshaw, was one of the elite big-wave riders of the North Shore. They knew what it was like to stare down a thirty-footer.

"Definitely coming up," confirmed Erickson.

"It's a northwest swell," said Bradshaw. "It's filling in behind the dropping north swell. Weather service was predicting eight to twelve feet by this afternoon. What would you say now, six?"

"If that. But it was smaller at dark. Definitely coming up."

I watched as a wedging wave gathered and pitched off Sunset Point. The thin trail of a speeding board traced down the long drop, then up the steep face. The wave appeared huge.

"Six?" I pointed. "That was a twelve-foot wave!"

Bradshaw pulled his square jaw and looked down his nose. "This is the North Shore." He gave my wide-eyed stare a hard study. "Maybe we should get out there before it gets too big for you."

We retraced the trail. Six!

Bradshaw has more boards than I have fishing rods, and I've been a professional fishing writer for thirty years. He rattled around his walk-in locker for the right equipment. I felt a flutter of nervous pulse and wandered to the car.

I had no real reason for going there other than it was parked in the opposite direction of the beach. The trunk was backed against a thorny tangle of kiawe brush—like mesquite back home. I rooted inside, ostensibly searching for a bar of surf wax or a bottle of sunscreen.

"Doggett! Where are you? Get out here!"

I crawled from behind the car, brushing twigs and leaves from my shoulders. He was holding his chosen board and scowling—and Bradshaw can scowl with the best of them. "Where have you been?"

"I thought I lost something."

"Yeah, your nerve." He paused, softening. "Look, a guy from California drowned yesterday down at Rocky Point. Do you want to go out or not?"

I took a shaky breath. "Yeah, that's what I came for." A greatness of surfing is that the terrible beauty has no limitation. The weekend golfer will not go to the Masters, and the club tennis player will not compete at Wimbledon, but any surfer, like any tribal warrior, can face a roaring lion.

We knelt on the beach and waxed the boards. Another surfer strolled up and stopped. He was not a big name, but he moved with the lazy grace of an expert. He was one of the faceless legions drawn each winter to the big waves of Hawaii. Bradshaw nodded an introduction, adding that I was, "a friend from Houston."

"You're always inviting those Texans over here. Do any of them survive?"

Bradshaw shrugged. "Hey, Don, how was Bali?"

"It was great, man. Padang was perfect, just cranking." I refrained from critiquing my most recent session in waist-high chop at Galveston's Flagship Pier.

Apparently the waves were not large enough, or the barrels were not opening wide enough, to suit the discriminating Don this morning. Bradshaw and I carried our boards to the rushing, surging edge of the ocean. Another wind-blown set detonated across the outside reefs, first at Sunset then at Kammie's. It was larger, meatier, than the previous sets.

"Definitely coming up," confirmed Bradshaw. "I can't give it eight, but maybe seven; see, it's starting to move out from the point. Sunset might be a bit tricky for you, shifting and all, so maybe we'll stick here at Kammie's."

I was jittery. Bradshaw attempted to allay my trepidation with temptation.

"Hey, check it out down the beach. I think I can set you up with her."

A gorgeous blonde was walking our way. She could have stepped from the cover of any swimsuit issue. I stared.

"No, no, not her. Down there."

Fleeting fantasy was replaced with glum reality. "Down there" was a rather matronly woman grubbing for pukka shells. She did not look like a Malibu Barbie, not even the mother of a Malibu Barbie.

I sagged, feeling the sun on my bald spot. "I dunno, Ken, maybe later." Bradshaw was frowning at my board.

"Geez, what is it?"

"I don't like that tail. Wrong design."

"This is a hell of a time to tell me the board's no good! What do you mean, 'wrong design?' You made it!"

"Aw, it's a squash tail. I was into squash tails last year. A rounded pin is better—more speed out of your bottom turn."

"Ken, I don't think the problem will be needing more speed or—"

"Let's do it!"

With a sudden whoop and crash, we were committed. I had no time to think or balk. Bradshaw charged the shorebreak, vaulting over the rush of foam. I followed, digging hard to clear the riot of turbulence, and the big board moved with authority across the confusion. We paddled over strange and swelling humps; they were not chop but restless surges. The North Shore was coming up, and mighty forces were at play.

Kammie's is the weak sister to Sunset, with less power and a more well-defined lineup, but the peak would be revered most anywhere else in the

Ken Bradshaw surfing Sunset Beach, North Shore, Oahu. December 1980. (Photo, Rick Doyle)

world. It's still the North Shore and, as my wild stare confirmed, bloody, freaking Sunset is right over there.

The distance to the outside was deceiving. We pulled up several hundred yards off the beach, where a cluster of waiting surfers marked the edge of the reef. The water was chopped and riffled from the gusting trades but clear and green. You could see the shifting bottom and the gray-brown contours of coral heads.

"Line up here," said Bradshaw. "If a set comes that you don't want, paddle for the channel right over there. If a set comes that you do want, paddle toward it; that lets you check out the first peak as it starts lifting, and it puts you in deeper water for an earlier takeoff. If you decide to go, dig hard; and if the side-off spray is bad, tilt your head to the right and squint your eyes. Whatever you do, don't get hung up in the lip."

We floated, bobbing amid the running chop. It was a fine morning, with bright beach sun accenting rain clouds against the far mountains.

"Set's coming."

Dark lines slid across the Sunset channel as the set of waves focused on Kammie's reef. The first swell gathered with frightening urgency, building and wedging. It became enormous. Heavy spray crackled from the top.

"Go, go!" chanted Bradshaw. I slid prone and paddled hard, sighting down the huge and sloping face. Up-rushing wind blew spray; blinded and scared, I aborted the takeoff and slid back as the wave threw forward. When I looked up, blinking through the salty sting, Bradshaw was gone. He had taken the wave.

I turned and felt a strange mix of exhilaration and fear. The next wave was looming—too big, too fast, too much. I paddled farther out, barely skipping over the lifting crest with a blow of spray and a gasp of breath.

The next wave was bending onto the reef. It was a legitimate North Shore set wave, rising with awesome and undeniable presence. I, alone, waited in the path of the peak. This was it—somehow I knew it would be a lonely moment.

The big board wheeled around and surged, chattering with determined effort. The bottom began falling away, and I sprang up and drove down the steepening face. The speed and distance were incredible; the board that once felt stiff and heavy now seemed like a splinter against the mass and power.

The initial drop and ensuing bottom turn covered the entire distance of a decent beachbreak ride. The board angled up the face, banked from the top, and dropped ahead of the pitching crest. The curling wave was a supercharger of compression that shot the board across the shoulder and into the channel.

Joe Doggett and Ken Bradshaw, North Shore, Oahu, 1990. (Photo courtesy of Joe Doggett)

I sat and panted, dazzled and stunned. How did I get so far so fast? And on what? The clean force of the big wave was a thrill, an ecstasy, that no rule book ever could judge. Bradshaw paddled over. He was smiling. "Not bad," he said. "Sunset's starting to look pretty good. You want to give it a go now?"

I looked north across the sun-sparkle and measured an onslaught of pitching peaks. Plumes of spray lifted high and the waves beckoned with regimented precision. "Let's do it!"

We began the long paddle across the channel. Again, the distance was deceiving. The climbing sun beat down, and I paused several times to rest—not a good sign. Bradshaw glanced back.

"You okay?"

"Yeah, just give me a minute."

The water turned from blue to green as we approached the vast Sunset Reef. We stopped and sat. A cluster of fifteen or twenty surfers waited about a hundred yards away.

"Not many guys out yet," Bradshaw said. A set gathered across the out-side shelf and the pack began scrambling and scratching. "There goes Michael Ho. There's Darrick Doerner."

Ho and Doerner! The big names legitimized the day. Watching from the edge of the channel was like viewing an IMAX surf movie. This was the real deal—pumping Sunset! I shifted and squirmed as the pointed nose of the board aimed at the waves. I took a shallow breath. Bradshaw studied my antsy behavior.

"Okay, I'm going to paddle over there and catch a few. You sit right here and watch. Keep those houses lined up and you'll be safe here in the channel. If you decide you want in, paddle on over but stay on this side. I'll be looking for you. And remember what I said: If you decide to go—go! Don't hesitate. And try not to drop in on anybody."

He spun and clawed like a lean, mean crocodile across the water. The pack adjusted as he entered the arena and several B-teamers drifted away.

Sitting alone, eyeing the distant houses, I felt the earlier resolve crumbling. The waves looked awfully thick, awfully fast, awfully powerful. And, as the paddle confirmed, my conditioning was marginal at best. I felt ten years too late.

Like the fat rat caught in the corner, I didn't want the cheese anymore; I just wanted my foot out of the trap. I looked up: *Please, just give me one wave and I'll go in!* Mighty Sunset started dropping. A prolonged lull settled across the reef, then two or three weak sets pushed through. The peaks were several feet overhead, almost crumbling as the frustrated surfers slashed and tore on pintailed guns. Several quit and proned to the beach.

I conjured the confident ride at Kammie's, resurrecting go-for-it momentum as another small set gathered off Sunset Point. Bradshaw caught the best peak and worked the peeling wall far inside. His head and shoulders climbed and dropped with clean speed. It looked fun.

I slowly stroked deeper over the reef and halted about fifty yards from the nearest surfers. The board drifted amid the running chop, and the bright morning was warm and reassuring. I craned to see Bradshaw paddling back out, then someone whistled at me.

I turned to face the Pacific.

Several monstrous blue-green hills were swinging wide of the pack and rising across my alley of reef. The other surfers were visibly irritated—the best set of the morning was aiming at a tourist.

I was terrified. I started paddling out, angling hard for the channel, but Sunset was having none of this chicken-hearted tactic. The massive humps blotted the path to deeper water. I rose over the first, leaving frantic, ragged punctuations.

The second wave was smaller, almost glassy. It steepened across the reef in predictable fashion.

This is the one, my wave! Catch it and go in a winner! Catch it and you can grow old telling the boys back at Galveston how you dominated Sunset Beach!

Surging adrenaline erased all fatigue. Two-armed digs pulled me forward as the wave lifted underneath. The slope was massive and nothing but open space hung below. Then, as the takeoff should have accelerated into certain glory, the wave backed off. The board hung at the top then slid down the backside of the unbroken swell.

I sat with my head down and exhaled with a whoosh. Then I turned again. My initial reaction was: *I'm a dead man.*

The next wave looked twice as large. It was fifty yards outside and already drawing and feathering with undeniable mass. The green face blotted the sky.

I was in the crucible of the classic Sunset horror story—caught inside. I sat with nowhere to go as the roaring crest came down, cascading almost in slow motion. In a final knee-jerk reaction, I "turned turtle," flipping the board and wrapping my arms and legs around it in a death grip.

The Earth slipped its axis. I have no idea what happened. The impact drove the board down and around, hurtling toward the beach. I surfaced, still locked around the rails amid the hissing and boiling of a billion white bubbles.

Bradshaw was paddling with serious intent from the channel. He didn't know whether to curse or laugh. "I can't believe you rolled that wave!"

"Hell, I was too scared to let go!"

"Well, here comes the next one. Let go now and let the leash take it. Dive for the bottom."

The rumbling, heaving white water was bearing down. I followed Bradshaw's lead and dove. The turbulence churned overhead, grabbing the board and dragging me underwater. When the tension subsided I reached for the leash and pulled hand-over-hand to the surface. Bradshaw was waiting.

"Here comes another one. You're doing fine; we're staying in the white water and it's pushing us to the beach. Take a good breath and dive again."

When the final wave subsided we were floating near the inside reef known as Val's. The sloping white beach and rustling green palms seemed almost close enough to embrace. I realized what the survivors of a shipwreck must feel like.

"I'm way out of my league," I said, gagging and choking, pulling myself back onto the board. "I need to get out of here."

"I figured as much." Bradshaw smiled. "Well, you gave it a shot. You almost had that first one. Hey, here comes a reform. Why don't you catch it and ride to the beach."

I turned. The reform from the first wave of a new set was approaching. The swell was head-high, with a gentle roll of dissipating white water along the top. It looked stately and forgiving, like the combers in the old Waikiki photos.

I slid prone and took several digs, then stood and turned. The board trimmed right, gaining speed across the peeling wall, then I cut back and rode the bounding, bouncing white water to the beach.

The sloping sand and straining grit felt excellent. I unstrapped the stressed, stretched ankle leash and wound it around the fins and looked across the water. I had my wave at Sunset—more or less, kinda sorta, well, not really. Screw it; at least I went out.

A big set hit like cannon fire across the outside reef. Erickson was right: definitely coming up.

Bradshaw dropped ahead of an avalanche. His turn was obscured by inshore waves, but he was out there somewhere and in his element. Then he reappeared high on the face, falling with the lip and disappearing again before jetting across the shimmer of green.

The Bradshaw Hawaii board felt strange again under my right arm. It was an Island board. Rough patches of sand clung to the deck and North Shore water dripped from the rail. I turned from the beach and began the long walk back to the rent-a-car.

Three Portraits of Sumatra

MATT GEORGE

The Crucible: The Indian Ocean vs. the Power of Australian Youth

Lance's Rights, Sumatra, 3:57 P.M. It was all building up to something. Something that could only be redeemed by fire. We'd been praying for it all week, and in the end, we paid for our sins.

None of us had any idea how big the surf was. All we knew was that our boat captain kept looking out to the horizon every ten seconds. It was a long dinghy ride in. In the soft late-afternoon light, the big, black backs of the waves were all we could see through the spume of the offshore blast. These black hills mutated and then flexed silver muscles that would gush clouds of leaden spit. Swimming pools of it.

There was a lull as we motored by, dropped off the boys, and set out for shore to establish a beachhead. We still had no idea. Not ten feet from the beach, the four of us in the dinghy turned our gaze toward the lineup. At first sight, we thought it was a cloud. It lumbered in through the mist, an animal sizing up its prey.

The "kids," the hottest seven junior surfers Australia had to offer, were fresh in the lineup, hair dry. They had no idea of her approach. A set hadn't moved through yet. Oblivious, Jay Thompson, 19, was sitting deepest. Nervous, he set himself up for the approaching wave's younger, smaller sister. From our vantage by the beach, we could already see that the bigger animal had started to smoke as the wind tore at its crest. Once we realized it was a wave, things got real quiet between us. The *Neptune*, our mothership a half mile out to sea, sounded her siren twice. The captain was heading for deeper water.

This wave wasn't going to break, it was going to occur. And there wasn't a damn thing any one of us could do about it.

Jay Thompson was already paddling for the first, smaller one. We could hear the hoots from the others as they scrambled up the face. It was taking them a long time. The thing reared up like a cobra. The hoots stopped short. This thing was loading up unnaturally. It couldn't be measured in size, only girth.

Terribly undergunned, Jay sketched into it. The wave bared its fangs and struck. Jay survived to the bottom before the whole Indian Ocean caved in on him like a coal mining accident. The rest of the crew blasted airborne through the lip and flew onto the back of the wave. The offshore wind was so strong that they wouldn't see the monster until it was much too late.

It would be the singularly biggest wave ever seen at Lance's Rights. And when it unloaded itself, lives would be changed. No fool, Western Australian Ry Craike, 17, dove for the bottom. He'd end up staying there for sixty-eight seconds. Nic Muscroft, 19, went for it, punched through vertically, then took the worst ride of his life into the hydraulic jackhammer . . . backwards. Later, he would say he fell so far he had time for two deep breaths. Nic would end up smashing into Josh Kerr, 18, who was pinned against the reef. Luckily, extraordinarily, Josh was still on top of his surfboard, hands on the rails, eyes closed. He would later look at the coral cuts on his knuckles and try to imagine if such a thing was possible. Nic and Josh would surface tangled in each others leashes. Adrenaline flowing, Nic would chip his tooth chewing through his leash to break free.

Jay Quinn, 18, was in no man's land. He dove off his board as the thing detonated onto the soles of his feet. He found things strangely still and quiet. What he didn't know was that he was being sucked up the face underwater. He actually saw trees on shore through the face and later described the instant as being "like some kind of glass elevator to heaven . . . then the world blew up."

Ben Dunn, the youngest at 16, was "trying to stay calm" and trying to get his leash off. He refused to look at the wave until he was free. Too little, too late, he took it right in the chops. Temporarily knocked unconscious, he was washed across the reef into the lagoon, impossibly unhurt, a good seventy yards from the lineup. He was so rattled that when he came to and surfaced,

The largest wave ever seen at Lance's Rights, in Sumatra, broke on Jay Quinn's heels. Onboard the boat, the *Neptune*, an hour after the wave, Jay (pictured above) had not yet said a word. He didn't take his eyes off the lineup until the sun went down. (Photo, Matt George)

he started calling out his own name. He wouldn't remember who he was for a full thirty seconds. His board was later found on the beach, in three pieces.

Shaun Cansdell, 19, rolled like a bowling ball so far in that when he pushed off the bottom for the surface, he hit his head on the bow of the dinghy.

By the time the surge cascaded over our dinghy, 8,000 dollars worth of camera equipment was at the bottom of the sea. Sure, at this very same time, the World Qualifying Series machine was dealing with full-tilt, fifteen-foot Teahupoo. We've all marveled at the photos of Tahiti. Sure, people are towing into sixty-foot waves all over the world. There are bigger waves in the world out there . . . but there are no bigger moments and no bigger hearts.

No veterans, these juniors, these kids, under twenty years old, gathered themselves up and attacked for the remaining hours of daylight. During that time, five other boatloads of surfers would show up to check things out. One of them chock full of B-grade pros. But not one other surfer wanted a piece of it. One by one, the other boats headed out to spots that "could handle the swell better." But everyone knew what that meant.

So our crew surfed it alone. Through torrential squalls, confusing tides, wild currents, through broken boards, broken dreams, and broken courage, they rode, defining a day for the future of surfing. These guys stayed out and made it happen because they wanted it. Not because they were being handed something, but because they wanted it. They wanted that feeling of not backing down but rather giving it a go. Any real Australian carries that desire like a tattoo.

Amazing Grace

A mean mosquito dusk falls over the tattered Sumatran island port of Sikakap. The day is done, the muezzin is calling the faithful over fuzzy speakers that hang from the crooked logs that spike the main drag like a whale's bones. The faithful, prostrate, face Mecca to the west and give thanks in this thankless place. Cerebral malaria and dengue fever will take half of the next generation here before they reach the age of three. This port, hell and gone, is home to a small, bustling wharfside quay that supplies petrol, water, engine parts, lightbulbs, oil, grease, sweat, and the odd prostitute to the wild array of tattered boats that ply these waters, both legal and nefarious. Perched on the edge of the world, if this place were to blow up, disappear from the face of the earth, the first people to care would be the illegal exotic fish dealers that regularly scrape the reefs for the Yakuza bar aquariums back in Tokyo. The

Jay Thompson, 17, in the tube at Lance's Rights. Though no photo exists of the giant wave, this shot gives an idea of the low-tide power the boys were dealing with. Water depth: four feet. (Photo, Matt George)

second to care would be the local, deadly pirates, and a distant third would be the Sumatran Government, which would simply shrug its shoulders and then shake its head once or twice like everyone else.

The last to care would be surfers because to them it is a fuel stop, and if Sikakap blew up, the surfers would shrug their shoulders too, and that would be that. There aren't any waves in this place, and hell, there's always a place around with fuel.

Funny how surfers have become a part of these forgotten places and don't realize it anymore. Like a virus, surfers no longer explore, they exploit. They find new breaks all over the world, take pictures, and lay the infrastructure for the hordes to follow. Once overrun, the surfers jump hosts, finding new places to commoditize, bringing their western influences of greed and selfishness—the strong impulses which drive their obsession to surf in the first place. They bring the worst of their own worlds with them. They sow cultural confusion, then they sell it on t-shirts. It's just the way things are.

And maybe this explains why a pack of Australian junior surfers, some of the hottest on earth, found themselves on shore in Sikakap, sweating in the mean mosquito dusk, sitting in a circle of chairs on the edge of the main drag with some locals who regarded them as Martians. In front of a bare-lightbulbed cigarette shop, they were drinking hot beer, smoking cloves, and plunking out a rousing version of "Amazing Grace" on a handful of ten-dollar guitars they had bought off the locals. For a moment, all of Sikakap stops to listen to this strange brew. Back on board the surfers' tattered boat the Sumatran captain listens, too. He hears this strange song rising over the shanty town of Sikakap, over the open sewers and through the clouds of mosquitoes, past the whale bones. It carries over the quay. He asks his first mate about the song. The first mate doesn't know, but the little girl bicycling home past the cigarette shop knows. She learned it at church. That new Catholic Church that was making her feel so different from her veiled friends. And she can't believe that all these tall white heathens sitting in a circle in front of the cigarette shop know the words to her new favorite song.

Cockfight

Three hundred bucks on Big Red—a veteran of twenty-six bouts. Blood covered its feathers and featherless skin—the scars from the razorsharp beaks that had slashed at him again and again. The cock of the walk. Big Red. Three hundred bucks.

It was a backyard affair on the outskirts of Padang. Illegal as hell. But surfers were there. Seven of them. The best juniors Australia could offer. With money in their fists, they sweated and screamed at the two roosters who fought for turf, fought for food, fought for chicks, fought for it all. They slashed at each other time and again. After three minutes of bloodshed, the owners of the roosters asked the surfers if they wanted the roosters to fight till one quit or till one died. "Death," the surfers said.

And so it went until the cops got wind of it. Things broke up pretty fast. Cash was lost in the rush, but the blood lust was still in the air. Half the crew elected to head back to the hotel, to air conditioning, showers, MTV, and the long wait for the flight home. Three others elected to drive four hours out of town, where it was rumored that a water buffalo fight was underway. Big horns. Big stakes.

Hours out, the road petered out to nothing amidst a vast otherworldly terraced planet of rice. With the van ground to a halt, the surfers jogged along the dirt path up the hill, past the mosque, to stairs that went up to nowhere, and finally they found the noise coming from the schoolyard. Two thousand Sumatran highlanders screamed in unison as the bloodshot eyes of two giant water buffalos glared back in rage. A rage as elemental as the dawn of man. The great beasts, surrounded by the throng, smashed and tore and lunged and swung, trying to open the other's veins. Down on the killing field, not ten feet from the rage, the surfers watched bug-eyed as the two beasts grunted and lowed and pushed and smashed and did their best to open each others throats. In the end, the biggest water buffalo chased the other through the crowd, with every swing of his great horns flinging wiry brown bodies into the air.

The three surfers ran for their lives.

Four Wipeouts That Changed the Way We Surf

MATT GEORGE

SUNDAY BLOODY SUNDAY
Banzai Pipeline, Hawaii — December, 1981

Clean Pipeline can hurt you. Dirty Pipeline will obliterate you. This, the almighty "Pipe Masters Disaster" occurred on a day that started out impossible and just kept getting worse. The main problem wasn't the crossed-up swell conditions, or the lowest tide of the year, or even the wind that switched directions every fifteen minutes. The problem was a lump of sand. About the size of an Olympic swimming pool, this "turtleback" had built up freakishly over the previous week and turned Pipeline's exit section into a pneumatic jackhammer, making the game of the day a quick drop, a quick pose of some sort, and then a forced ejection into the wild blue yonder.

By the time contestant Steve "Beaver" Massafeller made it outside, five top competitors had pulled out of the contest. Gerry Lopez had left the beach in disgust, and the lifeguards had warned everyone that they doubted they could get through the shorebreak if something happened. Massafeller had a lot riding on this contest. A recent transplant from Florida, he had to prove himself to the locals. There was also that prize money within his grasp. He took off on a monster. The thing doubled up wickedly. The wind held him up in the lip. Massafeller, board in hand, fell twenty feet and got pile-driven straight into the reef.

The impact mashed in the top right side of his skull like a boiled egg. Dragged from the water officially dead, he came away from the Kahuku hospital weighing a half pound more because of the steel plate in his head and with physical disabilities that linger to this day.

The day wasn't over yet. As Massafeller was being choppered to Kahuku General, Chris Lundy, the head of the infamous "Pipeline Underground," took off on the biggest wave of the day and committed suicide, hands over his head, in an enormous tunnel that crashed to a spectacular end into the dry sand. Rattled beyond sense, Lundy tried to stand up on the sand. The sight brought expressions of horror from the beach. From just above the knee, Chris Lundy's right leg was a ruined mass, twisted 180 degrees. He fell unconscious from the shock. The beach screamed. The lifeguards brought him to the beach. He would not walk again for over a year.

THE HOLY GRAIL
Jay Moriarity, Half Moon Bay, California—December, 1994

The die-hards in Santa Cruz hadn't slept all night. Hour after hour, the pounding swell roared against the cliffs of this surf town, where surfers are like Knights of the Round Table, and all that matters is your honor in giant liquid-nitrogen waves. He'd been told he was too young to go, but before dawn, sixteen-year-old Jay Moriarity cut school, lied to his mom, and hitch-hiked forty miles up the coast to play with the big boys. Paddling out alone before the sun, Jay sat outside and dodged elephants for an hour.

By the time the boys arrived, a strong offshore wind had picked up, obscuring the lineup. No one could believe their eyes when this little kid with the giant smile and the borrowed 9-foot gun went to catch a set. Because of his weight, the wind kept blowing him back. That's when Jay paddled deeper, determined to get under the lip. The biggest set of the day approached. Chris Brown, sitting in the channel, had a front row seat, so did photographer Bob Barbour.

Jay explained later that he couldn't see a thing. He just gritted his teeth and paddled as hard as he could. Blinded by the sun and the wind and fear, Jay stood up instinctively. What followed has been called the longest freefall any surfer has ever survived. Jay remembered the flight and the breathless fight for air that followed. Crushed by the lip, he was driven to the bottom. Bathometric measurements put it at four fathoms. He was lucky enough to hit feet first. Then the tornado touched down. Eighteen violent seconds later he surfaced in the channel, looking like a cat that had been attacked by a dog. No one would ever see his board again. Chris Brown would later say when Jay surfaced, he thought he was a ghost. Borrowing another board, Jay surfed for the rest of day and was the last one in at dusk.

By surviving this wipeout, Santa Cruz superstition said Jay would owe the Ocean his life for eternity. Three years later, Jay Moriarity, once again alone with the ocean, drowned in a big-wave training accident in the Maldive Islands.

BEDLAM
Shane Powell, Teahupoo, Tahiti — May, 2002
In World War I they called it shell shock. In the Gulf War, they called it Post-Traumatic Stress Syndrome. One too many brushes with death and the sounds of shells exploding could reverberate in a soldier's head long after battle. These echoes could cause out-of-character, aberrant behavior. Our tribe, too, shares these invisible battlefield scars. Take the strange story of Shane Powell in the 2002 Billabong Pro. Beau Emerton had just scored a perfect 10 on the previous wave of the heat. Shane was in battle, his blood up, his confidence high. He attempted to ride one of the biggest waves ever by a paddle-in surfer at Teahupoo. Two stories high and three thick, it was a black water monster of ocean muscle. As friends screamed at him not to,

Shane Powell dropping into the maelstrom that changed his life. (Photo, Steve Ryan)

Powell's ride looks perfect but one second later the Pacific ocean caved in on him.
(Photo, Steve Ryan)

Shane paddled for it, charged the machine-gun nest, and was cut down at the knees. Driven into the vortex, air punched from his lungs, he was caught in that zone of underwater terror where the wave seems to delight in not letting you go. Shane believed he would never breathe again. In the black depths, he swam not knowing if he was going sideways, up, or down. The water turned a light pink, he broke surface and got a quick breath as the next wave in the set crashed down. With his first burning taste of oxygen flowing down his throat, something had changed in Shane Powell—the kind of change that only a true brush with death can bring. For the rest of the contest, Shane had an aura about him. Native Americans call that aura "the shining," produced when one visits the spirit world and comes back alive.

On the plane flight home, Shane finally vented his madness. First there was screaming, then punches were thrown. The incident would be remembered as a drunken fist fight between a pro surfer and photographer. But perhaps it was a breaking loose from the trance of his wipeout, a shaking out of the demons, an outrunning of the hellhounds that had chased him since he fell into that stygian pit of roiling water and entered the airless place alone. Perhaps the fight wasn't anger at all. Perhaps it was a healing. Nonetheless, air marshals waited for Shane on the ground.

THE END OF THE WORLD AS WE KNOW IT
Photographer, Girlfriend, and Skipper, Teahupoo, Tahiti

The test will come, but you will never see it coming. And when it does, your true character will be revealed before all. Take the case of the photographer, his girlfriend, and the Tahitian skipper who found themselves caught inside a giant Teahupoo. An enormous wave approached. The boat was helpless, dead in the water. At the supreme moment of conflict—as the wave reared up like a deadly, fifteen-foot cobra—three things were observed. A skipper, determined to save his ship against all odds, hung on to the tow rope as the boat knifed into the approaching giant. A terrified, petite, bikini-clad woman (girlfriend to the lensman) clung to a bulwark with all her frail might. Her boyfriend, a surf-experienced ocean photographer, bailed out to save his own skin. With swim fins on, he headed for the safety of the channel, leaving his girl to fate. Her fate was a horror trip over the falls and into the maelstrom, followed by a dramatic rescue by a local lifeguard.

Ten Days

RICK DOYLE

I still have the Sony Walkman that saved our lives. I've always wondered what our fate would have been without it.

I've never had an easy boat trip while on assignment. My first adventure in search of surf was in April 1982 for *Surfer* magazine. I traveled with East Coast pro Greg Mungall to Todos Santos Island, located twelve miles off the coast of Ensenada, Mexico. The seemingly benign twelve-mile channel crossing became formidable as twenty-five-knot winds combined with a large northwest ground swell. We bailed water out of the tiny fishing skiff as fast as we could to avoid sinking. That was just a warm-up for what was to come in my surf photography career.

Later that same year, in what would be known as the great El Niño winter of '82-'83, I was part of a three-man crew on a 36-foot Islander sailboat named the *Raging Jean*. On a journey between the Northern and Southern California coast, we experienced nearly every disaster you could think of: two fires, mechanical break-downs, an encounter with a great-white shark, knock-downs, twenty-foot seas, storm-pushing anchor drags at night next to rocky cliffs, lightning, food poisoning, a near collision with a super tanker in pea-soup fog, and numerous sixty-knot gales that drove fierce rain.

I've found over the years as a veteran surf photographer that scoring great waves on a surf adventure is rare. All the variables—swell direction, wind, weather, and tides—must be aligned with the stars. Generally, I've had to make silk from a sow's ear to get photos published. Scoring perfect waves, I've found, is not the point of a surf trip. The point is to enjoy the moment, the journey, and the friendships that combine to form the experience.

I received a call on Valentine's Day 1997, from *Surfer* magazine photo editor, Jeff Divine, and the next day I was on a plane to the Caribbean. Assignment: Search for the perfect wave with Rusty Surfboard's international hot grom team. I had mentioned to Jeff during our phone conversation that my passport would expire in four days. "No problem," he assured me.

I arrived at the marina in Barbados as the crew loaded supplies onto our floating condo—the *Ocean Mist,* an elegant 60-foot power catamaran. I was stoked. The weather was warm. I took in the sights of colonial architecture, cinematic vistas, and strolling vendors selling their goods. A woman toting a monkey on her head sold bananas by the dock. I bought some for the trip. I didn't know then that bananas are said to curse a boat voyage.

Before leaving port, the captain's wife came onboard and spoke to him, "The wind's been blowing from Africa for two months. You don't know how big the swells are, and I don't think you should go."

Captain T.I. Bainfield, a former black-coral diver, stood with his twelve-

The Rusty grom crew gathers around a fruit vendor wearing her pet monkey. Barbados Marina, 1997. (Photo, Rick Doyle)

and fourteen-year-old sons and said, "We'll manage."

First mate Bruce the Irish said, "Like the skipper says, we'll manage all right."

Rusty's grom crew, managed by twenty-eight-year-old Darren Brilhart, was totally unconcerned with what lay ahead. American dynamos Dylan Slater, 15, and the Hobgood twins, CJ and Damien, 17; Spain's first hope for the world tour, Eneko Acero, 18; South African Junior Champion, Simon Nicolson, 17; and Aussie wonder-tike Jock Barnes, 15, were all amped for the waves of tomorrow. Filmmaker, Brad Anderson, 30, and myself, 43, were a bit concerned about the overnight voyage.

We set off before sunset into the Caribbean Sea, running downwind with a swell at our backs in pursuit of fun, sun, surf, and adventure. As the night pitched darkness, the bumpy seas grew large, keeping us all from sleeping. I lay holding my bunk frame, sweating for hours. I managed to drift off to sleep once for a moment, and then I awoke airborne, about to hit the deck of my double-berth cabin.

The open-ocean swell was running over twenty feet. According to the captain, the engine governor was set at nine knots, but we were reaching twenty-four knots each time we slid down a swell. We frequently fishtailed with the excess speed, almost rolling over broadside, or broaching, as it is called. This roller-coaster ride lasted fifteen hours as we traveled from Barbados to Tobago.

After getting tossed from my bunk, I made my way to the rear, where Dylan Slater was puking into the darkness. I climbed up a slippery ladder through swirling sea spray to the cockpit. The instruments' light cast an eerie red glow on the captain's wet face. Dawn was just breaking the horizon. The captain had fought the seas all night. "Rough passage," he said with a wry smile. I couldn't tell if he was stating a fact or asking me a question. "The wind never laid down," he said.

As we got closer, the island revealed velvet-green volcanic cliffs rising out of a turquoise sea. In the sweet and fresh air, we rounded the point at Mt. Irvin, our destination. The surf was head high, maybe a little bigger on the sets. The boys were ready to throw some tail. But first things first, we had to go through customs and refuel.

The immigration officer gave me a cold stare and leering smile as he stamped my rejection order. My passport was the problem. Next in line was Darren Brilhart. I started laughing hysterically when he pulled out a wrinkled-up photocopy of his passport, which had been stolen in Europe. Darren and I were both to be detained in a jail cell. After some hours of pleading by the captain, we were to be detained on board the *Ocean Mist* at Mt. Irvin. We were not to step foot on land, except to appear before a Special Inquiry officer a few days later.

Refueling was the next ordeal. The fuel dock had no pumps. We bought 100-gallon drums of diesel fuel at inflated prices from the townies, and the captain, puking intermittently, siphoned it into the tanks with a garden hose. This took hours.

Finally, we pulled up to our anchorage at the point in the late afternoon. A few American transplants were anything but thrilled to see six groms and two photographers paddling into the lineup. Disgruntled, they tried hard to spoil our party, but they could have more easily paddled home to New Jersey than ruin these kids' day. There were a couple of true locals that we befriended, such as Barry St. George, the cordial dive-shop owner. Like Barry, the locals were grateful to witness insane surfing in their normally tranquil front yard. Though the swell direction denied us Mt. Irvin's true J-bay potential, the boys found pockets of speed as they connected long rides from the point all the way to the shallow inside reef.

The boys' routine was set for the next four days: surfing, fishing, and diving during the day with dinner at nightfall, followed by a game of cards called "Thirteen." The winner staked priority in the line-up the following morning. They prepared themselves for bed with wrestling matches and screaming, while the old men played dominos over rum and conversation.

On day three, the surf diminished a bit. Jock volunteered to burn his underwear in a surf sacrifice. The ritual produced no immediate results, so the other kids tossed him overboard, fully clothed.

On day five, Immigration denied our appeal, so we headed north to the island of Grenada. Thirty-five knot winds and twenty-foot seas beat us up all day, but we reached Grenada at sunset and refueled. While locals stink-eyed us from the docks and thousands of gallons of fuel flowed into our tanks, the captain gave us a history lesson. "See those pock-marked buildings up there on the hill," he said pointing to the .50-caliber bullet holes. "Back in 1983, the Cubans had infiltrated the government and risen to power. They pulled a coup and executed the Prime Minister, along with one of his aides and some children. Then they took over. In October of 1983, a Caribbean coalition of allies led by the U.K. and the U.S. invaded Grenada and faced stiff fighting from Sandinistan, Cuban, and guerrilla troops. The initial 1,200 troops were repelled and 6,000 more were brought in to bring the island under U.S. con-

Barry St. George, local dive-shop owner, shows the Rusty grom crew how the locals rip.
Mt. Irvin, Tobago, 1997. (Photo, Rick Doyle)

trol." The kids nodded their heads in silence.

With full tanks, we headed up the chain to a small island called Beque, where we anchored for the night in steady thirty-knot winds. We hailed a water taxi from one of the Rasta boatmen and ate a dinner of fresh fish at one of the local restaurants while discussing the wind and swell. In the morning, we were to motor upwind into the driving swell to get back to Barbados. The captain was confident that the *Ocean Mist* could handle all that the sea could throw at her. I was skeptical, maybe terrified, and so was Darren. We offered to fly the crew home from nearby St. Vincent Island, where the boat could hide out until the wind and swell subsided. The captain looked at us and said, "There will be no insurrection on this boat." But, Ahab, I wanted to plead . . . the risks are not worth it.

Dawn broke loose with full-on winds. Small-craft warnings echoed out of the weather radio calling for forty-five-knot winds and heavy seas. We headed up the coast on beam before making our fateful turn at St. Vincent toward the northeast and Barbados. I felt like a lamb meekly herded to slaughter.

The open seas were life-threatening. Once again, we suggested to the captain that it might be a good idea to turn back for St. Vincent. He listened to us, pushed his throttle to full power, and then looked us in the eyes. I looked out at the sea. It was colored gray and marbled like bad meat. Looming walls of water were coming from every direction, battering us. Suddenly there was a thundering boom. The boat was swept bow-to-stern by an enormous wave which ripped through the wheelhouse taking out all of our navigation equipment, damaging the hydraulics, and opening a gaping crack in the hull. The *Ocean Mist* was sinking.

Water poured through the cracked hull into the salon, draining down the stairwells and filling the two forward double-berth cabins. I rushed down the stairwell to get our camera gear while Brad quickly beat it up to the wheelhouse to notify the captain and first mate of the disastrous situation: Water was making its way down to the engine room, threatening to electrocute anyone standing in water should the wiring get soaked.

The captain and first mate quickly patched the hole in the hull slowing the flow of water to a trickle. We were now stopped dead doing doughnuts in mountainous seas and lashing winds. We kept onward to Barbados.

Below deck, in the salon, the instrument panel flashed like Christmas lights as the bilge pumps strained to keep us afloat. I looked around. The galley was destroyed. The refrigerator and dishwasher had been ripped out of the floor and tossed side to side, ramming the entire salon into kindling. Food, debris, and broken wood were everywhere.

Brad, Darren, and I met with the captain, first mate, and his sons up in the wheelhouse. They looked whipped. "We've lost our navigation system, and there's no Coast Guard out here to save us," said the captain over the shrieking wind which sheared through the cockpit, stinging like buckshot. The captain continued, "If we're lucky, if I can navigate, and if the steerage system doesn't break, we'll make landfall before we run out of fuel and lose power. If we do lose power, we'll lose our bilge pumps and steerage. We'll float for awhile at the mercy of the sea until we sink. Prepare your gear just in case we have to abandon ship. The life vests are up front."

I thought, well here it is. Now, I know how I'm going to go.

"Do any of you have an AM radio?" he asked. I fished in my camera bag and pulled out a waterproof Sony Walkman. He put the ear phones in, tuned to an AM station, then straightened his arm and held the Walkman away from his body. He swung his arm around slowly, stopping at points, and slowly moving again. He did this several times, stopping in the same two spots, again and again. The spots were 180 degrees apart. Then he adjusted the ship's wheel. "I've located a radio station. I'm headed toward the source, which is in the direction of the weakest signal. I just hope that signal is coming from Barbados and not some other island," he said.

The *Ocean Mist* edged heavily burdened into the night, straining up the faces of massive swell at three knots. The crew struggled to maintain steerage with the loss of hydraulics. The seas rose up in huge dark mountains. As we crested each swell, the boat would go half airborne then slam back down, shuddering violently as though it were breaking apart. Soon, we would encounter a nonnegotiable wave that would take us out for good. That's what I thought for hours and hours.

Everyone on a sinking boat reacts differently. Most of the kids were lying around seasick or blowing chunks overboard. CJ and Damien shrugged it off as though they'd been through it before, but they were at that immortal age. I guess they figured it can't be as bad as getting caught inside by an angry four-story west peak at Sunset Beach. It can't be as bad as getting crushed in the shallows of backdoor Pipeline. The seawater was warm here, and if we did have to abandon ship, the kids knew they could float around on their surfboards. But probably, they didn't give it much thought. I, on the other hand, was an old guy. I knew we were in serious trouble, possibly headed for a watery grave.

Brad and I packed the film we'd shot into canisters and placed them into

L to R: South African junior champion Simon Nicholson (17), Dylan Slater (15), CJ Hobgood (17), Aussie wonder-tike Jock Barnes (15), Damien Hobgood (17), and Spain' first hope for the world tour, Eneko Acero (18). On board the *Ocean Mist*, Tobago 1997. (Photo, Rick Doyle)

Captain T.I. Bainfield (center) uses a waterproof Sony Walkman to navigate after the boat's electronics were destroyed. The radio reckoning technique saved the boat and all aboard. (Photo, Rick Doyle)

plastic food bags that we duct-taped shut. I joked that if we didn't make it back, perhaps somebody would find the film, and *Surfer* would run the photos in tribute. We then settled in and took an unmerciful beating for eight hours.

"Lights, lights, I see lights," screamed the captain. "We've made it! It's Barbados!"

We pulled in on fumes at 2 A.M. and docked at the nearest location, alongside the Greenpeace ship *Rainbow Warrior*. Our crew scrambled off the boat, and Eneko and a few of the other kids bent down and kissed the ground. Some of the Greenpeace crew came by to survey our damage, remarking that we were lucky to be alive. The *Ocean Mist* suffered $100,000 in damage that night.

I have not been on a boat since that trip. Looking back, I remember that I'd taken bananas on my first two disastrous boat rides, as well. Superstition or curse, I don't know. I think I'm due for the dream boat-trip that scores perfect surf in calm weather. But then I think, even without bananas, I might be pushing my luck.

Birds of Timor

CHRIS COTÉ

Surf magazine writers are a spoiled bunch. I, personally, am one of those spoiled few who frequently travel with the upper echelon of surfing royalty. A few years ago, I had occasion to visit Timor with a select group of pros including Andy and Bruce Irons, Dean Morrison, Jason Shibata, our friend Blair Marlin, and photographer, Brian Bielmann. We dovetailed the standard surf trip with a good bender—not an uncommon occurrence.

On our last morning spent in the sweltering heat, dive-bombing mosquitoes, and stench of Indonesian cigarettes, our crew suffered from the after-effects of a last-night-on-the-boat booze party. Hangovers in the tropics have a special zing that pinches the brain stem and causes terrible, shaky sweats. We were a sweating, stinking mass of grumpy surfers. After a ten-day boat trip, getting on land and into an air-conditioned room and stationary bed loomed like a dream, not to mention the thought of late nights in the full-service bars of Bali's Kuta Beach. We put the fun waves behind us, and looked forward to the comforts that waited at the other end of a short flight from Timor to Bali.

We loaded into the first six rows of the late-'70s DC-10 that was no doubt an American Airlines hand-me-down (faded AA logos were barley visible on the backs of the seats). We were all in first class, which was like last class on any other airline. We sunk into the seats and hid from the demons of the night before behind our dark sunglasses.

(Left to right): Jason Shibata, Bruce Irons, Chris Coté, Blair Marlin, Dean Morrison, and Andy Irons celebrate living to see another day (or night) in Paddy's, a Kuta Beach, Bali bar that was destroyed in the Bali bombings a few years later. (Photo courtesy of Chris Coté)

I said my little prayer for safety as we taxied down the runway, but God must've been on the other line, because as the plane reached its top ground speed and the nose lifted, an explosion rocked the fuselage. The cabin filled with a putrid smell: a mix of melting plastic and burnt popcorn. Black smoke filtered in. I wondered in terror who had shot an RPG missile at us, and why. The plane skidded, almost rolling over at one point, until it came to a halt in the bushes at the edge of the runway. Silence, screams, then more silence followed the blast. We sat in shock. What the fuck just happened? Are we dead? If so, heaven sucks; it's still hot, and now my headache feels like a heart attack.

My face was white, and my palms poured alcohol-scented sweat like a faucet. I looked around at our party; everyone had the same pale-faced expression of shock and disbelief. All I could do was sit and pray and work out in my head a way to get off the plane and back on the ground. The steward opened the door to let some smoke out. As he did, the passengers behind us lit up cigarettes. I guess surviving a near-death situation called for a smoke.

The same guy who checked our luggage, gave us our tickets, and drove the stairway to the plane, came out to inspect the damage. We all peered out the window in silence; the baggage handler reached into the engine with a puzzled look on his face and pulled out a mangled, burned bird the size of a small chicken. He tossed it to the side of the runway, gave the captain a thumbs-up, and the plane started right back up again. The revving engines spat out the remnants of the charred bones of the unlucky bird.

On our next takeoff attempt, the runway and sky were filled with birds. Maybe they were there before and I just hadn't noticed. Now, all eyes were on the flock of heron-like creatures flapping around. They suddenly became just as dangerous as sharks or terrorists. Just as the nose came up again, a small black flash shot by my window, about two feet above the engine. A bird being a smart-ass?

With pale faces, sweaty palms, and palpitating hearts we raced upward. The safety of the sky approached. Across the aisle from me, Bruce and Dean's seats broke loose and they fell into the laps of the Indian-looking gentlemen behind them. Maniacal laughter replaced petrified silence.

Needless to say, this was the longest one-hour flight of our lives. Once on the ground, I wondered who to contact about reserving passage on a boat home from Bali.

The Third Channel: Corsica to Elba

BUZZY KERBOX WITH **BEN MARCUS**

In the summer of 1990, Laird Hamilton and I paddled the Molokai Channel, the thirty-mile gap between the islands of Oahu and Molokai, unescorted. That went okay, but when we got back to our little shack on Maui, we began planning our European vacation with an eye toward channels we could paddle. We were headed to Europe in September to do some sailboard speed trials in the Canary Islands. Laird already held the European speed record at thirty-six knots, and he was amped to break that. We were looking at the map of Europe, and I said, "Since we're going to Europe, why don't we paddle the English Channel?" A mission had begun.

There wasn't enough wind at the speed trials to break a record, and when they ended, we met up in Spain for the start of our Europe '90 trip.

It ain't over 'til it's Dover

We didn't tell anyone we were going to do it, and we didn't get permission. We just paddled off from Calais beach in France and made for the white cliffs of Dover. We carried little emergency gear with us: duct tape and my Visa card—sometimes you can't get home without it. We also had a handful of candy bars and a bottle of Evian water each.

Twenty minutes into the paddle, things got interesting. We had entered the shipping lanes and now had to dodge huge tankers and cargo ships. One ship was on a collision course with us. We changed our course three times, and each time the ship also changed course. Things got serious. We went hard and just made it past the ship's path. I remember thinking, this is going to be a long day. Soon after making it into mid-channel, a boat from the Dover Lifeboat Station motored up to us and ordered Laird and me to get in the boat. With three hours invested so far and the cliffs in the distance, we both said, "No way! We came to paddle this channel and that's what we're going to do." We split up in different directions to make it harder for these guys to get us. Then the boat radioed the Coast Guard and got permission to guide us the rest of the way, leaving us a nice wake and diesel fumes to add to the briskly cold waters.

Laird made it to the beach first in five hours and forty minutes, and I came in twenty minutes behind him feeling delirious. I was totally hypothermic. The Coast Guard took me to the hospital where I warmed up from a core temperature of eighty-eight degrees.

An English official greeted us in courteous amusement. And as we left, an immigration guy filled out two forms for us to get back into France. In the box that asked, "Mode of entry into UK," he wrote: "Surfboards."

Able was I ere I saw Elba

We went back to Paris to check out the museums, the nightclubs and to hang out with some friends. The French flocked around Laird. They loved him.

Buzzy Kerbox and Laird Hamilton paddling from Corsica,
France to Elba, Italy, 1990. (Photo courtesy of Buzzy Kerbox)

Laird Hamilton takes a rest break on the Mediterranean Sea. (Photo, Buzzy Kerbox)

When we sat down to eat, Laird polished off three full entrees in one sitting. His appetite astonished his audience. After a couple of days of city life, we made off for the south of France to do some surfing. Then Laird came up with the idea of paddling from the French island of Corsica to Elba (the Italian island where Napoleon was exiled after his abdication in 1814). We looked at the map to see where we were in relation to these islands. Laird made arrangements with a French TV crew to shoot our mission from a helicopter. Perfect. The helicopter would meet us on Elba with a big bottle of Champagne for my thirty-fourth birthday.

We rented a little 8-foot-long Peugeot car and stuck our 12-foot paddleboards on top. Gerry Lopez made Laird's, and Harold Iggy shaped mine. Then we headed off for the south of France to catch the ferry to Corsica.

The ferry ride was easy because it was September and the French were

After the forty-four-mile crossing: celebrating Buzzy's 34th birthday with six entrees and a bottle of champagne. Elba, Italy, 1990. (Photo courtesy of Buzzy Kerbox)

back at work or in school. We drove around scoping out the island; the car was so slow going uphill, you could almost run faster than it was moving. We came across huge cliffs. Laird walked up to the edge, looked down and said, "Yeah, this looks good." I looked over the edge and way down below there were boulders clearly visible in the crystal blue water. Then Laird just jumped. I watched him fall, counting: one . . . two . . . three . . . four. Four seconds . . . and then he hit the water. Holy shit, that's a big jump, I thought. I had never jumped off anything that high. He was down there in the water waving his arms: "Come on! It's good! Let's go! Jump!" I was thinking, *no way!* I felt like I had to go, so I jumped. I could almost hear my dad as I was speeding toward impact, "If so-and-so jumped off a cliff, would you?" It was a major rush, free-falling. We swam around and decided to launch the next day at 7 A.M. from this spot.

Back at the hotel, we got out the navigational charts, and the distance from Corsica to Elba was "37." It didn't say thirty-seven what. So we figured, well, this is Europe, it's got to be kilometers. So that's equal to twenty-three miles. No big deal. We could do that easily. Cakewalk.

We talked to some people about weather and wind. They said the wind never, ever blows out of the east. They all said that emphatically. We were paddling due east, so this was good news.

Everything looked good. We had all our gear dialed in, some nice compasses and new batteries for our waterproof Sony Walkmans. We went back to the cliff early the next morning, hiked our boards down, and placed them on a rock just above the waterline. Then we climbed back up as the helicopter arrived. They loaded in our clothes, passports, money and a big bottle of champagne for my birthday. "We'll meet you on Elba," they said.

Laird told them we were starting our journey from the top of the cliff. We jumped together on "three" as they filmed it. After the jump, they yelled down, "That was great! We want to film it from another angle. Can you guys do it again?" Back up at the top, we felt a gust of wind and then heard a smash. Down below my board had been blown off its rock and into the cliff. We jumped a second time, and I swam over to my board. The last three inches of it were facing the wrong direction. I smashed it straight and hit it with five-minute epoxy. Then we got to it.

The conditions were nice: sunny, smooth water, and no wind. As soon as we started, my "waterproof" Walkman got wet and stopped working. So Laird and I traded his Walkman every now and then. About two hours out, we had an easterly wind straight in our face—the wind direction that never happens. We were paddling into the wind and progressing slowly with con-

Can we get a ride to the ferry? (Photo courtesy of Buzzy Kerbox)

stant sprays in our eyes. We paddled prone the whole time, and every so often we took a break, sat up, and had some bottled water or a chocolate bar. We could see Elba off in the distance, but it never got any closer. After four hours, I was thinking, uhh . . . we should be there by now. But we weren't even close. Five hours out and we're just paddling and paddling and the island is still looking just as far away as it did when we started. "What's going on?" I said to Laird during a break. "We've paddled five hours. That's well over twenty miles. We should be there now."

Laird, upbeat and positive, just pointed and said, "Well, there it is. Let's keep going."

The helicopter went by us to one side and didn't see us. They flew on ahead, hovering in the distance searching for us for quite a while. Then they flew past us going toward Corsica. When I saw that, I thought, well, they must have landed on Elba and left somebody to wait for us with our money and passports and stuff.

But, no, they bailed on us.

We weren't in any danger, though. The water was warm, no ships were charging us, and we had plenty of energy. I didn't hear until much later that the largest great white shark ever caught was in the Mediterranean, but we didn't see any. Six hours . . . seven hours . . . eight hours. We were still a ways off, and it was starting to get dark. We thought we were going to be there midday, but here it was well after sunset and we were paddling toward a little flickering light. I was getting a little nervous. I just wanted to finish the paddle, get to Elba, eat a huge dinner, and celebrate my birthday.

We finally got out at a boat ramp. It had taken us close to nine hours for our simple crossing. We walked up this big hill and there were two restaurants and nothing else for miles. There was no one there to greet us: no welcoming committee, no fanfare, no cameras, no helicopter—just Laird and me in our wetsuits carrying 12-foot paddleboards. We had done the paddle just to do it, because nobody had yet done it. We didn't care about the TV guys, but we did want the champagne and the ride back.

Luckily, I had my Visa card with our emergency gear. The first restaurant didn't take Visa. The other one had that little Visa symbol out front. Seeing that was like seeing an oasis in the desert. "Laird, come on, we're in!" The owner spoke English, and he was cool. We told him what we had done, and he said, "That's forty-four statute miles." No wonder it took so long! It was thirty-seven *nautical miles*, not kilometers.

No matter, we were here. I ordered us a fine bottle of champagne and six

Shoeless, broke, and wearing wetsuits, Laird and Buzzy make their way back to Corsica. (Photo courtesy of Buzzy Kerbox)

entrees to share. Laird never did pay me back for that.

Our next dilemma: how do we go back? We really didn't want to paddle it again the next day. "Can we catch the ferry going back to Corsica tomorrow?" I asked the owner.

"The ferry is closed. It's off season," he said.

"Okay, where's the airport?"

"The airport is also closed," he said.

"How do we get back?"

"You take the ferry to mainland Italy, then a long bus ride up the coast to Livorno, then a ferry to Corsica."

Great. Here we were with no clothes, no shoes, no money, no passports, and a few days of travel ahead of us wearing wetsuits and carrying 12-foot paddleboards. But the owner was nice. He set us up in a hotel behind the restaurant and gave me a forty-dollar cash advance on my credit card. With that money I bought us each a sweatshirt, and I had enough left over for the first ferry ride.

Wearing those sweatshirts, but still shoeless, we hitchhiked to the harbor on Elba and caught the ferry to mainland Italy. Then we caught a bus up the coast to Livorno. The boards barely fit underneath in the compartment on the bus, but we got to Livorno where we had to find a hotel and wait for the ferry leaving the next day.

Walking around Italy with no shoes was like walking around naked. People stared, jaws agape, at us. After a while, I couldn't take it. So I went to a shoe store to find some slippers or something. All they had were those expensive dress shoes, which would have looked ridiculous. We caught the ferry back to Corsica and then hitchhiked back to the cliff to get our car.

We were the second-to-last car to squeeze onto the ferry from Corsica back to France. Then, driving to our friend's house in the south of France, we hit a deer, veered off the side of the road, and flew off a four-foot ledge. The front corner of the car caught, and I thought for sure we were going to roll and crush our boards on the roof. But we just plowed through these head-high bushes and came to a stop. Laird pushed the car out and I got it going again. I looked at the car, and every single inch—and I mean every panel—was dented. We took it back to the rental place in Biarritz. Two French women were working there, and Laird said, "We need a faster car." They looked at the car, looked at us, had a little conversation, and then handed us the keys to a faster car.

Permutations of a Bohemian Bubble Chaser

MAGILLA SCHAUS

The universe does not behave according to our preconceived notions. It continues to surprise us.
—Stephen Hawking

My surf chants the night before were answered the next morning with a muffling layer of snow. The news showed a huge western isobar with curved jaws and barbed teeth sweeping across the Great Lakes basin. In the afternoon the snow changed from a diaphanous, snow-globe fantasy into a robust lake-effect storm. The wind howled and rattled my living room windowpanes. It was time to hit the waves. I placed my waxed board in the bag with a towel and my six-mil wetsuit. The chief at the fire station where I work called and offered me overtime pay to come in and do the day shift. Without hesitation, I turned down his offer. I'd rather surf the storm than make some extra money. I wedged my longboard into my car and headed over the Peace Bridge, just blocks from my house. The wind buffeted the United States, United Nations, and Canadian flags marking the border between Buffalo, New York, and Fort Erie, Ontario, Canada. Then the following conversation occurred between a Canadian Customs officer and myself:

"Where were you born?"

"Buffalo."

"What is the purpose of your visit?"

"Surfing."

"Are you that surfer who wears the Santa suit?"

"No, that guy's a windsurfer."

"Okay. Go ahead."

On the road westward the fullness of the storm and thunder increased. Lightning sent blue pulses through the whiteout. I parked in front of the aptly named Crystal Beach and watched ground-level clouds scud across Lake Erie. The water faded from gray to pure white and back. Horizontal spider webs of fire bolts veined the ivory sky. I turned up Carl Orff's *Chants Profanes* on the sound system and watched the snowy onslaught while the crescendo of medieval chants stirred the mood. I waited and waited for a break in the storm, and after some time had an epiphany: It was pointless to surf today. I couldn't see the lake. It was just a theatre of blowing white.

The drive back was like passing through an avalanche. At the approach to the Peace Bridge an official truck flashed warning lights and blocked my way. The road home was shut down. I switched on the AM radio. The voice tones were lower than usual: "A storm emergency has been declared in the city of Buffalo. All driving of private vehicles is prohibited. The City of Buffalo is asking that anyone with a snowmobile assist in transporting medical staff to work."

I turned off the radio, unzipped my jacket, and settled in for the long wait. Snowstorms bring an unusual silence to the city. I rolled my windows up and down to clear the snow off. I looked out at the distant Niagara River, and the flowing water placed me back in the summer of 1989, when I swam across Lake Erie handcuffed.

It was the image of one man stopping a column of tanks during the Tiananmen Square uprising that prompted my symbolic swim. The television showed this enduring image over and over along with shots of students and workers gathered around a 33-foot statue dubbed the Goddess of Democracy. This Styrofoam and papier-mâché student-made statue was based on, but not quite a replica of, the Statue of Liberty. The Goddess stood in the heart of Tiananmen Square and became the epicenter of a massive protest that called out for democratic reform and an end to government corruption. I watched the protest escalate for days on television.

On June 4, 1989, the media reported that the Chinese People's Libera-

Magilla Schaus riding in the ice flows of Lake Erie, Crystal Beach, Ontario, Canada, January 2003. (Photo, Chris Furminger. © Magilla Schaus)

tion Army ended the uprising with a wholesale massacre. I was stunned. A few days after watching this news, I had an engaging conversation with some graduate students from the Chinese Student Club at the University of Buffalo. As we stood in the street, with the Allentown Art Festival going on around us, I came up with the idea of doing a symbolic swim—ten miles across Lake Erie handcuffed in remembrance of those injured, arrested, or killed during the uprising. The swim would also send a message that this atrocity and human rights abuse could not and would not be ignored. I suggested that club members ride along in a support boat. They wanted time to consider the idea.

A week later Wei from the Chinese Student Club called to say that the club would support the swim. I was ecstatic and got right to work. First, I had to find someone to build a full-scale replica of the Goddess of Democracy. Next, I had to find a boat big enough to carry the 33-foot statue through the waters which catch much of the southwesterly prevailing winds. The lake bottom, littered with sunken ships, is testament to how quickly these winds can rise.

Finding a sculptor to build a 33-foot statue quickly and pro bono would not be easy. I approached a couple of artists and exuberantly explained my vision. Most were supportive but otherwise engaged. Finally Alice Dudko agreed to make the statue provided I buy the material. I took my father's one-hundred dollar donation and bought four rectangular foam slabs, similar in size to longboard blanks. I gave Alice a photograph of the Goddess of

The portrait of Mao Tse-Tung overlooking Tiananmen Square faces off with a statue erected in the square on May 30, 1989. The statue was dubbed "The Goddess of Democracy" by students from the Central Academy of Fine Arts, who modeled it on the Statue of Liberty.
(Photo © AP Wide World Photos/Jeff Widener)

Democracy.

With a hotwire cutting tool, she brought the foam to life. We interconnected the pieces with small wood dowels. The two dimensional statue stood with an unstable back and forth sway. The next day my friend Carl braced it in a wood frame, and the members of the Chinese Student Club painted the whole thing white. Our 20-foot Goddess was gorgeous, yet too large to mount in the 14-foot boat that would carry her. We decided to mount only the top portion—the head and raised arms clutching the torch. Upon completion of the swim, we would reconnect the two halves before the cheering crowd and media.

During our final planning meeting, a club member named Ming told me that years ago he completed a similar swim in a Chinese river pulling a floating placard of Chairman Mao behind him. Ming was amped to swim all ten miles with me. Other Chinese students also wanted to join. In the week prior to the swim, the students sent out press releases to the local media and contacted law enforcement offices for appropriate notifications.

The night before the swim, I was still ironing out logistical arrangements, and my phone rang until 4 A.M. I couldn't get any more than a short catnap. Sunday morning, August 13, 1989, we held a press conference at the Erie Basin Marina just after dawn. After completing these interviews, we boarded our power crafts and motored out into Lake Erie.

Though I'd arranged for three support boats, only two managed to show up on the day of the swim. Four Chinese students rode in the 14-foot boat with the Goddess, food, beverages, and their gear, while Carl Grimm, Dave Thines and Kevin King (my plumber/construction buddies) rode in Kevin's 16-foot boat, which was put in charge of navigation and swimmer safety.

The surface was calm and the wind light as we rode ten miles across to our starting point—my favorite surf spot, Crystal Beach. We conducted a second press conference for the Canadian media on the sandy shore.

After the interviews, Ming and I got into the water. Carl ratcheted the handcuffs over my wrists, which I'd wrapped in neoprene from an old diving glove. We set off swimming. Dave paddled beside us on my longboard with the handcuff keys on a chain around his neck. Kevin navigated his boat on point, warding off other boats that got too close. The Goddess waved to and fro above the Chinese students in the other boat. Our flotilla headed slowly for the distant skyline of Buffalo as Carl, Kevin, Dave, Wei, Wendang, and Xianglong rotated in and out of the water for solidarity swims next to Ming and me. At intervals, the support crew handed us sections of peanut butter sandwiches, Ginseng root slices, and sips of water.

The longer I swam, the better the quality of my strokes became. My handcuffed swimming was an interchange between a dolphin-like kick-and-glide and a double-armed cross-body stroke. The day became warm, and a light chop spread over the lake from the wakes of hundreds of boatgoers enjoying the mid-August sun.

About two miles from the Erie Basin Marina, we entered the part of the lake that is the source of the Niagara River. A light current pulled on us. I was in a trance-like meditation enjoying the cadence of my stroke when I heard someone scream, "The boat is sinking!"

In wonder, I replied, "What boat?"

I looked back and the student boat with the Goddess of Democracy listed at thirty-five degrees. The boat was swamped with water from a large wake that had rolled over its transom. The back end was taking on more and more water. The Chinese students scrambled through a forty-five-degree pitch to disconnect the securing lines from the Goddess statue. They freed the Goddess just before the boat hit ninety degrees and sank with grievous dispatch. Some of the students plunged into the water, and one hopped onto the floating Goddess. It was a glorious and symbolic moment to see the Goddess rescue a son of liberty in international waters.

I called off the swim, got my handcuffs off, and climbed into the surviving boat to size up our situation. Flotsam of plastic bottles, bags, jackets, and other junk surrounded us as we pulled the students into the support boat one by one. Remaining quietly in the water was Ming, blue-lipped and pale. He'd been swimming eight hours thus far and lost all his warmth during these last motionless moments.

"Get Ming out of the water now!" I yelled. "The swim is over."

A student slung Ming into the boat. Wrapped in a blanket, he shivered uncontrollably. We waved down the first passing boat and asked the driver to radio U.S. Coast Guard to tell them one of our boats had sunk. We also asked the driver to bring Ming ashore as a precaution should his hypothermia advance. Carl accompanied Ming into the other boat and went to the Erie Basin Marina.

On our crowded vessel, a scuttlebutt broke out over whether we should head directly in, or rescue the Goddess now floating away. There was no question. We motored over, tied a line around her and dragged her toward shore. Carl returned in the other boat to report that Ming was feeling better. We thanked the skipper for his help, and as he departed, the Erie County

Activist, firefighter, and surfer Magilla Schaus, Crystal Beach, Ontario, Canada.
(Photo courtesy of Magilla Schaus)

Sheriff's Department boat came up beside us. The police demanded that all the Chinese students come aboard. We explained the symbolic swim, our press conferences, our prior contact with the Coast Guard.

"This was a freedom swim," I said to the officer.

He didn't care and again demanded that the Chinese students come aboard. The students complied and the police boat zoomed off with the students in custody.

Demoralized and awakened to the turning nature of our swim, the remaining four of us motored towards the shore. But no sooner did a U.S. Coast Guard boat intercept us and order us to follow them. On arrival at their base, Carl, Kevin, Dave, and I were separated and interrogated. I could only assume that the sheriff's department had contacted the Coast Guard and told them about the Chinese nationals they had in custody. The officer kept questioning me about how I knew the Chinese people. I told him the entire story: from the images of Tiananmen Square, to meeting the Chinese Student Club members, to the press conferences, to the boat sinking. The officer appeared suspicious and asked again and again about the Chinese students and the boats. Finally I said, "Listen, who in their right mind would smuggle Chinese people into the United States from Canada in a boat with a big statue that looks like the Statue of Liberty . . . and, I might add, hold a press conference in both countries before proceeding? There are less obscure and obvious ways."

Eventually the officer saw the logic and released us. We left their base and motored to the Erie Basin Marina, our final destination. Everything I had purposed to do had fallen apart in the ninth hour. I felt like I had wiped out on a big wave, and now I was in for a long hold-down, just chasing bubbles trying to get to the surface. We tied up at the Hatch restaurant, left the Goddess floating on her line, and climbed the ladder to the dock. In the adjacent park, our families, friends, and supporters applauded and cheered as we walked over. Ming came up to us with a big smile. The applause surprised me. We dispatched a friend to get the club members back from the sheriff's department. A long time later, a car with the Chinese students returned. As everyone gathered around, I announced that in several weeks I would swim the lake handcuffed again and successfully complete it.

After I made the announcement, I heard a voice say, "Here, this is for you." I turned around, and an Erie County Sheriff handed me a ticket for operating an unregistered boat.

The next day wire services picked up the story, and our swim became national and international news.

At my court appearance, I pleaded guilty. The judge asked to hear the circumstances of the violation. I told him the whole story. He dismissed the charge, turned to the sheriff, and said loudly, "I can't believe you gave this man a ticket."

On Sunday, August 27, 1989, I successfully completed the handcuffed solo swim with support from Tom Schneeberger and my four brothers Steve, Kevin, John, and Joseph. At the end of the swim, I was met by supporters, the Chinese Student Club, the Goddess of Democracy and Chinese Embassy officials who were "documenting" the event. I felt a simultaneous victory and defeat: Victory for completing the ten-mile handcuffed swim and defeat for jeopardizing the club students' future back in China.

My ambivalence soon turned to full-on defeat as the networks reported a massive stadium trial underway in Beijing for all those involved in the Tiananmen Square uprising. At the time, reports claimed that the convicted students and workers were led out side-doors and executed on the spot with firearms. The parents and families of the condemned were reportedly each sent an official bill from the Chinese government requiring them to pay the cost of the bullet used in the execution of their child or relative. Though it was unsubstantiated, I nevertheless believed it.

A revving noise pierced the silence and startled me out of my memories. The truck in front of me began to move. My time in stasis had come to an end after three hours of waiting to cross the Peace Bridge. As I crossed the bridge, the snow stopped falling.

United States officials halted me, saying that all of Buffalo was shut down. But when a line of cars grew behind me, they let me pass. The blade of a plow had not yet touched the three-foot-deep snow on the roads. I left my car parked in the street in front of my house and post-holed a track to the side door to get my shovel. It took strategy and planning to figure out where to stack this much snow. Four hours later, with seven-foot snow walls around me, I had cleared the driveway to the side door.

I unloaded my board and gear from the car. Some days are like this when you surf in Buffalo. I went in and had a bowl of soup and a Canadian beer. Then I fell asleep on the couch exhausted.

Miki Goes to the Movies

BRUCE SAVAGE

When I arrived, Miki was resting on the stoop of his grandma's West Hollywood bungalow, around the corner from Barney's Beanery. He was nattily attired in beige Sy Devore slacks, accented by a salmon-colored alpaca over a white-on-white sport shirt. His Morris-the-Bootmaker loafers shined like patent leather. Clutched in his left hand was a parcel the size of a cigar box. He gracefully stepped off the porch and settled into my red ambulance. We motored south to Hermosa Beach.

I was one of the select few appointed to chauffeur Miki Dora to and from surfing functions. I'll never forget Wednesday, June 6, 1960, the day of my first assignment. Greg Noll's *Search for Surf* was playing that evening at Pier Avenue Junior High in Hermosa Beach, and I was to help deliver Dora and his parcel.

The moment Miki entered the auditorium, the South Bay regulars spotted him. Instantly the clamor shifted from hoots and hollers to boos and hisses. Miki openly aired his condescension toward the South Bay gang—in his eyes, they were a bunch of country bumpkins. The ridicule from Noll's fans became intense, then someone heaved a water balloon, narrowly missing Miki's head. Nonetheless, Miki maintained his usual aloofness. Completely composed, he said to me, "These South Bay clowns are nothing but water buffalo. Stay at my side; we're going to act fast."

The novelty of his arrival soon wore off, and the movie began, following a warning from Greg Noll. "We must all act as ladies and gentlemen," he said, "because we want to use the hall again for future showings. Thank you." After that request, Noll called for the house lights to be dimmed, and the proceedings got underway, accompanied by the dissonance of full-on screaming.

Miki and I sat in the last row of seats watching the first ten minutes of red-hot surfing. Even with all the excitement, I couldn't help but notice the chick seated in front of us, squirming uncomfortably in her seat. Finally, her husband, a big-wave rider, adjusted his arm around her in a reassuring manner. Peeking over her shoulder, I saw her stomach. No wonder she wiggled in her seat, her gut was the size of a huge casaba melon. Sitting back, I whispered the news to Miki. The bird must be nine months pregnant.

"That one there?" said Miki, pointing to her.

"That's the one." I nodded.

"Well," he said, "I'll take care of that."

He opened the small parcel he'd been carrying, revealing a gigantic 35-millimeter thunder-cracker with a ten-inch fuse. Leaning forward, he placed the explosive directly beneath the expectant mother's seat and lit the fuse. The roar of the crowd was so deafening that no one was able to hear the hissing fuse. Miki and I took our leave.

At the exit stood several L.A. County lifeguards moonlighting as bouncers, Miki smiled, nodding to each one as we passed, and we were gone. Outside, the explosion was earth shattering. We sprinted to my car and speed-shifted out of there.

I learned afterward that when the thunder-cracker exploded, the concussion catapulted the impregnated girl into the aisle where, in the middle of a smoke screen, she lay writhing in pain. Her lifeguard husband kneeling at her side was in tears. "Who the hell did this?" he screamed. "Why? Why? Why?"

The crowd picked up the chant: "Dora! Dora! Dora!" The woman immediately gave birth to the infant. Greg Noll leaped onto the stage and gripped the microphone, ranting, "I want Dora. I want him at all costs." He paused momentarily. "Bring him to me, my friends. This can go no further," he bellowed. "Dora is a maniac. He must be stopped!"

The next day posters surfaced throughout the South Bay. "Wanted! Miki Dora! $25 reward." Because of the bizarre event, all surf movies scheduled to be shown at Pier Avenue Junior High were suspended indefinitely.

Months went by before Noll's next presentation, *Tiger on a Hot Balsa Board*. This time he was forced to book the high-rent Santa Monica Civic

Years later as friends, Greg Noll (left) gestures the unknown; Miki Dora
wears a clear plastic mask. (Photo courtesy of Greg Noll)

Auditorium—and that was more or less Miki Dora's backyard. Realizing this,
Noll beefed up his county lifeguard bouncer squad by importing "Knuckles"
Edmundson as a precautionary measure against Dora's presence.

The morning of the screening, I received a phone call from Miki request-
ing my services. On the way to his house that evening, I convinced myself he
was out of his mind to go. I thought about suggesting he just stay home. Noll
and his lifeguard bouncers would surely annihilate him if he were detected.
Nevertheless, I made the drive to West Hollywood. This time Miki wasn't on
the front porch, so I made my way to the door and pushed the buzzer. The
door creaked open and Miki, his head barely visible, did this Count Dracula
gig.

"How are you, my friend? How nice to see you." He drew out his words.
"Come in, please."

I followed Miki into the parlor where these two fellows sat on the dav-
enport, each with a death-grip on a pint of sour-mash bourbon. I recognized
the two, but I was beside myself when Miki introduced me to my heroes,
Tubesteak, the King of Malibu, and Jimmy Fisher, Makaha big-wave charger,

Original poster for Greg Noll's *Search for Surf* movie series. (Poster courtesy of Greg Noll)

who had showed up at Malibu one day, watched Dora's style, then imitated him doing thirty-two tweaks on a juicy wave from First Point to the pit.

Both men were outfitted in full surfing-movie paraphernalia. Miki disappeared into a bedroom and after a few moments emerged with a bulging satchel in his right hand. "Drink up, my friends," he said, "for it is time to go."

The four of us departed on what I thought was a suicide mission—Greg Noll's big night at the Santa Monica Civic Auditorium. The place seated 5,000 people and Noll would have it packed.

I turned my customized fire-engine-red ambulance into the Civic parking lot. Miki ordered me to head for the rear door marked: *Artists Only. Keep Out!*

"Over there! Over there is where I want out," he said.

Miki, carrying his black leather satchel, slipped unnoticed into the inner sanctum of the massive auditorium. I uttered a silent prayer that neither Greg Noll nor Knuckles Edmundson would get their hands on Miki, for it would mean his certain death.

The atmosphere was somewhat different inside than at the Pier Avenue Junior High. The crowd seemed more sophisticated—but, of course, this was Santa Monica not the South Bay.

It was a grand feeling to be ushered in with Tubesteak and Jimmy Fisher. There I was, at a surfing movie for which I didn't have to pay, and being introduced to the likes of the Incomparable Lance Carson, Tom "Dr. Standing Island" Morey, Mikey "Messerschmidt" Doyle, Dewey "The Little Man on Wheels" Weber, Peter "Mr. Big Wave" Cole, the Masters Velzy and Jacobs, Johnny Fain, and so many others it made my head spin. I made up my mind right then and there that if I never did anything else in my life, I wanted to be a surf star and maybe, just maybe, a surfing legend.

The lights dimmed, a signal for the obligatory hooting and hollering to begin. Greg Noll sensed he had the audience in the palm of his hand and smirked.

Seven minutes into the first reel, Tubesteak nudged Fisher, pointing toward the orchestra pit. The big-wave segment was under way and all eyes were glued to the screen. A figure emerged from the bowels of the stage, made a beeline up the west aisle, and headed in our direction. He wore a black opera cape, a Scottish tam, and horn-rimmed glasses with a fake nose and moustache. Not only did he look like Groucho Marx, he even walked like him.

He sat down in the empty seat behind us, leaned forward, and unzipped his leather satchel. "All right, my friends," he whispered, "I am ready." With that, he unscrewed a two-gallon mayonnaise jar chock full of crazed gypsy moths and placed it on the floor. Then the four of us nonchalantly departed.

On the way out of the auditorium, Tubesteak and Jimmy Fisher smiled at the lifeguards. "Later, boys," said Fisher. "It's party time." Swaggering in front of head bouncer Knuckles Edmundson, Miki Dora, in his Groucho Marx disguise, wiggled a two-dollar Havana in Knuckles' face. Then he said to Knuckles, "Say the secret word."

We were gone. Back inside, the moths whirred out of the wide-mouth jar, gathered in a pyramid formation, and zoomed from one side of the auditorium to the other, finally zeroing in on the movie projector's beam of light. Greg Noll stood at his pulpit watching as the screen grew cloudy.

"Focus!" he yelled. "Focus!" But to no avail. Three thousand gypsy moths had entirely shrouded the projector's eye, plunging the Santa Monica Civic Auditorium into darkness.

"Focus, dammit, focus!" Noll yelled. He was livid. "Lights! Lights! He's here! I know he's here!"

The house lights came on. The auditorium was bedlam. Noll sprinted up the center aisle. "Where is he?" He bellowed, "I'll kill him. I'll kill the bastard!" But we were gone, while Noll was left facing thousands of surfers chanting, "Refund! Refund! Refund!" Above them the three thousand gypsy moths held a tornado-funnel formation.

Across Main Street in the Cherrio Bar and Grill, Miki Dora, Jimmy Fisher, Tubesteak, and I peeked out a window observing the disturbance. We doubled over with laughter. Once we regained our composure, Fisher announced, "In celebration, gang, I'm taking us out for dinner, drinks, and a real show, Jimmy Fisher style."

RF

BEN MARCUS

On one picture we went to Hawaii and lived on the North Shore for two and a half months. We did something that had never been done before. Big-wave riding was filmed in 35 mm. They wanted to capture the atmosphere surrounding the many surfers who make the annual winter trip to the Islands to ride big waves. I had faith. I wanted to make this thing a success, not only for them but for me, also. We had to leave for the Islands so fast that I didn't have time to collect equipment, and all I could get when I arrived was a 10′ 4″. I rode the beast at Sunset, the Pipeline, and Waimea. It was murder. . . . I was psyched out! My hair began to fall out. I got stomach ulcers. The Pipeline was a little scary, but Waimea had the biggest waves I've ever seen in my life. Under all this pressure I had to ride these waves, and every time they hit the button on that camera it was a hundred bucks—like it was judgment day. I'm paddling, trying to get going, and these guys are in it even before it stands up on the reef. They're driving and I'm just getting into it . . . by choice, I'm a four-feet-and-under man!

—Miki Dora, from "Surfing's Angry Young Man," *Surf Guide*

There isn't a day that goes by that I don't think about that asshole.

—Greg Noll on Miki Dora, March 2005.

Buy or rent the DVD version of *Riding Giants*, go into "Special Features" and click on the "Writer and Surfer's Commentary." As the movie flashes by, writer Sam George guides surfers Greg Noll, Jeff Clark, and Laird Hamilton through their own personal, behind-the-scenes, in-the-lineup narrative on Stacy Peralta's documentary on the history of big-wave surfing. Those four invisible talking heads say some good things all the way through, making an enjoyable movie doubly enjoyable as four guys with a lot of knowledge and experience give the inside scoop on boards, babes, and balls.

In Act One, close to the seventeen-minute mark, there is a shot of two guys with elephant guns wading into the water at the keyhole end of Waimea Beach. The guy on the right is carrying a board with orange and white panels. He is tall, dark, and wearing orange and white surf trunks.

On the narration, Sam George interrupts himself to identify the guy in the orange and white.

SAM GEORGE: Hey, that's Miki Dora there.
GREG NOLL: It is Miki. You're the first guy to pick up on that, Sam. I stole his trunks that day. He hung them on the side mirror of the car. It was pretty tough to steal anything from Miki Dora, but he hung his trunks there, and they were just asking to be scooped.

At this point the image changes to a group shot of the lineup at Waimea. Greg Noll is sitting farthest outside, recognizable in his black and white striped trunks. There's about a dozen other men and one woman in a lime-green bikini sitting in the lineup.

Greg's story about Dora's trunks is interrupted by Sam ("See the girl in the lineup there?"). The woman in the bikini is never identified, and then that thought is interrupted by something else, as the narration goes bouncing off on other tangents. And that is a shame, because Noll's story about stealing Miki Dora's surf trunks has its own weird and wonderful tangents and is worth telling.

That shot of Miki Dora strolling into the water carrying an elephant gun under his arm came from the winter of 1963-64. Dora was in Hawaii working as a surfing double for pop singer Fabian Forte, who was acting the role of surfer Jody Wallis—one of three mainland surfers who flew to Hawaii to challenge themselves on the North Shore.

Ride the Wild Surf premiered in New York City on August 5, 1964. Although *Beach Party* had come out the summer before, this was Hollywood's second semi-serious attempt to make a surf movie after *Gidget* in 1959. Unlike *Gidget* and *Beach Party*, *Ride the Wild Surf* didn't have any surfers breaking into song in front of their girlfriends, and this movie wavered from cool to corny and back again, with the emphasis on corny.

Ride the Wild Surf was shot first and acted later, bending a story around surfing footage captured during that winter of 1963-64. The waves are howlers and so are some of the words that come out of the surfers' mouths. John Milius, Greg Noll, and many others see *Ride the Wild Surf* as a serious but failed attempt to capture the mood of the North Shore at the time. Although it came out rated "C" for Corny, Contrived, and Commercial, *Ride the Wild Surf* launched a few careers and a thousand clichés that would reappear over the years in movies such as *Big Wednesday*, *North Shore*, *Point Break*, *In God's Hands,* and *Blue Crush.*

Cliché number one was "the surf trio" and cliché number two was "*haoles* to Hawaii." In *Ride the Wild Surf* the surf trio was Fabian, Tab Hunter, and Peter Brown, but in *Big Wednesday* the trio was Gary Busey, William Katt, and Jan-Michael Vincent. *Blue Crush* did a gender switch with Kate Bosworth, Sanoe Lake, and Michelle Rodriguez, and you could also argue that *Point Break* was a trio movie made of interchangeable characters: Patrick Swayze, Gary Busey, Keanu Reeves, Lori Petty, John Philbin, and the other surfing bank robbers.

The "*haoles* to Hawaii" device would pop up in *North Shore* with Rick Kane flying from Arizona to Oahu to get his feathers ruffled, and it appears again in *Blue Crush* with Kate Bosworth.

But the biggest cliché launched by *Ride the Wild Surf* was the "life or death ending in giant surf." *Ride the Wild Surf* ends on a big day at Waimea, with surfer after surfer getting picked off until one guy remains to take that "one last ride." What seemed corny at the time actually came true a few years later, as Greg Noll was the last man standing on that December day in 1969, when he scratched into a giant wave at Makaha.

The "life or death ending in giant surf" thing would appear over and over again in a number of movies. In *Big Wednesday*, Katt, Busey, and Vincent are reunited for a fifteen-foot day at Malibu which almost kills all of them. In *North Shore*, Rick Kane faces his fears on a giant day at Pipeline and survives to win the heart and mind of Kiani. In *Point Break*, FBI agent Johnny Utah travels all the way to Bell's Beach on the trail of psychobabble-spouting bank robber Bodhi, who is there to face his fate in the swell from the fifty-year storm. After a knock-down, drag-out fight at the water's edge, Johnny Utah puts the bracelets on Bodhi only to do the ultimate bro gesture by letting Bodhi go to take that "one last ride"—a stunt memorably achieved by Darrick Doerner.

At the end of *In God's Hands*, Matt George's Mickey refuses to ride giant waves using an infernal combustion engine, and he pays the price, going to Davey Jones' Locker, never to be seen again. And in *Blue Crush*, Kate Bosworth's Anne Marie Chadwick faces her fears on an epic day at Pipeline and snags a perfect-ten barrel.

Ride the Wild Surf is the movie that launched all those clichés. It begins with three mainland guys getting off the plane in Honolulu, then driving across the island to challenge the big stuff on the North Shore of Oahu. Steamer Lane (Tab Hunter), Jody Wallis (Fabian), and Chase Colton (Peter Brown) arrive wearing suits and ties accessorized with a variety of social, physical, and philosophical chips on their shoulders. They make it to the North Shore looking groomed and groovy, but the North Shore ruffles their feathers pretty quickly. Hurling themselves into the social scene by land and sea, they meet chicks and get in fights and are constantly challenged by man and nature to prove their manhood.

The *wahines* in *Ride the Wild Surf* are played by Barbara Eden, Shelly Fabares, and Susan Hart and they are Babealonians. The supporting cast includes James Mitchum as Eskimo, a big, gruff, no-nonsense guy with a Roman nose who rides the biggest stuff wearing black and white striped trunks.

Sound like someone we know? Greg Noll says he was a victim of circumstances. "Hey, I was just out there surfing, you know, because it was good Waimea that season," Da Bull snorted. "I kind of knew there was something going on because Miki Dora was out surfing Waimea, and he had never done that. He didn't really like the big stuff, but I knew he was getting paid and so was Mike Hynson. Well, Miki and I were kind of friends, and I wanted to see how he would do and maybe keep an eye on him. We rode a lot of fun Haleiwa and Sunset and fifteen- to twenty-foot Waimea, and I caught so many waves in those stupid black and white trunks, they created the Eskimo character, gave him some black and whites, and wrote him into the movie. I was totally bummed to be portrayed as a Hollywood jerk-off."

There is a backstory to this incident, one that goes back to the early '50s, when an exotic surf trip for Dora and Noll was a long drive through the citrus orchards on a summer day. "I first went to San Onofre," Greg Noll said, "when I was about ten years old or something, maybe eleven, and Miki was there. He was the only other kid on the entire beach. We hung out and surfed and it was kind of a friendship. I would call it a friendship or relationship or whatever it was. Dora didn't have friends in the normal sense."

The next summer Dora and Noll were at San Onofre again. By the time they were in high school, Noll and Dora were going mobile by hitching rides and then getting their own rides, and they would all meet again at Malibu.

When a south swell hit, Noll would jump a ride with Velzy or one of those guys and meet up with Dora at Malibu or at the Manhattan Beach pier. It was on and off like that. "We went on a few surf trips together before he stole everything I owned."

Noll is only half-joking when he accuses Dora of stealing from him. Dora is well known for being something of a sociopath, someone who lived for the scam.

Miki Dora didn't have a lot of friends, but Noll was about as close to being his friend as any surfer has been, and he has some ideas on how Dora became known as a conman. "There was a time when I could trust Dora a little bit," Noll said. "When we were kids hanging around San Onofre and Malibu he was somewhat normal. He started living with his grandmother. She was Hungarian and talked with an accent. He picked up her accent and used it in his everyday life, and it became one of Dora's trademarks. I will say this for Miki Dora, he had an incredible sense of humor. He could make something out of nothing. He was the brightest guy I've ever seen when it came to humor."

Noll says that guys burning each other was just a part of the *zeitgeist* in California and Hawaii from the '50s into the '60s. Noll calls it "ratfucking," and he says it was just what guys did, in another time, 50 years ago:

> What people don't understand is that period of time from about the '50s to, I don't know. . . . Something happened . . . something changed and it was just a strange time. There were a bunch of guys who surfed up and down the coast, and everyone was RFing each other. Some areas were worse than others.
>
> Here's kind of a bad example. I was a lifeguard and worked relief sometimes. I would go to another guy's tower to relieve him for fifteen to twenty minutes. Well, automatically I would check and see if he had any lunch. And if he did, I would eat his lunch. It was just a normal RF. It was a normal thing to do. It was a different mindset. It was continual from the time you opened your eyes to the time you went to sleep. And, you know, sometimes it even worked after we were asleep.
>
> We were surfing the Cove one time . . . it was me and Bing and Bev Morgan. Bev was driving because Bing and I weren't old enough, we were like fifteen, I guess. Bev had this old shitty Model A, so we took it up and surfed the Cove, and when we were done we found this dead skunk lying in the middle of the road somewhere up in Palos Verdes. The thing

reeked to high heaven and where most people would have avoided it, we thought, "Here's an opportunity!"

We couldn't put the skunk in the car because the car would have stunk forever, so we put a rope around the skunk's neck and tied the other end to the bumper of the car and dragged that sucker all the way back to the Manhattan Pier. When we got to Hermosa we pulled up at the bus stop and the skunk landed at the feet of these old ladies sitting there at the bus stop. They shrieked and carried on and we pushed on to Manhattan. We got there and couldn't figure out what to do with the skunk until we saw the sleeping bags.

Back then we all slept on the beach and we had our sleeping bags all lined up in the sand. We would do whatever all day and then crawl into the bags at night. Well Dale Velzy had a bag about twenty-five to thirty yards from Bing's. We moved it a little farther away than that and then inserted our friend the skunk into the bag. Everyone crapped out whenever, but Velzy was a notorious ladies' man. He came back around 2:30 in the morning with a friend, and they crawled into his bag. All of a sud-

With an original and brilliant advertising campaign, Miki Dora taunted and belittled potential customers of his signature model surf board. "Da CAT's Theory of Evolution" clarifies who is most evolved. Appeared in Surfer magazine in July 1967. (Courtesy, Greg Noll)

den there was this terrible shrieking that woke everyone up in time to see Velzy and his gal running bare-assed down to the water, the moon shining off their cracks as they jumped into the ocean to rinse off that stink. Velzy never found out who did it. He would have killed us. So that is a lot better than stealing some shitty lunch, huh?

Terry "Tubesteak" Tracy agrees with Noll on all of this. He spent time around Dora and knew he was a sophisticated guy who took his RFing to new levels: "Some guys would go to a party and steal lawn furniture. Dora would walk into a party and steal an Oscar. He did this, and I saw it, at a party at a writer's house in Los Angeles, near the Veteran's Cemetery. He walked in and walked out with an Oscar. I think he got caught and gave it back."

Anything could be an RF: women, money, booze, boards, wax, lunch, waves. From the '50s on, "it all went to hell," according to Greg Noll on the *Riding Giants* soundtrack. He was referring to the transmogrification of surfing from a sport of kings and gentlemen into the pursuit of rascals and rats.

And out of the '50s into the '60s, Miki Dora, Da Cat, was also King Rat. A good part of Dora's problem was that he was bright, perhaps abnormally so. Greg Noll says that Dora was a genius when it came to humor, and anyone who knows anything knows that humor is just a side effect of intelligence, a

I have been asked by several leading Universities to clarify the various stages of evolution in the history of surfing. Much time and research has gone into these studies and the final results. *Mickey Dora*

Mickey Dora / da CAT

717 VALLEY DRIVE
HERMOSA BEACH,
CALIFORNIA

GREG NOLL
Surfboards

*distributing the
Greg Noll Surfboard
exclusively*

SPORTSWAYS
INC.

7701 E. COMPTON BLVD.
PARAMOUNT, CALIFORNIA
NEvada 6-9771

MAFIAS
ANA POINTIS

DECENTUS
INDIVIDUALIST

HOMOSAPENS
MICKEY DORA

will survive only as
its food supply lasts.
the earlier stage of
with their dull wit
worship. This form is
ognized by its pleasant
gaudy outfits. It is
sell out to any side.

Easily recognized once it is spotted. Although this is a very rare form it is serious and intelligent in its action. He possesses skill and cunning, and his type probably led to the final stage.

The peak of perfection has all the qualities of the latter stage plus more advanced knowledge and ability. Uses only one model . . . da Cat . . . a very rare form, the only one known.

pressure release for an overburdened brain. But the guy who is smart is also determined to prove it, to be on top, and Dora not only wanted to be the best surfer in the water, he also wanted to be the top ratfucker on land.

And so he gained his reputation as a con artist—someone who would steal Oscars and push guys out of the way on waves at Malibu. Dora RFed everyone, Greg Noll included. By the winter of '63-'64, Noll and Dora had lots of history between them, and the game was on when they came to Hawaii.

"*Ride the Wild Surf* was shot in 1963, or something like that," Noll said. "By then we had put in a lot of miles down the road together. I don't know if Miki and I were friends then, but I guess there was a sort of wary respect, because I knew I couldn't turn my back on the guy, and Miki was maybe a little worried about what I would do physically if he got carried away. All of that lead to us being in the water at the same time at Waimea. They were shooting that crappy movie, and I was vaguely aware that something was up, because Dora didn't really like big waves. But there he was in the lineup at Waimea on a pretty big day. He didn't want to be there, but he had obligations to the movie people paying him, and he certainly had his pride when it came to being a good surfer. Dora was in over his head, so he was sticking close to me, using me as a lineup because he knew I had put my time in at Waimea and knew I would be in the right spot when a set came."

The entertainment value of *Ride the Wild Surf* goes *way* up as you watch it forty years later with Da Bull. "Oh my God, look at these guys!" Noll roared at the sight of Fabian, Brown, and Hunter checking the lineup at Waimea. "A suit and tie? At Waimea? Look at the hair. It's perfect! Look at the car. No rust! No wonder we didn't hang out with these guys. They're a bunch of Hollywood dorks. A bunch of phonies. I avoided them like the plague, and the other guys hung around because they were getting paid."

Forty years later, Noll can barely watch the movie, but perks up at the surfing scenes. "That's Haleiwa there, and who's the guy in the stinkbug stance at Sunset? There's L.J. Richards on that wave and that's Ricky Grigg. The backside guy is Butch Van Artsdalen. I remember that style. Check out Jeff Hakman! What is he, eight years old there? Here's a big wave. That's Mike Stange taking off behind me at Waimea and wiping out, and there I go wiping out so maybe Mike wouldn't be lonely when he went over the falls. Oh, and now I'm claiming it there on the shoulder. Okay, it's starting to come back to me now. I remember the camera guys wanted some good wipeouts, so they kept an eye on me, because that's what I did best."

Noll watches *Ride the Wild Surf* with one hand over his eyes and one

Noll (left) and Dora (right) with a second generation DA CAT model surf board. Crescent City, California, 1998. (Photo courtesy of Greg Noll)

Greg Noll's Eulogy to Miki Dora at the 2004 Waterman's Ball

When I was coming down here on the airplane, I started thinking, "Geez, what can I say about this guy that's nice."

Miki was just a hard guy to be nice to. Our relationship goes back to when we were just kids and the relationship was a bit like two dogs circling, growling at each other most of our lives. Miki came over to the house, just before he checked out. We had a great time; I took him to the woods and we did a little hiking, and he put his arm around me at one point and asked for a picture to be taken, which he just hated violently—having pictures being taken.

And I asked him, I said, "Man, you're really caving in here. What? You're getting old? You want your picture taken? You want to put your arm around me—get away from me." I think he might have known then that he was looking at the end of the tube. The big kickout.

I called him the day before he passed away. I said, "Miki, how's it going?" I had no idea that he was going to be gone the next morning. I said, "How you doing?"

He said, "Well they just gave me a shot of morphine and an enema. When I am through with this conversation, I am seriously considering doing a wall painting."

One thing you can say about Miki Dora, the guy took his humor right to the end with him. I said, "You know we've been shitty to each other and taunting each other for almost forty years." I went to hang up the phone and I don't know why this just jumped out of my mouth. I said, "I love you, man." There was a little hesitation and he said, "I love you too, pal."

I hung up. It was really personal. I didn't think I was going to say it; it just came out.

Then I'll be damned if the next morning he doesn't die. I swear, I'll spend the rest of my life trying to figure out whether he was putting me on or not.

hand on the remote control. When the phony Hollywood actors are on, he fast-forwards to get to Barbara Eden's parts (if you know what we mean). When Eden and Peter Brown buy New Year's Eve fireworks from Mr. Chin, Noll nods and says, "Well they got that part right, anyway. The North Shore on New Year's Eve has always been World War Four."

After the fireworks, with the "high surf alarm" echoing all over the North Shore, the Chase Colton character attempts to jump-start his manhood by diving from a high rock at Waimea Falls. As Barbara Eden clasps her hands to her lovely bosom and implores her man not to do it, a stuntman in a straw hat and hula pants does the dive. Ricky Grigg thinks the diver might have been Butch Van Artsdalen, while Fred Van Dyke is pretty sure the diver was Chuck Quinn. Speaking from Pacifica, Quinn said he dove off Waimea Falls a lot, but doesn't remember doing it in a straw hat and hula pants with the camera rolling. Must have been Butch.

Noll has no idea who did the dive, but he said that part of the movie was realistic. "Diving from the jump rock was a big deal back then. I did it, and I'll tell you when you got to the top of that plateau there and looked down, it really made your butt pucker. I jumped feet-first but never went headfirst. I think Muñoz dove and I remember Pat Curren doing a huge belly-flop from up there, and we thought he was dead. So they got a few things right in this *Ride the Wild Surf*. But, holy shit, did you see that guy's hair? Nobody's that perfect."

Dora wasn't perfect at Waimea, but he did awfully good for a guy making a quantum jump in a season. When Dora takes off at Waimea, Noll is proud of how his friend held up: "Look at him take off on that wave, a little fade at the top and a big drop," Noll said as he watched Dora on the small screen, forty years later. "Look at him there in front of me."

The wave that laid the foundation of the friendship between Greg Noll and Miki Dora is not on film, but Noll remembers it vividly, because it led to so much down the years:

You know, I distinctly remember riding behind Dora on that one wave at Waimea. I was behind him and he knew I was there. When I put my hand on the small of his back, I could tell he thought he was about to get ratfucked. Every muscle in his body was like crystal glass. He thought I was going to shove him like he had shoved millions of guys. But I didn't. I knew the wave was going to get me, and I was stoked for Miki going out and charging some big waves, making a big jump in a day.

He was a ten-foot-and-under guy and there he was riding waves over twenty foot. How many guys could have done that? So instead of pushing Dora off, I gave him a big shove that blew him through the impact zone, just before that wave ate me alive. I didn't know what happened to Dora. When I came up I saw that my board had popped out. I was swimming over and Dora paddled over and got my board and brought it to me, which was really unusual. Normally, he would have paddled it out to sea and left me with my ass hanging. But this time Dora got my board and pushed it back to me as he was slobbering at the mouth: 'That was the nicest thing anyone has done for me in my life!'

I didn't think much of it, but Dora never, ever forgot it through the years and right up to our last few weeks together. It was like removing the thorn from the lion's paw. After that, Dora and I were as close to being friends as you could be with him.

That wave at Waimea lead to Noll and Dora teaming up to produce the Da Cat model. Miki Dora's signature model surfboard was marketed with one of the most original, controversial, brilliant advertising campaigns of all time. In his magazine ads, Dora slandered the surf industry, and his competition and all but dared the kooks, cowboys, valleys, and hodads to buy one of his boards. And it worked. Noll and Dora produced Da Cat from 1964 to 1967, and made a nice dollar. Twenty-five years later they made another deal in the '90s to produce quality recreations of Da Cat.

These boards sold for big bucks and led to the arrest and conviction of a guy for selling knockoff copies in 1994:

I should tell the whole story about that some day, about the second time we made a deal to produce Da Cat model boards. The first time was bad, but this time was like the Great Alaskan Land Deal. Miki had this lawyer whose tie was on sideways and his hair was messed up and he looked like he was in the middle of a seven-day drunk. Dora just knew he was going to get RFed on this deal and he demanded everything. He demanded that the printer sign something promising to print only so many labels, and he demanded to be paid in $50 bills sealed in manila envelopes before he would sign the labels. He demanded everything and it went on and on and on, and finally it was all set and the papers were before him to sign. There was nothing else he could demand but he just knew he was going to get RFed, and you know what he did? He started hyperventilating, like he was going to take off on a big wave. And he wasn't joking. It was that hard for Dora to sign a contract, and this was with me. I had RFed him in the past but never when it came to business. Finally he signed the thing and it took me like four days to get over the whole ordeal of watching Dora have to trust someone. But we did okay on Da Cat model, both times.

Greg Noll produced those second generation Da Cat boards from his home near Crescent City, where he escaped to in the '70s. These days, he works out of a Geppetto-class woodshed filled with exotic hardwoods from Hawaii and California, using the tools of a serious woodworker: planers, glue, templates,

DA BLUE CAT AWARD: One of many abusive advertisements written by Miki to promote the "DA CAT" model surfboard. Appeared in *Surfer* magazine in January 1967. (Courtesy, Greg Noll)

clamps. There is a lot of history hanging from the rafters of that woodshed—including several of the elephant guns that Noll rode into history at Waimea and Pipeline.

Get Noll in the right mood and he will dig into the archives and bring out an icon from another era. They are a pair of surf trunks, with orange and white panels, recognizable as the surf trunks Miki Dora wore during the winter of '63-'64 when he was doubling for Fabian in *Ride the Wild Surf.* They were Miki's trunks, but Greg Noll has them.

"I stole them from Dora," Noll says and his face lights up like a rascal. "Not many people can say they RFed Miki Dora, but I did and here is the proof. After that day at Waimea when I shoved him through the impact zone, I went in and Miki went in and we were standing up on the road. Miki was babbling and pretty excited because he had just ridden the biggest waves of his life, fulfilled his obligation to the filmmakers, and got pretty stoked, you know? So we're hanging around and Miki is so jazzed he hung his shorts on the outside mirror of my car. He was so stoked from the surf that he let his guard down. As soon as I saw that I grabbed his trunks and drove away. I could see him in the rearview mirror, standing in the middle of the road in a towel, shaking his fist at me."

Those trunks probably belong in a surf museum or a movie museum somewhere, and Noll has been offered a fair bit of money for them over the years, but he isn't selling such a personal trophy. "For twenty-five years Dora talked about that one wave at Waimea and for twenty-five years he asked me to give back his trunks. I never did. Fuck, no! Why would I do that?"

Capers in the Key of "T": Trestles Memories

STEVE PEZMAN

The brief, undulating two-mile strip of California coast running from Cotton's Point south to San Onofre holds a miraculous run of surf breaks including Upper Trestle, Lower Trestle, Middles, and Church. The breaks are soft, surfable things with long, tapered walls sloping at the bottom to let you around sections and with enough push so that a special mindless freedom can occur there—which is all you can ask of a surfing wave. The marsh and reeds that creep to the sand and the mesquite smell in the air give it such a distinct identity, that if deposited there blindfold, I'm sure I could sense where I was. Those who have frequented Trestles over the years have a trove of experiences to cherish. Most of mine come from the time when the US Marines owned and controlled the area. I offer these to celebrate an era and perhaps to humble today's crew with the knowledge that their time, too, will pass.

Summer 1951

The story goes like this: two precocious teenagers spent a summer frequenting the beach at San Onofre. The remarkable surfing skills of each had attracted attention at their home breaks, but they were quite different from

David Nuuhiwa (from Huntington Beach) going left at Lowers in 1964. (Photo, Leo Hetzel)

one other. The dark complexioned one from up north was with his eccentric stepdad, Gard Chapin, perhaps the best surfer on the entire coast at that time. The other, a lighter-skinned blond, hitched a ride up with some older guys from Oceanside. At this time, surfboards were in profound transition—from heavy planks and kook boxes to foiled, fiberglass-coated, finned, light balsa chips, capable of new, and as yet, unthought of stuff. Both youngsters had shown signs of departing from the surfing norm of that period. Being kids surrounded by older guys, at a beach ridiculed by some as the bastion of the status quo, they were looking around for some excitement.

Noticing a point with white water about a mile to the north, they asked Burrhead what the deal was. "Oh yeah, that's called the Trestles (named after a series of two low railroad bridges over San Mateo Creek and one at San Onofre Creek). So and so dragged his plank up there in '37 and tried it out. Said the waves were too quick—that he pearled on every try. Said 'Nofre was way better."

The "too quick" part attracted them. So the two walked up to the distant point, carrying their forty-pound balsa chips on their heads. There they discovered the waves to be quite suitable for the kind of surfing they had in mind. It is said by some that the two naturally competitive kids conducted an impromptu, mano a mano, radical maneuver duel to constantly top each other in the snappy curls at Lowers (then known as Middle Trestles), which they had completely to themselves every day—and that the two youngsters invented most of what is now done on a modern surfboard during that summer. One of them, much later in life, was said to have commented that for him, it was all downhill after that.

Summer 1955

Dale Velzy opened the Velzy & Jacobs shop on Coast Highway in North San Clemente where he produced hippy, highly maneuverable balsa "pig" shapes, and drew hot surfers from all over California and the Islands to work on and ride his sticks. Such luminaries as Rennie Yater, Kemp Aaberg, Del Cannon, Dick "Tiny Brain" Thomas, Donald Takyama, Kimo Hollinger, Duke Brown, and the Hawk himself soon took advantage of afternoon glass-offs at the kelpy, pristine points of Uppers, Lowers and Cottons. The Marines, who occasionally noticed the young men at play while they practiced war, were amused by their presence.

Summer 1957

A young and rambunctious member of a visiting crew from Malibu, in a wanton act of rebellion not untypical of that time, performed a stylish head-dip while dropping his trunks around his ankles and pointing his bum at a passenger train that was rolling by. The sight of that famous surfer's bare ass is said to have outraged the train's conductor and various passengers who reported it to the proper authorities upon arrival at the next station. They in turn complained to the Provost Marshall of the United States Marine Corps base at Camp Pendleton, California, shocking that gentleman with the fact that young men within the purvey of his jurisdiction were engaging in lewd public conduct. Wanting to clearly establish that this aberrant behavior wasn't coming from his corps, and that the provost was, indeed, firmly in control of his turf, it became the sworn duty of the United States Marines, from that day on, to keep Trestles free of surfers. Little did they know that it would become a battle that would challenge them unlike any other.

Summer 1961

By the third day of an eight- to ten-foot, main-event swell, maybe thirty surfers would have traveled from their home breaks to converge on the point break at Lowers. Some of those in attendance would include such period notables as Bing Copeland, Tim Kelly and Tom Sweeney from South Bay; Rusty Miller and Mike Hynson from down south; Robert August, Mike Haley, Bill Fury and Tim Dorsey from Seal Beach; "Chucker" Burgess and Lewis Tarter from Huntington; Mike Lutz, Chris Marseilles, Kent Halworth and Mike Marshall from Newport; John Graye and Don Young from Long Beach; L. J. Richards from Oceanside; Mike O'Neill and Linden Whitemore from P.V.; and Mike Doyle from Westchester. The talent pool of surfing styles was rich and diverse. Trestles had no locals at that time. We were all visitors and we coexisted well. Even though the crew was often numerous and red-hot, the pre-leash carrying capacity of the break could handle the load. Only maybe five to eight guys would be at the takeoff zone at any given time, while another handful were paddling back out, some swimming for their boards, and a dozen others rested on the beach.

Generally, most swells passed by lightly surfed, and many were completely unattended. On some swells, both Uppers and Lowers would be good, but the handful of surfers present on any given day were friends, and they'd choose one break, leaving the other unridden.

Upon arrival at the Trestles area, the initial approach usually included reconnoitering for the enemy from the Basilone Road surf check, which often would reveal Lowers and Uppers both glassy, anywhere from three to six feet and with no humans in sight. The burning question would then become, were the Marine's MP jeeps visible on the beach? Whether we could see any or not, our heart rate would soar as anxiety took over, because we could never be sure we were going to make it through to those empty, glassy, perfect waves—until we were actually out in the water. We'd usually trot, nonstop from where we parked the car, all the way to the beach, carrying our thirty-pound longboards underarm like they were feathers. The unknown of whether that day would be a disaster or a victory made every successful session at Trestles a sweet adventure.

Summer 1964

Bill Wetzel and I were lounging on the hot sand between leisurely go-outs on a three- to five-foot day just down from the point at Lowers. We were the only ones there, and then the Marine MPs suddenly showed up. True to form for experienced Trestles' veterans, our 10-foot boards were stashed back in a clearing (called a sunbowl) in the reeds. So as the MP jeep pulled to a stop fifty yards away and the two jarheads got out and ran towards us shouting, "Y'all are under arrest for trespassing on a military reservation! Stay where you are!" We merely stood up, stretched, looked over at the two uniformed kids about our age with a grin, shouted back to them, "Right, pal!" and stepped into the reeds, disappearing from sight. We waded into the marsh another fifteen or twenty feet and then stood there in silence, calf deep in the brackish water, totally hidden from anyone standing on the beach.

"Y'all surfers. We know you're in there. Come out. Now!"

Silence.

"Y'all better come out!"

Wetzel and I glanced at each other.

"Y'all surfers think you're smart, we'll get you."

We were pretty sure they wouldn't get their boots wet. Suddenly, a round beach rock the size of a grapefruit came arching through the air like a slow motion shot put, bending the reeds as it splashed with a thud ten feet away. Wetzel and I had to keep from cracking up and revealing our location. For the next few minutes, missiles continued arching through the air like mortar shells, bending the reeds as they ascended in a slow-motion barrage. We watched a stone lift to its apogee and then head back to earth and splash not more than a foot away. We silently leaned out of its path without moving our feet. The jarheads were now standing just fifteen feet from us, but didn't know it. They were swearing a blue streak and lobbing the biggest boulders they could heft. Theirs was a futile effort unless they lucked out and hit one of us

Marines arrest two surfers and await the photographer, Leo Hetzel, as he sneaks a photo. The Marines and the surfers were the same age, but the Marines were heading off to Vietnam; the surfers were going to the beach. The Marines were envious, perhaps resentful. (Photo, Leo Hetzel)

with a boulder. Did they really want that? This was just a game ... wasn't it?

In between the intermittent barrage and their profane shouts, it was quiet and serene in the marsh. The beginning of a light westerly breeze was swaying the tops of the reeds in rhythmic pulses. Bill pulled a baggie with a joint and some matches out of his wax pocket and showed it to me with a grin. I nodded. He lit it, took a toke, and passed it to me. I took a hit, held it down, and passed it back. Suddenly, I felt something nibbling on my lower legs right at the waterline. Looking down, I saw a flock of baby ducklings bobbing in the wavelets created by the splashes of the rocks. Wetzel and I grinned at each other, savoring the irony of the moment. The jarheads would be gone soon, and even with the freshening wind, the inside faces would still be glassy for our second session.

Summer 1968

Wetzel, Leo Hetzel, Steve Shearers and Stu Herz, and I called ourselves the "T-Key Club." Shearers drove a '48 Dodge which we brush-painted camouflage all-over, chrome included, so we could hide it in the jungle behind the tracks at Lowers. Before the San Diego Freeway had been built, there was a produce farm on the inland side of northbound 101 across from the Trestles. We cut a link out of the farm gate and put our own padlock on it. We'd open it, drive through and re-lock it, then drive along the farm dirt road on the inland side of the highway, past strawberry, tomato and lettuce fields and stooped, uncaring workers. We'd drive under the 101 bridge, over San Mateo Creek, then back along the Marine's main dirt road paralleling the highway. Around the middle of the valley floor we'd turn hard right and floor it over a small soft dirt berm that had been bulldozed to ineffectively close off an old track into the jungle. After another 150 yards along the track, snaking this way and that, we'd finally power the car into a dense thicket close to the railroad tracks that ran about 75 yards from the beach.

We'd leave our lunches in the safety of our car, climb up and over the raised railroad bed with our boards, and then trot Indian-style, single file with boards under arm, springing lightly over the soft spongy footpath through the reeds to the beach. We swore each other to secrecy about our access method. If too many people found out, the strategy would be ruined. When we'd leave, we'd make a big show of walking out along the beach taking some conventional route before cutting back into the jungle. But no matter how careful we were, our number grew as a result of giving different guys rides.

On good summer days there would be up to four cars tucked into the jungle near the tracks. The Marines got wise to this and began waging a war of subterfuge. They would park their MP cars out on the main dirt road and comb the jungle on foot looking for our vehicles. Upon finding one of our cars, they'd flatten our tires, take our valve stems or coil wires, and do other nasty deeds. Once, when returning to our cammo car for lunch, we happened upon two MPs leaning under the hood of someone else's car. We quietly sprinted around them to the main dirt road using an alternate path. Sure enough, there sat their MP vehicle, unguarded. We tried their driver side door and amazingly found it unlocked. Releasing the hood latch, we had soon stripped their car of spark plug and coil wires and flattened all four tires. Later, on the way home, we envisioned them trying to explain how their patrol vehicle had been sabotaged while they were off disabling our cars. By the middle of that summer's surf season, at least half a dozen of our friends had figured out our ploy and had their own locks in operation. Finally, the farmer blew his mind over all the locks on his gate and cut them off.

Summer 1967

One sunny afternoon, Stu and I had walked in along the northern Coast Guard Loran Station fence, up on the boundary line on Cotton's Point, when suddenly a young MP jumped out from behind a bush. He raised his night-stick, announced that we were trespassing on a military reservation, and then began striking Stu on his arms and shoulders. Stu dropped his board and began fending off the blows while screaming at the guy, "What's wrong with you? We're just going to the beach to ride waves. What are you doing? Are you crazy?"

The MP stopped beating on Stu and backed off in a dazed fashion, mumbling, "You don't understand. You don't understand. I just came home from Nam two weeks ago." It turned out he had been guarding an ammo dump against Viet Cong, and now he was guarding the trail along the fence at Trestles. He hadn't made the transition yet. Stu's arms were a patchwork of black and blue splotches for a couple of weeks.

Summer 1962

Wetzel and I drove down to Trestles from Huntington Beach on a dubious day of one- to three-foot wind junk. A tall, lanky girl surfer from Huntington named Mary rode along. She was a tomboy member of the Pier crew (meaning she was normally treated like a guy by the rest of us). She had an artistic bent and during that hippy period had painted most of the "flower power" surf shop signs that graced Huntington Beach's Main Street. When we finally got down to the sand at Trestles, we saw that the surf was poor, but since the break was empty, we all went out to catch a few lackluster waves and eventually came in.

The sun was warm so Bill and I took our soggy trunks off and hung them on sticks stuck in the sand to dry and then ran around naked for a while, trying futilely to interest Mary into doing the same. She ignored us. We only managed to embarrass and then bore her. We all lay down in the hot, midday sand, pulled it up around our chests and snoozed off.

Unbeknownst to us, Chuck Lennin and Ray "The Malibu Enforcer" Kunze had left Huntington about thirty minutes behind us. When they arrived at the beach, seeing the lack of surf and all of us crashed out with the two of us nude, they decided there was a better game afoot. Chuck and Ray crawled across the sand on their bellies, removed the trunks from the sticks then slithered back into the reeds and left.

Half an hour or so later, we awoke to find our trunks had disappeared. Had they blown away? Where the hell did they go? Oh well. Not to worry. We'd improvise. Wetzel found a tattered nylon windbreaker and forced his legs through the sleeves. He pulled the hood up in front to cover his unit, tied it around his waist using the drawstrings, and pulled the body of the jacket back between his legs and up over the tie strings to cover his butt. I found an old towel remnant and made a sort of loincloth arrangement using twigs to fasten it together at the waist. In that makeshift garb, we boldly marched out of Trestles, along busy Hwy. 101, boards carried atop our heads, to my '51 Ford woody and drove back to Huntington Beach unaware of what had happened until we arrived at Vardeman Surfboards on PCH. There in the window of Sonny's shop were two mannequins on display in the window—wearing our trunks. Surfers in town had heard the story by then and gathered in the parking lot to laugh at our arrival. But of course, we acted like it was no big deal.

Summer 1962

It was low tide on a hot and glassy six-foot day with twenty to thirty guys out, mostly from Huntington and Newport Beach. The Marine MPs were there too, waiting on the beach for us to lose our boards. This was well before the advent of leashes. But the waves were too good for us to just sit there bobbing in the swell until the jarheads left, so we were riding carefully.

Hot Huntington Beach goofyfooter Tom Lonardo lost his board, and it came to rest against a rock in six inches of tidal wash. He was twenty feet from his board and an MP was thirty feet away. They both began running, Lonardo racing barefoot over the rocks and the Marine splashing through the water in his combat boots. When the Marine saw he was going to lose the race to the board, he stopped running and began lofting big rocks at Tom's board. One rock landed nearby and ricocheted at his board with a wicked crack of a blow. Outraged, and in retaliation, Lonardo lofted a sizeable boulder of his own at the jarhead. To the shock of those of us who were watching from the lineup, Lonardo's missile made a direct hit, bounced off the Marine's collarbone and then the side of his head, causing him to fall flat in the water, face down. Lonardo retrieved his board and paddled back out. Two other MPs ran down and grabbed their buddy under the arms, dragged him back to their jeep, and sped off.

That spooked us, but the waves were glassy, and we weren't about to leave conditions like that, so we kept surfing. Sure enough, about twenty minutes later, a truck of MPs arrived on the point at Lowers. They piled out and started shouting at us through a bullhorn, but we pretended they weren't there and kept riding—only more cautiously than before. Then Lonardo lost his board again. As he swam after it, we could see that this time he had no chance. The MPs got it by one end, dragged it bouncing over the rocks to the sand and threw it in the back of their truck. So Lonardo swam right in, walked up the beach to the jarheads like he'd done no wrong and boldly asked for the return of his board. This obviously took them back a bit. So they started telling him about one of his buddies out in the water who had done this heinous act of violence with a rock to one of their compatriots. Lonardo told them he knew the jerk who threw the rock, that everyone in the water was pissed at the guy, and if they'd just give him back his board, he'd paddle out there and get everyone to force the offending jerk to turn himself in on the beach or they'll all pound him. Well, that sounded so reasonable to the jarheads that they actually gave Lonardo his board back. We couldn't believe it. But what really blew our minds was when Lonardo got about twenty feet off the beach, he turned around, and while giving the MPs the finger with both hands he shouted, "You dumb assholes! It was me! It was me!"

Summer 1961

A small group of us from Huntington were leaving Trestles after a nice, but not memorable day. As we came to the entrance of the path back through the reeds, Mary flicked a cigarette butt into the undergrowth. By the time we reached the top of the embankment, we could see smoke rising from the reeds at the beach's edge. Several of us ran back along the path to the fire slowly spreading in damp reeds. There was nothing nearby with which to put it out, so we emptied our bladders on the blaze to no avail. With no further firefighting options, we fled the scene. Luckily, the fire burned itself out after consuming about an acre of reeds. The next day, we heard that Peter Van Dyke's board that he kept hidden in the reeds during the summer had been consumed in the blaze. In an issue later that summer, *Surfer* magazine ran a shot of glum Peter standing next to the charred remains of his treasured balsa stick. Up until now, the origins of that fire have been kept a mystery.

Summer 1967

It was just Wetzel and me out at Lowers on an excellent six-foot early afternoon. The tide was medium low and out-going; conditions had improved greatly after a momentary midday south wind had caused everyone else to

Ronald Patterson (from Dana Point) doing a cutback on a lazy, uncrowded day in 1964. In the '60s there were hardly any surfers living nearby. The regulars drove in from as far away as South Bay and San Diego. But since Trestles became a California State Park in 1971, the crowds have grown worse each year. With localism rampant and population booming, it is now the poster child for violent surf breaks. (Photo, Leo Hetzel)

leave. We were having a great time when a truckload of Marines pulled up on the beach. An officer got out, dropped a ramp in the back and out jumped a whole squad of GI-rines in red sweatsuits. The officer formed them up into two rows on the beach and had them doing calisthenics—jumping jacks and squats.

Bill and I were just dumbfounded by this display. We couldn't figure out what they were up to, so we were watching and riding, warily. Then the officer blew a whistle, and on cue, the squad stripped down into red Marine Corps swim trunks and waded out through the rocks. At the time, the rock beds were covered with spiny urchins and the poor guys realized this as they picked their way out through the obstacle course without benefit of a board to lean on.

Wetzel and I figured out what they were up to and we were incredulous. They were coming after us, swimming! We shouted, "Watch out for the urchins! Watch out for the urchins, they'll wreck your feet! You can't get them out. They have to cut them out at the hospital." Most of these guys were probably from the Midwest and slightly terrified of the ocean, and we rapped it down to them as if we were truly concerned for their safety. They glanced nervously back at the officer on the beach, but he was blowing on his whistle and stridently pointing out to sea. There was no doubt what he wanted, and for them there was no turning back.

They divided into two groups of swimmers—one would come straight at us, distracting our attention from the other expeditionary force which would then circle around behind. The only flaw in their military science was that we were on 10-foot surfboards and they were swimming. Our strategy was to let them get oh-so tantalizingly close, say within three or four feet, while we "talked" to them, then we'd take an easy stroke and glide further out of reach. Using this method, over a period of forty minutes, we lead the two groups out to sea about a quarter mile. We stayed just beyond their reach, all the while telling them that it was impossible to catch us. Then I said, something like, "I sure hope y'all don't have to go to Nam with that guy as your officer" (they were, and he was). "He's gonna get you killed. He's gonna send you on hopeless missions just like this one, except we're just harmless surfers. You better accidentally frag that idiot first chance you get."

Finally, the officer blew his whistle and signaled them to turn around and swim into the beach. They climbed back into their truck and drove off down the dirt road. We surfed for a while and when we were starving, cold and sure they were gone, we paddled in. Sure enough, they were waiting for us in the bushes and jumped out and nabbed us cold. It ended up that Wetzel's gift for gab was so golden that they fed us lunch and then cut us loose.

The Provost's Collection

In the '60s, if you got caught at Trestles the Marines generally took your board. No one carried IDs in their wet trunks, so when they asked your name you could say anything you wanted. Famous guys like Phil Edwards, Dewey Weber and Lance Carson were in deep shit cause everyone used their name. When the MP records showed that Phil had been caught over twenty times in one year, they began confiscating boards. They kept the boards like political prisoners in a barbed-wire enclosed compound down at the Oceanside end of the base by the Provost Marshall's office.

After a year or so, they had well over a hundred boards in their possession. To get a board back, you'd drive down to the Oceanside gate, tell the MPs standing gate duty what you were there for, and they'd let you drive on the base to retrieve your property. When you arrived at the Provost's office, you presented your ID to a uniformed MP, who took you down to the compound and asked you to identify your board. There was the largest collection of the cherriest sticks you could imagine. Guys didn't take anything to Trestles but their best equipment, and there it all was. Some guys were actually afraid to go get their boards back, so they were just left there.

As we'd be inspecting the board stash for our own stick, we'd say, "Oh, there's Johnny's board. Johnny moved to Texas and his mom asked us to get his board for him." The Marines were dubious, but sometimes pliant, and on more than one occasion we were able to depart with "Johnny's board" as well as our own.

To this day, a few of us speculate that the Provost's office may possibly have the world's biggest and best collection of classic, mint condition, '60s longboards as a bizarre hangover from that period.

Summer 1962

Five of us (a full carload for optimum gas money) were walking in along the old middle trail, when we came upon four pup tents pitched in a semi-circle in a clearing under a dense canopy of shrubbery, halfway between the train tracks and the old Coastal Highway. Sticking out of one of the tents on the far side of the clearing was a pair of boots attached to some legs. The rest of the squad was obviously out reconnoitering in the area, perhaps looking for us.

Out in the open sat a .30-caliber machine gun with an ammo belt feeding from a metal ammo box. We all stood there silently, taking in the bizarre little military diorama when the lead guy of our group (who will remain anonymous) suddenly stooped down, picked up the .30-cal and the ammo box and motioned us all to continue. We proceeded to the beach. The surf was crummy, so he fired a few bursts of the weapon, which made a hell of a lot of noise. Scared, we tossed the machine gun into the reeds and left the beach at a fast trot by another path.

On the way home, we realized how bad we might have screwed that poor summer soldier. A machine gun stolen from the campsite while he's asleep on guard duty, whew! He might have even gotten time in the stockade. We guessed he probably had to pay for the weapon.

Summer 1965

Seal Beach surfer Bill Fury set the all-time flat tire record for a Trestles round trip, a distance of about sixty-five miles. Driving his 1951 humpback Mercury (which was later abandoned to Federales in Mazatlan, Mexico, and after that was seen serving as a taxi for several years), he experienced six flats on the way down and back, all with no spare. After the fourth flat on the homeward leg in Laguna Beach, all passengers finally threw in the towel, abandoned ship and hitchhiked home. It took another day for Fury to make it.

On the way home from Trestles in my '51 Ford woody, northbound on the Coastal Highway from Laguna Beach to Corona Del Mar, we were stuck in bumper-to-bumper traffic and creeping slowly along. Next to us in the lane to our right was a straight-looking guy in a family sedan sporting out-of-state plates with his wife next to him and his mother-in-law in the back seat. As we passed him, we were checking him out and he mouthed to us, "Daddy's car!" We were outraged. This woody was a surfer lifestyle statement and the geek thought that we were borrowing it from Daddy. (In truth, he did buy it for me.) In an act of revenge, the surfer next to me riding shotgun dropped his surf trunks and stuck his hairy butt out the window, "browning them out" in the grossest manner, testicles dangling, for at least ten full minutes of unabated horror. Because of traffic, they were trapped next to us the whole time. The women in his car were in shock, and the guy was powerless to do anything other than cringe.

Mike McClelland from Newport Beach used to boldly drive his Chevy Nomad where no man had gone before, somehow getting on to the dirt service road and up the beach to Lowers where he'd tuck it into a big bush which grew right on the point. In between surf sessions, Mike would disappear into the bush during which periods loud rock 'n roll would come thundering out of the bushes from his car stereo along with clouds of smoke. The MPs would cruise out to the point, stop and try to figure out where the music came from. They never did figure him out. Too improbable.

Trestles Tactics

On somewhat crowded summer days, the MPs would suddenly show up in their jeeps, with red lights blazing. They'd jump out and try to catch groups of surfers who would grab their sticks and run down the beach towards the Cotton's Point line or into the myriad paths that led through the reeds and across the tracks into the jungle. While the normal urge to escape involved running away and being chased, we would just slowly gather up our stuff and walk away down the beach. They preferred to chase those who ran rather than we who walked. In that fashion we would get about a hundred yards down the beach, well away from the fracas when they would suddenly notice us and scream, "Halt! Halt!"

We'd just wave and acknowledge their shouts by shouting back, "We're leaving, thank you, we're leaving," with no apparent panic. It almost always worked. Our motto became, "A dog will always chase a thrown stick."

When a group on the beach was comprised of veteran Trestles riders, and the customary solo jeep with two MPs would raid us, by pre-agreement, we'd all just get up and slowly walk off in different directions. There'd be maybe fifteen of us on the beach and we'd be leaving in six or eight directions, and there'd be only two of them and we'd be melting away before their eyes. They'd drive off in frustration, and we'd just reappear like the fog.

There were two times that Hollywood productions rented the beach at Trestles for making movies. They found that they could rent the beach from the Marines, but they couldn't clear the water of surfers. They finally figured out how to get us in. They offered everyone in the water an all-you-could-eat free lunch from their deluxe catering service. It was a little like heaven—surfing Lowers, catered.

Summer 1969

While President Nixon was in office, the old Cotton's Estate became the Western White House. When he was in residence there, no one was allowed within a mile of Cotton's Point, and this effectively closed Trestles to surfers. One day, when the President was coming in, the Marines swept the Trestles area clear of all but two knee-boarders who were out and thoroughly enjoying the

No one out! Howard Cooney, just inside the railing of old Highway 101 (this stretch was known as Slaughter Alley) eyes a Marine MP patrol rumbling past as the surf at Lowers beckons in 1964. (Photo, Leo Hetzel)

empty, perfect six- to seven-footers. Try as they might to get them out of the water, the kneeboarders weren't likely to lose their boards, and so, short of shooting them, the MPs could do nothing but watch until the boys damn well felt like coming in.

The scenario escalated as a Coast Guard cutter, drawn up as close to the Point as it dared, joined the Marines. The forces were soon joined by the Secret Service, and they all waited impotently as the boys continued to rip, ignoring the blaring bullhorns and flashing red lights. Eventually the kneeboarders paddled up coast to San Clemente Pier under cover of darkness, but they were followed and apprehended when they came in. The session ended up costing them each a cool five hundred dollars—about twenty-five dollars a wave.

Summer 1970

I'll never forget the time a small but tough Asian Marine Master Sergeant grabbed hold of the tail of my surfboard to detain me at the bottom of the steep bank along the side of the old Coastal Highway. With him holding onto my fin, I pulled him all the way up the side of the embankment and along the freeway towards where we were parked while he screamed, "Negative! Negative!" Finally, with the freeway commuters gawking and me laughing so hard, the sergeant became so flustered and embarrassed that he let go and ran down the bank back to his MP car and drove off. It was always a gamble for us that while we were passively resisting, they wouldn't snap and pull their weapon.

One day with a group of us out in the water, fairly far outside on a six-foot day, two MP jeeps pulled up and ordered us out of the water with bullhorns. As usual, we ignored their demand and began surfing more conservatively so as not to lose our boards. In between sets, we were huddled outside on our boards when we heard a crack. Then another loud boom. Off to the side of us geysers erupted in the water. Shit! They're actually shooting at us! The Marines on the beach had their side arms out and evidently were trying to scare us into paddling in. We were outraged that they would fire .45-caliber handguns in our direction. At that range, that type of weapon loses accuracy, and they might have actually hit us, which we were sure they didn't want any more than we did.

In the Reeds

"Sunbowls" were small areas, maybe ten feet across, where we'd smashed down a circle of the pithy reeds usually by doing back flips into them—they cushioned your landing and that pressed them down. These reeds grow in dense groves fifteen to twenty acres large in the marshy areas between the beach and the Coastal Highway. In these softly carpeted clearings, we'd hang out between surf sessions surrounded by the thickets of upright reeds. We'd stay out of sight of the Marine jeep patrols, soaking rays, listening to the sounds of the surf and reading the wind by watching the tips of the reeds bending in the breeze. After coming in from a surf session, we'd eat our lunches and smoke our doobies (stored in glass jars) in these protected little cloisters. Then, rested and refreshed, we'd pick up our boards and, hooting, dash back out of the thicket, across the beach and into the surf, past startled surfers sitting in groups on the sand who hadn't known anyone was back there.

War Machines

The Marines used Trestles to practice amphibious landings twice that I remember, and as luck would have it, the surf was six to eight foot on both occasions. The funny thing was, as uptight as the MPs could get about keeping surfers out, when those landings were going on, the soldiers practicing combat didn't ever bother us. Plus, any surfers that pulled up to the overpass and saw the beach and surf zone littered with huge landing craft figured that the place was history for them that day and split. So we got to surf alone. I mean with only metal war machines in the lineup. The jockeys of these boxes got a kick out of motoring alongside us in the lineup.

The Death Knell

I remember sitting out at Lowers on a nice but unremarkable late afternoon about twenty years ago, marveling about how many swells I'd surfed there over the years, about all the different days, people, and things that had happened up to that point, and I thought I certainly would surf it for the rest of my days. Being out there felt like home. Now, twenty years later, although I live five minutes away, I no longer consider myself a regular. I do get out occasionally, but other priorities prevail. The truth is, very few in today's lineup would know me. Since I sat out there lost in thought that afternoon long ago, there have been several generations of younger surfers to have those same feelings of familiarity. When I do show up, I must be quite a sight, as some kid will invariably make a remark—something like, "Wow mister, I sure hope I'm still surfing here when I'm your age."

While Nixon was being forced out of office, he needed a popular act to help his image. So he pressured the Department of the Navy to lease the Trestles beach and valley to the state, which it named San Onofre State Park and opened to the public in 1971. When the State of California took over the Trestles beach, that was its death knell. The State Park's own mission is to promote the area's "highest and best" use, but they don't have enough money to protect it from the hordes they enable to use it. To offset operating cost, they've allowed Lowers to become a surf-contest rental stadium.

So ended Trestles' days as a relatively pristine surf break, used only by those willing to take some chances. The area has gone from one of California's most aesthetic surfing experiences to a symbol of overcrowding and aggression known throughout the surfing world. The Marines, supported by U.S. Congressman Ron Packard, have built 128 officer's housing units on Cotton's bluff overlooking the marsh, the beach and the surf breaks. The new toll road will finish it off in a few more years. That highway will come out of the San Mateo Valley behind Trestles—ploughing and grading its way through the site of the first baptism in Alta California in 1769—and connect to Interstate 5 southbound. An elevated concrete overpass will arch sixty feet above the current level of the freeway and seventy-five yards closer to the beach, providing the flowing traffic with a marvelous vista of the waves and the lineup, as surfers gaze up at the roaring traffic.

The new kids won't mind; they won't know any different. But the older surfers will remember the past when driftwood littered the beach, when there was no trash or plastic junk. Maybe there were a few C-ration cans, and an occasional shell casing, but that was it. And the sand was clean, not greasy with human oils as it is now. The older surfers will remember and shed a tear. Eventually, the toxic runoff from inland developments that the toll road facilitates will wash down San Mateo Creek causing future generations to accept surfing in their own excrement, just like those who ride off San Juan Creek at Doheny now do. Fifty years ago, both creeks used to support plentiful steelhead trout runs. These days the fish are gone. They know better than we do. The sad truth is, if the state really cared about maintaining the sanctity of Trestles, they'd give it back to the Marines.

Lost Cause in El Salvador

The Filming of Big Wednesday

BY GLENN HENING

I was trying to say it all about surfing: the camaraderie, the flawed heroes, the presence of awesome and mighty forces, and the rite of passage from bravery to wisdom as the old guard gives way to the new. I was in a position to do just about anything I wanted, so I decided to do a film about the most important thing in my life: my surfing days at Malibu.

—John Milius, director of *Big Wednesday*

In 1976 I was living in El Salvador, working as a kindergarten teacher up in the capital city while surfing world-class waves near my home on the coast near La Libertad. I had been introduced to the country by Robbie Dick, Malibu surfer and master shaper, back in 1975, and soon I was making a good living as a teacher while surfing the best waves of my career, a situation that lasted more than five years.

I frequently wrote to Rob about the great waves at Punta Roca. Well, turns out that Denny Aaberg, another Malibu legend, was talking to Rob one day about the making of a film based on the old Malibu and trying to figure out where to shoot the surfing sequences. "You know," said Robbie, "Hen's been raving in his letters about how consistent it's been in El Salvador. Why don't you guys go down there?"

John Milius was hot. With the success of *The Wind and the Lion* and the buzz surrounding his screenplay for the eagerly anticipated *Apocalypse Now,* Warner Brothers wanted to be in business with him no matter what. "I had a green light to do anything I wanted, so I decided to film the story of what I saw growing up at Malibu . . . the heroes, the legends," he said to me in an interview I recorded with him on the twentieth anniversary of the film's release. "So I made *Big Wednesday.*"

In April 1977 an armada of rental cars, filming equipment, actors, and surfers rolled into La Libertad. Peter Townsend was surfing for actor William Katt, Ian Cairns for Gary Busey, and Jay Riddle teamed with Billy Hamilton to surf for Jan-Michael Vincent, who played the movie's hero. Gerry Lopez played himself as the vanguard leader of the incoming shortboard revolution. Greg MacGillivray was second unit director, with George Greenough and Dan Merkel doing water shots. They had the best cinematographers, surfers, and equipment, but the six-week shoot turned into a waste of money and a pile of footage they were never able to use.

The first day of filming, the waves were four to five feet at Punta Roca, and MacGillivray decided to get some helicopter shots right off the bat. For almost two hours the chopper followed wave after wave as Peter Townsend and Jay Riddle elegantly longboarded the surf old-school style. Then Riddle took off too far up-point and got raked over "death rock." Bleeding and slashed up, he had to be held down by several crew members while a medic squirted disinfectant into the deep gashes left by the barnacles. Meanwhile, a Salvadoran colonel, with his armed brigade behind him, ordered the helicopter to come down immediately. The helicopter was brought in, and the colonel tried to commandeer it. He figured he'd better get it before the rebels did, and so MacGillivray did some hasty and hefty negotiating to get out of a jam. He called it quits for the day. They never used the helicopter again.

The next day the point went flat, and for six weeks Punta Roca was either not breaking or lacked the light quality needed to film. Every day, the crew went out looking for waves from their headquarters at the Club Atami, about twenty miles up the coast from La Libertad. But even with surf-cinema master MacGillivray in charge, and the skills of Dan Merkel behind an enormous 35-mm water camera built on-site by George Greenough, they couldn't get any usable footage. The wind would come up, the tide would change, and the light would get shifty, forcing the crew to call it quits for the day.

Bloodied extra during the filming of *Big Wednesday*. (Photo, Anthony Friedkin)

Back at the hotel, the crew slept in small rooms with thatched walls and low ceilings. In the weeks before the first rain, nights were a tortuous ordeal of stifling heat, very high humidity, and no breeze until just before dawn— and then it was a south wind that put a lump in the surf.

One day the crew showed up at Sunsal, a fun wave up the coast from La Libertad. While trying to get some footage of Gerry Lopez, Mr. Pipeline lost his cool after being repeatedly cut off by a local. Lopez started to berate the kid, who turned out to be an entitled son of El Salvador's *Los Quatorce*—the fourteen families who owned and controlled all the land in the country. Thirty years ago, like now, the locals who surfed the breaks around La Libertad were the *Quatorce* kids, who speak perfect English and act like perfect gentlemen, unless you cross them. The guy went after Lopez, chasing him out of the water and threatening him in no uncertain terms.

A few days after the Lopez incident, a swell was rumored to be on the way. The crew approached Bob Rotherham, longtime owner of the restaurant at the base of the point in La Libertad, to see what he thought of this idea: pay the locals to stay out of the water during filming. Bob said it was a pretty stupid idea as most of the surfers were from ultra-wealthy families. In the end it didn't matter, the swell never showed up.

In the downtime that followed, I decided to throw a party at my house to celebrate the *Primero de Mayo*—the first of May marked the beginning of the rainy season, but also doubled as the leftist International Day of Revolution. Had the military interpreted us as a bunch of celebrating rebels, then the evening could have gotten dicey. The country was under martial law at the time and all gatherings of more than ten people were prohibited.

But we were surfers, and we were just as radical as the characters Milius tried to portray in the movie. I invited the surf stars, left-wing revolutionaries, right-wing oligarchs, locals, and the entire movie crew for an afternoon of rum, music, and a fairly combustible combination of Latin America's more esoteric libations. Everybody got along just fine, and the place was on the verge of getting wild when the local police captain, who had been having a great time, let me know that everyone really had to go. The soldiers had orders to "shoot to kill" on the highways after 9 P.M.

A week went by and the surf began to show some promise. The cast and crew thought the worst was over. They hadn't counted on the rainy season, which now came on strong, flushing all of the country's waste- and sewage-filled ravines into the ocean. With the brown waters came *Mal de Mayo,* or May's Disease, which downed many of the crew members with amoebic dysentery.

One night in mid-May, I was up at the film crew's basecamp delivering a load of peanut butter (I made up hundred-pound batches—creamy and chunky—and sold it to American surfers for years). I ran into a restless Ian

The Malibu Wall, recreated for the filming of *Big Wednesday*. (Photo, Anthony Friedkin)

Cojo Point. Location used for the filming of *Big Wednesday*. (Photo, Anthony Friedkin)

Cairns, who was obviously not having a good time as the rain came down hard. He hadn't surfed in a week and it showed. He asked when it was going to stop.

"Stop?" I said, "The season is only just beginning."

He immediately walked me over to MacGillivray's room. Ian told me to tell him about the rain. MacGillivray, looking a bit pasty with stomach issues, just rolled his eyes when he heard my forecast.

The next day I went up to the city to teach. I drove by Punta Roca early in the morning; its blown-to-bits waves looked particularly depressing under a heavy mist and overcast skies. The weather continued to be bad all that week, and I stayed with friends up in the capital without giving surfing a second thought.

Finally, the weekend arrived, the sun came out, and a solid six-foot swell came up clean and sunny at Punta Roca. But the stars were not in the water. They had packed everything up the morning after my visit. The entire cast and crew had taken the first flight back to Hollywood, where, to add insult to injury, the little usable surfing footage they did get had to be trashed because the surf doubles were not Screen Actor's Guild members. Hollywood was a union town at the time, and the use of non-union actors got the attention of the Teamsters very quickly. In the end, they used one shot of some beach scenery along with a few seconds of helicopter footage showing Peter

Townsend at Punta Roca.

So the crew had to start filming all over again at Cojo on the Bixby Ranch, north of L.A., and then later that year on the North Shore where Jay Riddle and Billy Hamilton surfed Sunset Beach for the film's climax. Finally the film went into postproduction, where the ideas of Milius and Aaberg conflicted with the editing priorities of Warner Brothers. Milius did not have final cut on the film.

The film premiered in July of 1978, fifteen years after the period it depicts. Although hype was high in the surf community, nobody knew exactly what to expect. But one thing was for sure: nobody expected the film to flop as it did. Certainly the timing was not good, as it was released within a week of blockbusters like *Grease, Animal House,* and *Jaws 2.* Unlike those films, *Big Wednesday* played to empty theaters and was panned by the critics, with comments like: *Only nostalgic surfers with more than a little patience will enjoy this ode to the beach set and that perfect wave.* The picture was withdrawn from distribution after only a one-week run in major markets.

Milius came in for heavy personal criticism for spending a fortune (twelve million dollars, or about sixty million in today's money) on what was judged to be little more than a vanity piece about his lost youth. Despite some absolutely classic scenes, such as the boys faking injuries and mental conditions before the draft board, the film was crippled by mediocre acting, overblown music, and a story line that may have been great on paper, but when edited turned into a patchwork of loosely connected scenes that failed to guide viewers through the peaks and troughs of drama. Critics considered it a boring film made excruciating by its epic aspirations to tell the inside story of California surfing in the late '60s.

In hindsight, Milius says that he did the film because he saw where he was going with his career and that surfing would cease to be a part of his life. In Milius' own words, "When the film wrapped, I basically stopped surfing. Years later, in 1982 or '83, we paddled out at eight-foot Pitas Point, but when I saw a young kid eat his lunch, I realized that I wasn't ready for that, and I paddled back in."

His final abandonment of surfing mirrors the ending of the film, when the hero turns his back on the ocean and limps off into the sunset after basically failing, although surviving, the challenge of his life. The hero gives away his surfboard and his surfing days come to a sorry end. What does the audience get out of watching a life of surfing and camaraderie being thrown away? The empty ending, reinforced by the overly dramatic "Three Friends"

Filmmaker George Greenough on the set of *Big Wednesday*. (Photo, Anthony Friedkin)

closing theme song, left audiences feeling deflated and indifferent.

Perhaps with a bit more period music here and there, some recutting of key scenes, and an upbeat return-and-triumph-of-the-fallen-hero ending, the film would have made more sense. Audiences needed a reason to invest in Milius' take on surfing, and Milius never delivered.

Given the success of his previous films, the flop of *Big Wednesday* was a close-out set for John Milius. He got worked worse than his hero did at Sunset Beach at the end of the film. His standing as a bankable director was quickly brought into question. The public's rejection of the film haunted him twenty years later.

"Sometimes," Milius said, "I think my career has always been a bit clouded by *Big Wednesday*. When it flopped, it was a classic fall from grace: suddenly no one would return my calls."

Over time, friends such as Steven Spielberg would comfort him with sincere compliments about the film, and Milius was occasionally surprised when, out of the blue, he would find himself being highly respected for his efforts, such as the time a group of major Japanese businessmen wanted to meet him (and not Spielberg, who he was accompanying on a promotional tour for the movie *E.T.*). Many Japanese saw Milius as a true man of the sea and had immense respect for his portrayal of a unique, fleeting period in a culture, a portrayal that buttresses the California myth of a pure, carefree life saturated with the energy of the ocean and its waves.

When I asked him about a sequel, Milius replied, "I don't know what more there is to say about surfing. I don't think a sequel would make any sense."

Postscript

When I saw the movie at a twentieth-anniversary showing in the Santa Monica Civic Auditorium at a Surfrider Foundation benefit, the evening was eerily reminiscent of exactly what happened when the film premiered. Everyone was stoked going in, but when the final credits rolled, there was little applause. The hero ended up soggy and dazed, defeated by the sea and giving up surfing forever. Now, how is that going to play with people who are surfers for life? It didn't.

Today, there are many who see *Big Wednesday* as some kind of classic cult film. To me, the $800,000 wasted in El Salvador said it all about what happens when someone gets to spend a lot of money telling the story of their youth as if it were some kind of mythic quest of heroes. I saw a planeload of heroes on a lost cause in El Salvador, and their surf odyssey—like the hero's, and maybe even that of Milius himself—came to a soggy, limping end that said little, if anything, to me about the true spirit of surfing.

Laughing to Disaster

Rat on a Stick, Backless Wonders, and Sacred Incan Sexual Fantasies—Chillin' with the Buddha in the Ruins of Peru

STEVE BARILOTTI

Peru—June, 1996.

"Look, Gerr . . . Llama shit!" Cupping a handful of the fragrant black pellets, I proffered them to Brad Gerlach with infinite idiot joy and wonder.

Gerr, whose bald head, moon-shaped face, and wide sensual mouth gives him the look of a vine-strangled stone Buddha, gazed at my treasured turds. His expression alternated between puzzlement and disgust.

Then his mouth twitched. He giggled, then laughed, and finally collapsed in great gasping howls on the ancient garden terraces of Machu Picchu.

"Christ, Barlo, are you kidding me?"

In the wake of his echoing laughter I laughed too—one of those ecstatic soul-cleansing laughs that border on weeping. There was nothing left to do but laugh. We'd been through so much hard, existential slogging to get to this moment, in which I stood atop the Andes in a ruined Inca temple and extended pungent little pellets of alpaca poo to a former world champ runner-up. Pausing for a moment to regain my breath in the thin, rarefied air, I reflected on the last, schizophrenic year—the loss and the rage and the spiritual meltdown of my own life.

And I laughed again.

Around us stretched the sprouting walls and stepladder ziggurat of Machu Picchu, the sacred lost city of the Inca, "discovered" in 1911 under a thick blanket of jungle growth by American explorer Hiram Bingham. Two thousand feet below us, the Urubamba river rumbled its way past snow-capped mountains into the Amazon. Across the ruins a huge red hawk swooped in rising lazy eights around the glowing jade cone of Huayna Picchu. Above us I heard the plaintive whistle of a *quena*, the traditional Andean bamboo flute.

Loosely gathered around the Hitching Post of the Sun was an eclectic, eccentric band of New Age seekers from around the world. They'd trekked some fifty kilometers from Cusco up the Inca Trail to this legendary power vortex to blow on flutes, chant, hold sacred crystals, or scatter ashes of loved ones into the twelfth-century planter boxes where, it is thought, the Incan high priests had once grown their sacred coca leaf.

The ancestors were all around us, watching, whispering. I heard them all: the vanished royal Inca, the fierce jungle Antis, Francisco Pizarro's murdering conquistadors—their ancestors, my ancestors, my drowned sister. I felt an ethereal energy charging this mystic ravaged village. No doubt there were copious middens of antiquated Inca bones, golden erotic fetishes, and fossilized twelfth-century llama turds lying directly beneath our feet.

Gerr picked up his pack and continued down the steps toward the Temple of the Sun. I remained, carefully stubbing out my last precious clove Kretek on a stone step hewn by long-dead Incan hands.

We were seekers, too, although we had not originally come to Peru for its archeological wonders. Our winter pilgrimage was intended to exploit the legendary Peruvian power surf waiting along 1,500 miles of wave-rich desert coastline. But a lack of rideable surf, plus travelogue romanticism, had seduced us up to this ancient pagan shrine on the edge of the Amazon.

A month of hard floors, paltry surf, and seedy third-world motels had taken their toll on our little band. A week ago, down to just fifty dollars apiece, Gerr and I had sold all our boards in Lima to buy wool ponchos and train tickets. The night before, I'd narrowly escaped an indefinite stay in a stinking Peruvian holding tank for the blunder of sparking up a roach in a Cusco disco. Three weeks, thousands of dollars spent, and only one roll of decent surf action burned on the magazine's behalf. A textbook skunk-out.

And how many planes and cars and cups of *maté de coca* did it take? How many of our intrepid crew did we sacrifice on the ascent? Cordy—gone.

Brad Gerlach in the ruins of Machu Picchu, a mountain-top city of the ancient Incas that sits at 8,000 feet in the Andes, Peru. (Photo, Steve Barilotti)

Kahea—gone. Tom—gone. Even the indomitable Magoo was left moaning deliriously on his sickbed in Lima.

Such high hopes we had at the start, such bright beginnings! At LAX a month previously, we were singing schoolboys off on a summer holiday, joking, bro-slappin', and wallowing in our good fortune.

Now at 8,000 feet and 200 miles from the coast, Gerr and I were the only ones left. We lacked sleep. We lacked digestible food. We lacked baths. Our guts were in bloody flux after the Mancora debacle; open sores festered and green mud flaked from our itchy, vermin-ridden scalps.

Yet I felt weirdly elated.

Surf trips can be wondrously strange that way.

At Lima International Cordy was quivering and quoting scripture to no one in particular. *"Do not be afraid, Abraham, I am your shield; your reward shall be very great."*

We'd begun to worry about Cordy. Cordell Miller, the tall, young, blond shaper-savant from Newport Beach had checked out days ago, retreating into his dog-eared Bible and an endless loop of Christian-rock standards on his yellow Sony Walkman. The poverty of Lima had him zoned. The legless beggars had him freaked. The food had him sick. And the impending third-world flight via an aging surplus 737 to Southern Peru had him close to the rail and ready to jump. Cordy suffers from a rare affliction among surf pros. He hates to fly. Scares him shitless.

And the last taxi ride from hell via Lima, at lethal speed down wrong-way streets, over sidewalks, blazing through red lights and *alto* signs, had finally made it impossible for him to hold on to the delusion that he was somehow still in Southern California, freeway-close to his beloved spiritual home, Disneyland.

The rest of the crew was still buzzing from the ride. Gerr, Kahea Hart, and our Peruvian host Magoo de la Rosa laughed over having cheated death in such a spectacular fashion.

"Are you kidding me? That was insane—just like the movies!" chortled Gerr in disbelief as he paid his airport tax.

He was right. In fact, this whole trip thus far had been just like a bad Monkees' rerun from the '60s. Mad, slapdash rushing about to no apparent purpose other than to take our outlandish act to another spot for the bemused locals to have a good long gawk. Mad Max Gerr with his blond mohawk; mute, grinning Cordy with his neon-blue leggings and bearded Christlike visage; Kahea, ultracool behind black shades, perpetually bandana-wrapped and bare-chested, resembling nothing less than a Hawaiian Axl Rose. With dapper Magoo and Tom Servais as our managers and photo entourage, we looked like a boy band on a low-rent bar tour.

Two days into the trip we were having a great time. Expectations were running high. The biggest swell in three years was pounding the Peruvian coast and reports were that Pico Alto was cracking twenty feet. Surf shaman Sean Collins' advice: "Get on it. Quick."

But Pico Alto and other well-known spots had already had heavy play in past Peru articles. We wanted to discover our own breaks, perhaps even name a couple. So, at our request, Magoo was guiding us south, far from the tried-and-true Peruvian breaks.

Magoo, the sole Peruvian ASP contender during the 1980s, was a great host and invaluable trip *bwana*. A hell-hot surfer with the *cojones* of a former matador (his original boyhood training), he'd been dubbed "The Peruvian Tom Carroll" for his compact structure and steely-eyed courage while pulling into certified death barrels. Of course, Magoo pointed out that in Peru Tom Carroll is simply known as the Australian Magoo de la Rosa.

But it was Magoo's unflagging enthusiasm and generosity with traveling surfers that earned him enduring legend status. No request was too outrageous, no question too stupid. So when we asked him to take us to some never-photographed spots, he responded with his typical Latino stoke and gave us wide-eyed promises of plundering virgin Peruvian tubes: "Guys, you gonna blow your minds! *Puta*... I'm gonna take you to places where they never even seen surfers."

He was absolutely right.

Bulging board bags were stacked three-high atop a vintage Chevy van, held down with leg ropes and ties. We spent countless hours slowly shuffling down fifty klicks of potholed dirt road patrolled by fat vultures and school-boy *indios* brandishing scarred old AKs—no doubt recently pried from the rigor-mortis grip of some rotting, fly-blown Shining Path partisan.

This was no blue-water-and-babes glamour tour. We rolled by miles of huge, lethal closeouts bashing against a barren, desert coast. We lurched past a series of copper smelts spewing gray, sulfurous plumes into a horse-blanket sky and leaching a toxic red menstrual flood into a leaden ocean. We shook and rattled along in a sleepless, prickly torpor, breathing dust and each others' sundry body exhalations.

Magoo stared morosely out a dust-caked window from behind a red bandana, no doubt feeling somewhat responsible for leading us down this unproductive hell coast. The rest of us had collapsed into a sullen forced-march silence while Gerr, our spiritual leader, tried unsuccessfully to raise morale up out of the dirt.

Tom Servais, world-jaded surfari vet and master of accreting his personal comfort zone in any unpleasant pig-latitude scenario, had finally lost patience with the endless hassle of third-world travel. Missing the biggest swell in three years to chase phantom waves in a cramped van down a bleak dirt road hadn't improved his mood any. His digs at Gerr, the trip's organizer, were pointed and wickedly sardonic.

"Gee, Brad, this place looks just like Big Sur," observed Tom in a dead-as-ashes voice—"after a nuclear holocaust."

Since the beginning of the trip there'd been a battle of wills between Tom and Gerr for the hearts and minds of our squad. Tom, as the man responsible for bringing back the visual meat of the article, as well as the eldest and most experienced of the group, was the natural leader of the expedition. But Gerr had organized this trip, and Tom didn't want to be seen undermining Gerlach's judgment.

Thus far, however, we had been consistently skunked by poor advance information and a swell so diabolically huge that we'd driven half of southern Peru in vain looking for a spot that could produce a rideable wave. Mutinous thoughts began to bubble to the surface.

Tom, who was on the verge of pushing the abort button for a quick return back to Dana Point, couldn't resist taunting Gerr for his boneheaded choice in bringing us down to this nightmare coast and the shortcomings of Latin America in general. But Gerlach, determined to prove Tom wrong,

Cordell Miller slowly gives Gerlach a mohawk with sideburn trimmers while Kahea Hart watches, Iquique, Chile. (Photo, Steve Barilotti)

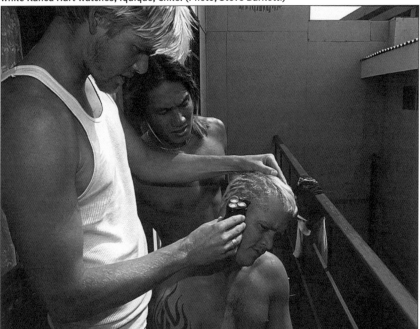

returned fire by poking holes in Tom's crusty psychic armor with his lethally accurate parodies of Tom's dour, finicky nature.

Meanwhile, Kahea, our resident good-time Hawaiian and sex-symbol frontman, gamely tried to keep a smile and a cheerful attitude in the face of off-tasting meals, endless bitching, and an equally endless chain of dismal, mildewed motels. Kahea, who treasures his Hawaiian heritage, would spontaneously begin singing Hawaiian songs or give a masterful show of Tahitian slap dancing to the delight of the locals. Down south a little too far, however, his happy songs had devolved into some sort of Polynesian death chant as he pined for his green island home and his Tahitian fiancée.

Kahea was glumly thumbing through the back pages of a dog-eared sex mag when he came upon an ad for a discount grab bag of sundry latex sexual appliances. Attempting to lighten the mood he read aloud: "Hey, listen to this: 'Four-and-a-half-inch anal stimulator delivers high-speed action to you at the peak of excitement!'"

A few obligatory half-hearted chuckles. Then silence.

Gerr, however, was momentarily distracted from Herman Hesse's *Narcissus and Goldmund*, and picked up the thread of humor. He was soon on a roll, extolling the virtues of using a battery-powered butt plug with that "special" lady. From there he seamlessly segued into imagining one of the Top-44 innocents mistakenly receiving a box of sundry latex sexual appliances addressed to the notoriously deviant Todd Chesser: "Oh jeez, Cheeze, what's this? Look, a butt plug! Wow, that feels neat. Wait 'til I show my girlfriend! Whoa ... sheeze!"

That raised some giggles, but Tom, sensing an opportunity to needle Gerr further, began to grill Gerr on the particulars of anal sex.

"So, Brad, where do you keep your butt plug? Do you wash it off after every use? How do you measure for it? Do you offer it to the girl first, or after?" Tom grilled Gerr with endless questions that eventually had Gerr squirming on the ropes. But Tom was going for the kill and wouldn't let up.

Finally Gerr, in exasperation, indicated testily that perhaps Tom should stop being such a one-position-wonder and experience the full spectrum of sensual delights, if only for his lady's sake.

Tom flared at this and shot back, "Hey listen, Brad, I've had the finger up the butt plenty," as if listing his qualifications for the presidency.

Dead silence as all eyes turned to Tom. Gerr stared for a second in disbelief at the rich vein of humor that Tom had inadvertently opened up for him. This would be good for weeks. Unable to even comment at the magnitude of this gaffe, Gerr giggled uncontrollably. The laughter quickly spread like the Ebola virus through the clanking van until we all bled from the ears, gasping and coughing up a lung.

And poor Tom, temporarily beaten, retreated into his headphones with a grumpy scowl and a weak, "fuck you."

We were still chuckling hours later as we passed a bloated cow being torn to shreds beneath a black, flapping crowd of flesh-headed buzzards.

In lieu of intelligent action, we boarded a flight for Chile. By now we had the drill down cold. First, show up at the airport about the time they were rolling the gantry away from the plane. Next, plead, cajole, and charm the check-in girls into letting us and thirty surfboards onto the aircraft ten minutes after the posted departure time. Then run full tilt down the tarmac to a steaming, screaming, straining jet, and jump aboard, sweating and panting under the comely flight attendant's disapproving glare. Fly thirty minutes to the next disappointment. Repeat endlessly throughout South America.

But, in the end, our manic determination saved the trip from being a total write-off. Epic waves were ridden, barrel rides recorded, new boards tested, and pretty pictures taken. But only by accident. And only for an eye-blink.

After landing in Iquique, a small fishing village being reincarnated as a multinational free port under Chile's NAFTA-fueled economy, we piled into a cheap beach motel across from the city breaks and waited for the swell to come up.

It didn't.

That night, giving into the despair of never finding a decent wave along the length of South America, we got reasonably drunk on Cristal ale at a Chilean Chinese restaurant. For laughs, we timed our watches against the "Largest Clock in the World," a digital readout beamed against a whole mountainside behind the city.

The next morning, after a cursory dawn-patrol check revealed a flatlined swell across the street, we cursed the sun and blotted it out with our ragged motel-room drapes. If not for Kahea weaving out early for his morning jog, we'd have never known about the eight-foot Backless Wonder breaking a hundred yards up the beach.

By the time we rallied crew and gear down to the beach the wind was threatening to turn onshore at any moment, so Tom ordered the quartet out into the water immediately. The Backless Wonder, nearly invisible from the

Magoo de la Rosa and Brad Gerlach looking at surf in Iquique, Chile. (Photo, Steve Barilotti)

beach, turned out to be a fearsome beast when viewed up close. A double-overhead left, a sucking claw of a wave described in the Surf Report thusly: "Critical takeoff . . . actually breaks below sea level. Experienced surfers only—probably the heaviest wave in South America."

Even the experienced surfers had a hard time with the heaviest wave in South America. Because the Backless Wonder broke in open water, lining up was problematic and ultra-dicey. The wave had a fast, unforgiving go/no-go takeoff, and anybody daydreaming on the lip got slapped on the shallow rock shelf like a fat fly on a kitchen counter.

But for all the trouble getting into the wave, it quickly stubbed itself out in the channel after a cursory tube and spit. Kahea got pounded badly twice before he figured out the drop. Gerr and Cordy, too. Magoo, of course, as the sole goofyfooter and local, rode the deepest and got pitted ridiculously.

By the time Tom came in to change rolls, however, the Backless Wonder had disappeared under the rising tide and freshening wind.

Thirty-six frames and an hour later, we had checked out and were rolling for the airport.

Back in Lima, Cordy was the first casualty. After nine turbulent, God-beseeching flights, the idea of getting on yet another diabolical flying death trap was such anathema to him that he was seriously considering renting a car and driving the 3,000 or so miles through Latin America back to Costa Mesa, California. We sent him home, Bible in one hand, Walkman in the other, babbling.

After a day's rally back in Lima we decided to go north to the border territories. Magoo promised it would be sunny there (a prerequisite for Tom since most of the Peruvian coast is shrouded in low overcast for nine months of the year), and if there was any swell left at all we could score one of the best barreling lefts in South America, Cabo Blanco.

"You guys," exclaimed Magoo, pursing his lips and sucking air, "it's gonna be sooo good. *Puta!*"

A half-day later we arrived in Mancora, a dusty little fishing village reminiscent of Baja and straight out of the pages of a Gabriel García Márquez novel.

As guests of Maki Block, Magoo's tour buddy and longtime friend, we were put up in the palatial vacation palapa of Pitti Block, Maki's father and one of the notorious Peruvian playboy surfers of the '60s. The elder Block, a soap baron and champion Formula One racer, had built his house on the desert point as a tropical Hawaiian Eden, complete with tapa prints, sliding screens, hammocks, giant macaws, and fruiting coconut palms growing right through the second floor. Down below, next to the workout equipment, was a well-maintained stable of vintage and late-model longboards to be used on the long, looking-glass Malibu left peeling gently off the rock point out front.

I trunked it that evening in the balmy seventy-degree water and met Nuño, a genial Portuguese surfer who bore an uncanny resemblance to Tom Curren. As we shared the head-high waves, he told me of his recent adventures through Ecuador and how he and his buddy Joao had drifted down to Mancora a few days earlier. He said the prospects looked good for catching Cabo Blanco firing. The ambient stoke level rose perceptively.

That night in the village we sipped frosty Cusqueñas and devoured heaping mounds of freshly made ceviche at Restaurant Cesar while a children's parade for the upcoming *Corpus Christi* celebrations marched past. Each child carried aloft an intricate stick-and-paper lantern, lit from within by a single votive candle. The lanterns were in the most fantastic shapes, representing the child's patron saint or just personal preference. Here a St. Francis, there a Star of Bethlehem, over there a Huey attack helicopter.

We soon learned that most all the food in Mancora was either an aph-

(Left) Brad Gerlach and Kahea Hart in the mud pits of Barra Verde, Mancora, Peru; (right) the author with a handful of the trip's treasure. (Photos, Steve Barilotti)

rodisiac or a cure for impotence. At the restaurant, Magoo encouraged us to slurp up the dregs of the octopus ceviche, saying the locals called it "Panther's Milk." It was guaranteed to jump-start a tired sex life. A molasses and herb extract called Algarrobina Especial was sold by the liter in the village market as a sure-fire sexual tonic. This drink was derived from a local tree that is a favorite of the wild donkeys that run the dusty arroyos. That's why there were so many donkeys, swore the locals, and they indicated its effectiveness with a fisted arm held stiff and erect at crotch level. And about a half-hour's drive out of town was the fabled *Barra Verde*, the source of the medicinal green mud that would cure everything from cancer to crabs.

We ventured up to the mud baths one night, more as relief for our twisted, travel-spavined bodies than lack of lead in our underutilized pencils. Covered in mud, howling at the southern stars in the warm Mancoran night, we shaved Gerr's head as a sacrifice. Things just had to get better after this.

The next day, following another dusty, fruitless morning foray for waves, we inched our way down miles of dirt track to Cabo Blanco. The bedraggled little fishing village was famous for two things: 1) Hemingway once fished for marlin there, and 2) it has a screaming, dredging left that peels like G-Land in front of the anchorage. Hemingway and Cabo Blanco also had other features in common: both were legends, both had their pictures tacked to the restaurant walls, and both were quite dead that day.

That was it. Tom's official tour of duty was up, and he was out on the next flight, dreaming of his Floridian surfer girl and a big wedge of Chart House mud pie back in Dana Point. Kahea, in stoic agony from severe mosquito bites and shellfish poisoning, gratefully shipped out with him. With our lensman and half our crew gone, the trip was officially over. But Gerr and Magoo vowed to continue if the swell filled in as predicted.

That night, however, Gerr succumbed to a plate of tainted mussels and was confined to a hammock the next day, scarlet and moaning in delirious toxic dreams. Then Magoo, after surviving the Backless Wonder without a scratch, impaled his knee to the bone on a rock while riding a one-foot wave out front. He limped in white and whimpering.

"You guys," he said, sucking wind and wincing, "I'm really fucked up."

Puta.

Part 2

"If you try to leave, the door will be locked for you."

Despite the heavy accent and awkward syntax, the dwarf bartender made it absolutely clear by the way he smirked up at me and crossed his arms over his keggy bulldog chest that he was a patient man, a consummate professional, and I had fucked up big time. His gold earring winked fractured disco rainbows at me.

The problem wasn't that I'd sparked up a joint on his shift, the problem was that I was a stupid gringo who'd tried to bullshit him. That pissed him off. But he wasn't going to create a scene among all the paying customers tonight by calling in the boorish *antidroga* squad to arrest me on the dance floor. He could wait until closing time. *Go ahead, gringo. Finish your drink. It will be your last.*

Things had gotten real weird, real fast. One minute I was drawing on a sweet Kretek and trading long looks with a petite Brazilian temptress, the next I was being chased around the undulating, strobe-lit dance floor by an enraged waitress and a midget bartender with serious attitude. I slumped next to a bank of bass speakers thumping out Beck's "Loser."

I was alone, deserted at the first sniff of trouble. Across the room, I saw Gerlach dancing, oblivious and ecstatic, with the cute little Israeli sharpshooter in the well-rounded tank top. Bad Bruno from Lima was also writhing mindlessly, obviously feeling no pain after draining the pint of Cuban *anejo* rum he'd smuggled in to avoid paying for drinks. Louisiana Lou, with his Cajun drawl and corny jokes, had vanished like a rat down a hawser.

I contemplated my sinful backsliding ways and the retribution that was about to drop like an axe. I remembered the armed guard at the door and the ever-present squads of Kevlar-vested *Policia Federal* stationed on every corner of this sixteenth-century conquistador party town. I recalled the dire postings in Spanish against drug trafficking that up to now had been merely humorous diversion while we waited for our bags to come off the airport carousel. It wasn't supposed to be like this.

Gerr and I were supposed to be on the Inca Trail, early in the A.M., with the other seekers, trudging to enlightenment one step at a time in the frigid Andean air. Now it looked like I'd be spending quality time with the *antidroga* boys in some dank colonial inquisition cell. I could almost feel the plastic bag slipping over my head and the electrodes being clipped to my abused testicles.

But one can, and does, get distracted. By the waveless sea, noble motives have no chance against pagan desires.

How did I get in this situation? After pulling the plug on Cabo Blanco, Gerr and I decided to travel on to the ancient ruins of Machu Picchu as we had planned months ago back in California. Perhaps by veering away from the coast we could sprinkle the rare spice of true experience over the blinkered, rushed photo-ops that pass for media surf adventures these days. Only problem was, we were broke—down to financial seeds and stems. With help from our Peruvian host Magoo de la Rosa, however, we held an impromptu garage sale, selling off our boards and wetsuits. When the dust had cleared we counted out over a thousand dollars. Suddenly flush, Gerr and I booked passage to Cusco, the sixteenth-century Spanish colonial city built over the bones of the bygone Incan empire.

The plan was to join a backpacking expedition and hike the entire forty-eight kilometers along the Inca Trail to the Lost City. It would take three days and a lot of sweat, blisters, and coca leaves, but other seekers who had done the trek spoke of the experience with an ethereal, blissed-out look in their eyes. We were determined to have that hard-earned psychic jolt of high-altitude nirvana.

We arrived during an inauspicious phase of the moon, full of chaos and conflicting gods. Cusco was in the throes of the week-long *Corpus Christi* celebrations, a raucous cannon-firing time of fireworks and spontaneous parades where Cusco's nineteen parishes competed against each other to create the best bloody martyred saint float. Fifteen-man squads, fortified with equal amounts of prayer and *pisco*, would hoist the heavy, flower-draped statues on their shoulders for a trot around the brooding, cathedral-lined Plaza de Armas, a popular site for public executions of Inca rebel leaders during colonial times. We stood on the sidelines clasping cold Cusqueñas cheering on the crowd favorite, St. Jude, although the Virgin was obviously the perennial contender for the beatific heavyweight crown.

That night the local brewing companies set up food tables in the narrow, white-walled cobblestone streets, and all of Cusco became a rollicking Peruvian Oktoberfest, complete with roasted maize, succulent broiled chicken, and juicy mounds of rat on a stick. The fried rodent was actually guinea pig, a local Quechua *indio* favorite, but impaled on a bamboo skewer and sporting bared teeth and charred tail, its resemblance to a well-fed sewer rat was fascinatingly repellent. We strolled around the square listening to *zampoña* pan pipes under a chilly winter moon, making unbelievable deals on handmade alpaca fur goods and sacred Inca erotic pottery.

We also found the discos. It was predestined, no doubt. Gerr is by nature a gregarious animal and craves the press and funk of human contact. With his llama-wool poncho and newly-shaven head, Gerr resembled a newly fallen Tibetan monk debauching his way into the material world in a gleeful decadent rush. My stamina was taxed to the limit, requiring endless cups of coca tea, espresso, and barely legal herbal tonics sold in the stalls near the plaza.

Despite our higher intentions, we were soon spending our nights happily embalmed in a pulsing womb of smoke and loud music, drinking rum and writhing toward nirvana in creaking colonial fleshpits.

Cusco has become the Catholic Kathmandu, a rowdy staging area for all manner of adventure treks and New Age expeditions. These days, since Fujimori's government crushed the Maoist *Sendero Luminoso* (Shining Path) and their terrorist—or at the very least anti-tourist—ways, one can safely raft the Urubamba, paraglide through the Amazon, or mountain bike down the Sacred Valley. Cusco, once called the "Navel of the World" by its Inca builders, has transformed into a new age Dodge City, filled with a motley crew of healers, shamans, hustlers, global drifters, and good-natured scam artists.

We met a squad of Israeli youth, recently discharged from their army duty. Gerr was particularly taken by the spunky, close-cropped *sabra* lass with a nose ring—her specialty was stealth warfare and sniper training. She could slit a man's throat, she said, with a playing card if necessary.

"Cool!" grinned the bald, laughing Buddha Gerr.

We also hooked up with Louisiana Lou and Bad Bruno. Longhaired Lou, a newly clean ex-junkie with a trust fund, was dutifully making the Cusco cathedral tour with his mom and sisters during his supposed rehab, but at

night he'd sneak out of his room and prowl the discos for a little secular action. After we fronted him a couple rounds he invited us down for Mardi
Gras, singing the praises of sultry Creole women and "Nawlins" pubs.

Bruno, a suave Lima urbanite just back from a failed marriage in Miami,
surfed occasionally and was stoked to meet the infamous Gerr. To show his
friendship, Bruno promptly produced a bottomless bag of Amazonian jungle herb which didn't attract so much as a smirk from the management. In a
crossroads bar such as Mama Africa it seemed certain youthful indiscretions
were permitted, within reason.

But tonight something had gone wrong. As soon as the joint was passed
to me, it promptly fizzled out. While attempting to re-light it I felt a tap from
behind. It was the cocktail waitress. I told her I was okay for the time being but catch me in a half-hour. Another tap. She seemed to want some. No
problem, just wait your turn. Another tap, an impatient demand, and an angry face. Okay, chill out, bitch!

By then my drug- and rum-addled brain had done the math and could
see that she was demanding the contraband for evidence. Stalling, I played
the Clueless American. Err, *no comprendo.* Meanwhile, under the table, I
handed off the reeking roach. It quickly got lost in a triple-blind cut-out
worthy of a Ludlum novel—Bruno to Lou to Gerr, then gone. The waitress, a
cute *rubia* local in a tank top and tight skirt, became furious at the deception
and ran off to get the manager.

Bruno indicated in pointed tones that we should split up and evacuate
immediately. In my panic to become invisible I blindly stumbled into dancing couples, knocked drinks off tables, and generally made a bumbling, babbling ass of myself. Then the midget appeared like the Lord's own knee-high
summoner.

"If you try to leave, the door will be locked for you."

I eventually escaped that night by disguising myself in a hooded poncho
and wrapping myself around one of the Peruvian party girls hovering near
the crowded entrance. We waltzed past the police and disco guard who was
busy arguing with two drunk Germans over the cover charge and tangoed
gracefully into a waiting taxi.

Once well away from the Plaza de Armas, I tipped the cabbie and the girl
heavily for their discretion. I returned solo to our hillside pension, stashed
my passport and cash in a daypack, and prepared to bolt over the rooftops
and hide out in the Amazon rainforest if necessary.

Gerr crawled in at daybreak, stinking of cigarettes, sweat, and gamey wet wool. He told me in breathy detail about all the insanely sexy Indian girls he danced with after I mysteriously disappeared. The girls led him to fantasize himself as an Incan king in ancient times, pleasuring scores of vestal virgins who waited in line for his godlike favors.

Irritated, I cut him off. "That's beautiful, Gerr. I barely escaped a Peruvian torture cell, no thanks to you. While you were out dancing, I was fleeing for my fucking life."

"Jeez, Barlo," he said kicking off his scarred boots, "you're having a bad night tonight, aren't you?"

We split Cusco on the first morning train.

Nuño was waiting under a dripping verandah in Aguas Calientes. He had just finished his fried river trout and rice and was having a cold beer for dessert. He smiled from the trackside La Chosa cantina as we disembarked from the two-car tourist Especial. He waved us out of the pouring rain to his table.

It was good to see him again. We'd been running into Nuño repeatedly at the oddest times and places throughout Peru since we first met in Mancora, and he always proved good company. Under his rough, swarthy stubble and sunburn it turned out he was a gentrified antique dealer who owned a one-quarter interest in a chic Lisbon disco. He'd work for eight months, then travel and surf for the rest of the year.

We ordered beers and Nuño filled us in on his day-long hike around Machu Picchu. He'd just come back from the ruins and was raving about them. He had the high-voltage look of a true believer. "Absolutely amazing, my friends! But you must see them at sunrise."

Then the train rumbled through and he was gone. Across the way a crew of solemn Inca Trail porters waited stoically on the tracks in the rain for the local, less expensive chicken train to ferry them back to Cusco for another load of cook kettles, dome tents, and Trail trekkers.

Aguas Calientes was one of those hodgepodge Lonely Planet frontier towns you see growing like a symbiotic mushroom around natural or manmade phenomena. Think Kathmandu, Kuta Beach, Puerto Escondido, or Puerto Viejo—eclectic, low-rent global villages catering to the self-serve tourist.

As soon as we sat down under the drumming tin roof we were besieged by swarms of brightly clothed street *ambulantes* hawking bales of alpaca mittens, cleverly woven pot holders, neon knit caps, cigarettes, traditional me-

Brad Gerlach and porters sit on the train tracks, which also act as the only street in
Aguas Calientes, Peru. (Photo, Steve Barilotti)

dicinal herbs, and all manner of cheap gaudy trinkets. Ramshackle hostels
lined both sides of the track, along with food stalls selling everything from
fruit smoothies to *Makdonelds hamburguesa con queso*. There's a case to be
made that there is no place so remote in the world these days that one cannot order a pizza, even if it's made with goat cheese and industrial-strength
Greek olives.

On the half-day train journey to Aguas Calientes we'd followed the
Urubamba river northwest to the "Eyebrows of the Amazon," a dramatic
transition from the dry coastal plain we'd been traveling through for the
last month. Deep jungle growth covered the dark gorges as we chugged up
the valley sipping sweet, yellow Inca Cola and eating ham sandwiches. Gerr
mind-surfed the miles of rapids, charting the relentless wild flow and pulling heavy imaginary reos over twenty-foot boulder drops. He was keen to
try rafting soon. We'd met some master river men back in Cusco, and they'd
seduced Gerr with tales of endless river barrels and death-tempting Class V
rapids.

He'd particularly bonded with a Puerto Rican architect-in-training
named Luis who surfed and was leading rafting expeditions for the sum-

mer. Luis was fascinated with the architecture of Cusco because to him it represented the reason why Latin America is such a political and cultural nightmare. "Look around you," he said, pointing to the brooding cathedrals surrounding us in Cusco, "you've got the rigid dark oppression of Spanish colonialism married to the rock foundations of animistic Indian beliefs. That's why there's such an underlying feeling of rage here—it comes from the people; it comes from the buildings themselves." Luis' quest was to develop a hybrid architectural form that took the best of both cultures and promoted an evolved way of living. He called it "healing architecture."

Up the hill from the hostels was a group of natural hot springs after which the town was named. After checking in at the nearest hostel, where we secured two monkish cots and a cold shower for five dollars a night, we grabbed our baggies and hiked up to the springs to cleanse ourselves for our last assault. Nuño had strongly advised hiking the road up to the ruins before dawn to get the sunrise coming over the Hitching Post, an amazingly accurate celestial calendar.

Soaking in the steaming concrete bins of geothermally heated river water, we met a quartet of young American women who had just finished the three-day hike into the Lost City and were melting their pack-twisted backs and tortured feet in the healing hot waters. They had all just finished a two-year hitch with the Peace Corps in Peru and were well-versed in a wide variety of basic third-world development skills including bridge-building, composting, and rural prenatal care. When they found out that Gerr was a world-famous professional surfer they were intrigued, if not a little baffled.

"So . . . just what the hell are you doing up here, anyway?" asked one of them politely.

Exactly. While they had the leached, utilitarian look of nuns out of habit, I was jealous of their unwavering integrity and determination. They had all made the trek without a second's hesitation and now had "the experience" to share with each other for the rest of their lives. Also, they had a legitimate reason to be here: they were here doing some real good, not stumbling around this long-suffering country on a decadent, though aborted, surf search.

At midnight they turned off the hot spring lights and Gerr and I returned in silence to the hostel. We set our alarms for 4:00 A.M. and fell asleep listening to the river's ceaseless rumble.

In the end, we overslept and took a bus up to the ruins. Looking back, it was the best move we'd made yet. The ascent from the gorge was eight miles of muddy, switchbacked road that would have given a python back problems. And, by catching the first bus up the mountain, we had the whole Lost City to ourselves for the better part of that cool, overcast morning.

Once through the gate, Gerr and I quickly drifted apart. After the initial wonder of hiking among the ancient stones and zenned-out alpacas, we soon began exploring at our own whim. I decided to make the ascent of Huaynu Picchu, a steep two-hour ordeal on a goat-wide trail that left me sweating, dizzy from high-altitude hypoxia, and close to cardiac arrest.

The view was sublime. The entire valley was laid out below with a toy train snaking along the bottom. In the distance was a chain of sugar-frosted Andean peaks, the Cordillera Urubamba. Legend has it that the Inca, the royal ruling class, would fly on ingenious wings of golden cloth from village to village, saving days of hard travel through the steep jungle terrain.

I tried to see this place for my sister, to show her with my earthbound eyes all the beautiful places she missed in her unwavering duty to her marriage and daughter. A love-filled loyalty that had been returned with years of abuse, and finally, when she tried to leave, with her death. I watched this particular hawk for a long time, watched how gracefully and lazily it sky-surfed from peak to peak, and realized that perhaps from now on she would be showing me.

By the time Gerlach and I hooked up again it was late afternoon. Stray beams of sunlight poured through the ancient stone portals leading down to the Sacred Plaza. An animated Gerr told me he'd had a mountaintop epiphany. He saw his whole life plan—career, surfing, marriage, family—laid out like a glowing spider web before him as he sat in a secluded terrace overlooking the city. He'd just spent the last few hours furiously taking notes and was buzzing at the prospects.

Gerr had come to an important decision—he was staying in Cusco. California, he reasoned, was no doubt suffering through another dismal overcast summer of crowds and mediocre gray waves. By contrast, the possibilities here seemed unlimited. He planned to mountain bike, river raft, learn Spanish, and do high-altitude aerobic training in preparation for his impending World Tour assault next year. Cool?

Cool.

My own spiritual breakthroughs were a little more fuzzy, but no less profound. By the time I'd hiked down off Huayna Picchu, I'd come up with this: noble intentions are fine, but in the end it doesn't really matter if you trek, drive, swim, or paraglide your way to enlightenment. What matters is to be able to share a joke, or perhaps a stiff drink on the way . . . then enjoy the view once you get there.

It had been the worst surf trip of my life, and I was sad to see it end. I hadn't laughed like that in a long, long time. And perhaps in these abandoned ruins I found the foundations for the healing architecture of my own soul.

Aftershock

NATE LAWRENCE WITH NATHAN MYERS

ASU ISLAND, INDONESIA—March 28, 2005.
Violent shaking threw me from my bunk. Some massive force jerked our eighty-ton vessel like a toy on a string. I staggered into the hall, collided with other surfers in the darkness, and made my way to the upper deck. Others were already there, bewildered, frightened, and half-asleep.

"That was an earthquake," said Captain Flint. "A big one."

And then we saw the lights onshore, flashlights and lanterns bounding through the jungle and pouring out onto the beach. The villagers of Asu Island cried out to our boat in Indonesian, *"Tolong! Tolong!"* Help! Help!

And there was something else, too. Barely visible in the pale light of a cloud-shrouded moon, barely conceivable, the tide was dropping. Water receded off the beach at an unnatural rate. We'd all seen the tsunami videos from December 26, 2004. We'd all become mini-experts on this irregular phenomenon. And so now, without a doubt, we knew a tsunami was coming.

Ten days earlier, we'd stood on the tarmac of the Jakarta airport watching as our commuter flight leaked oil in a rapid drip. A kindly attendant explained that the flight would still be leaving; it just wouldn't be as safe. It was then that six California pro surfers—Nate Tyler, Jesse Evans, Micah Byrne, Jesse Colombo, Ryan Augustine, Sean Peterson, and two up-and-coming Indos, Dede Suryana and Marlon Gerber, and I, the lensman—swapped our one-hour flight for an eight-hour taxi ride. Dusty and weary, we arrived at the dock in Medan. Our photo trip for *Surfing* magazine was now just starting.

The plan was to scout new, post-December 26 reefs to surf and, while doing so, deliver our own tsunami relief package to an isolated village in northern Sumatra. We loaded the deck with surf and aid supplies—thirty-some surfboards, mountains of camera gear, boxes of first-aid kits, mosquito netting, toiletries, candy, clothes from the surfers' closets, and gear from their sponsors. The 70-foot *KM Nauli*, a steel-hulled former oil-tanker service ship out of Mississippi was ready to go, but was now stuck on a sandbar in the harbor. We waited six hours, and then the tide set us free. But just as we left, an engine caught fire, reducing our maximum trip speed to a four-knot, single-engine putter. But we were on our way—sort of.

Spirits aboard the *KM Nauli* were bleak and distant as we sputtered deeper and deeper into the vast blue unknown. Straight off, I crushed my trigger finger beneath a load-bearing ladder. There was no swell running in the open ocean, but even if we found some, I wouldn't be able to shoot.

Days slipped by in a Vicodin haze. I remember clutching my numb and mangled finger while Micah Byrne paced the deck ranting, "I can't believe we're already out of peanut butter. It's only the third day. How can we possibly be out of peanut butter so soon?" But it wasn't just the peanut butter that was missing. Each reef we passed revealed perfectly shaped waves ideal for four-inch tall surfers.

Captain Mark Flint, a sun-charred Aussie, had neck hair so thick he tied it up into his graying ponytail. He picked the target island for our homespun aid operation. Flint has been running charters in this area since before half our crew was born. He often navigated the complex island chain by sight alone. If the island he picked had a name, I never heard it spoken. Flint assured us that it had been hit hard by the tsunami and was too remote to benefit from the larger relief effort. We set course to the unnamed island.

When we got to the island, a village chief came aboard, examined our goods, and invited us ashore. The villagers swarmed us on the beach, but the distribution was surprisingly orderly. The chief gave out each item based on need.

The people's expressions of gratitude were more payment than we needed. Nevertheless, the next morning gifted swell. We took the instant karma and surfed nine hours straight at a virgin right-hander. With my finger on the mend, I managed to squeeze off a couple of rolls of water shots. The boys were surfing, I was shooting, and our little aid mission was a pretty solid suc-

Indonesian surfer Dede Suryana finds cover before the quake. (Photo, Nate Lawrence)

cess. It felt like our luck was finally turning.

The swell continued—respectable if not epic—and we meandered away from the nameless island, drifting reef to reef, island to island, until we wound up anchored offshore of Asu, an island with a peeling left that two-time world champ Tom Carroll once proclaimed was his favorite wave. We surfed this wave all day, and then watched the sun go down like a burning peach. As night set in, we shot flash photos, ate a comfortable meal of rice and fish while a brief squall blew through, called our loved ones on an unreliable satellite phone, and then we all went to bed around ten o'clock.

The earthquake struck an hour and a half later.

Captain Flint had the dinghy in the water before any of us even knew what was happening. His actions were calm and decisive, without a moment's hesitation. The rest of us merely stood and watched as Flint made trip after trip to the shore, loading the terror-stricken villagers onto his ship.

They came aboard crying, bleeding, screaming or shell-shocked beyond expression. One woman, covered in sweat and cradling a huge belly, was hauled aboard by four men. Her husband followed, saying in Indonesian, "Make way, make way, just given birth." The woman passed out on the deck and the man sat down on a pile of surfboards, watching over her and holding the newborn, weeping into the infant's still-unformed head.

Another man came aboard ranting, his eyes wide with panic. The ground's movement had been so violent that he couldn't walk during the quake. He couldn't reach his children as his house came crashing down around them. Now, his children clung to his legs, burying their frightened faces into his sea-soaked pants. He seemed unaware of the bedlam aboard the boat, as though he were still stuck in that terrible moment on land. The quake had lasted almost four minutes.

As Captain Flint evacuated the island, we stood on the sun deck and watched the water level drop further and further down the beach. "We've gotta get outta here!" one surfer was screaming. "Forget these people! The tsunami is coming."

"If we wait much longer," another campaigned, "we won't be able to leave at all. We'll be dry-docked."

Some were silent. One surfer laughed wildly, another went down and tried to sleep. Getting the island's entire population, about 100 people, on board took about a half-hour, but it felt like forever. We pulled anchor in maddeningly slow motion. Then, in a moment, we were gone, puttering at our wounded-snail's pace toward the safety of the open ocean. The boat was at full capacity, loaded with desperate, weeping, bleeding, puking villagers who had just witnessed their world shaken down for the second time in almost as many months. Their eyes bulged with fear and sadness.

All aboard: the chaotic post-rescue scene on the *KM Nauli*. (Photo, Nate Lawrence)

We were only two minutes out to sea when Captain Flint said, "I'm getting something on the radar." I looked over his shoulder and saw a mass of water blipping a wide green line across his monitor.

"This is it," he said. "Get ready."

I put on a life jacket with many of the others. Some huddled in sheltered nooks. Some did nothing. One surfer held his board at the ready. I climbed to the upper deck and peered out into the darkness. There on the horizon, we saw it—just a squall: a thick, low belt of a storm that brought rough seas, but not a tsunami.

Our relief was drowned as the sudden storm lashed wind and rain at us from every direction. Waves crashed over the lower decks, drenching the stricken refugees. We brought as many people inside as would fit. We emptied our suitcases to clothe our guests from the chill. Some huddled inside our board-socks and coffin-bags. Meanwhile, part of the cabin engaged in a sopping and disorderly makeshift triage, bandaging and cleaning wounds suffered in the earthquake. I helped pass around food and water and offered a smile where I could muster one. I listened to their stories, even if I did not understand a word of them.

"All we can do now is try to get some sleep," Flint said, putting his hand on my shoulder.

At dawn we returned to Asu and set anchor. Forty yards of pristine beach had appeared overnight. The reefs had risen nearly ten feet out of the water, with fish flopping around on the lifted coral heads. The night before, when we had watched the water recede, it wasn't the water receding at all. The ocean had not sucked out, but the ground had risen before our eyes. We had watched it happen, but couldn't comprehend it as such.

The villagers refused to go ashore, refused to go home. Delegates went and retrieved what heirlooms and valuables they could salvage. All but two structures had toppled during the 8.7 magnitude quake.

They requested to be taken to Sirombu, a village of Nias where a refugee camp had been established after the previous quake. Along the way, we stopped to help another village, but surrounding reefs had risen out of the water here as well, fortifying the island against any boat access. People waved and called from the island, but we were loaded to capacity. All we could do was motor on.

At Sirombu, good-byes were tearful and heartfelt on both sides. For us surfers, the trial was nearly over. For the villagers of Asu, it was just beginning. They had nothing now, and what would they find at the refugee camp?

Would there be enough food? Shelter? Water? Would they even be allowed to stay there?

On the beach they gave us more hugs, and we gave whatever food and supplies we had left to give. Then they made their way through the mud and rubble of the deserted town—abandoned since the tsunami—toward the refugee camp and some uncertain future.

We sat there on the beach, drenched and burdened in secondhand sadness, and then, *boom!*, an aftershock knocked us from our makeshift bench. Santa Cruz surfer Jesse Colombo looked at me wide-eyed and said, "All right, time to go."

On the long boat ride back to Medan there was no talking, no laughter, no drinking or game playing. Everyone kept to themselves. When I closed my eyes, I saw their faces, heard their moans. I thought back to a conversation from the night before, something a deckhand had helped translate. I asked one of the villagers what they thought was happening with all of the recent earthquakes. "They believe they need to respect the earth more," the deckhand replied. "To try to keep it more clean so Mother Nature will not get angry at them again."

News crews awaited us at the docks of Medan. Some surfers sold footage

All shook up: Pro surfers (L to R) Nate Tyler, Jesse Evans, Dede Suryana, Micah Byrne, and Sean Peterson visit a devastated village the day after the earthquake of March 28, 2005. (Photo, Nate Lawrence)

Not low tide: this canoe got dry-docked as the submerged reef suddenly rose twelve feet out of the water. (Photo, Nate Lawrence)

of the rescue that they had captured on their compact video cameras. I sold a few digital photos of the post-quake destruction.

Captain Flint stood apart from our little media circus. He stared out toward the islands that we had left behind, and I felt a moment of shame for the insignificant amount of money I'd just made selling pictures to a local newspaper. The images were so far removed from the reality of the people, their integrity, their displacement, and their fear of returning home. In a week or two, the world would turn its gaze toward the new flavor-of-the-week tragedy, while the ongoing suffering of these remote islanders would be forgotten.

As we shouldered our mostly empty bags onto the docks of Medan, I noticed the hollowed expressions on the faces of my fellow passengers. We would never forget.

Under the Buzzard Wing

The University of South Florida's 1994 Surf Club Trip to Costa Rica

REX WITKAMP

I sat in the Orlando airport, the bowels of Florida, daydreaming about crank-ing turns off the lip, sending huge fans of spray out over a full year's worth of frustrating, lack-luster Florida waves—our inter-collegiate contests had been held in knee-high surf. Pollo, our club president, was still out in the arrival zone doing paperwork with the lady who rammed his truck while we'd been unloading it. Kracke, club VP, was hot-faced and bitching about the way security roughed him up and removed him after he screamed for the twelfth, perhaps fifteenth, time, "Why the fuck did you do that, lady? Are you retarded?" And Kentinental, club secretary, was plugged into some tunes. So began the University of South Florida Surf Club's 1994 spring break trip to Costa Rica.

Then the counter lady spoke the words, "six-hour delay." There were no thoughts as to what we should do. With our wrecked truck being towed out of the departure zone, Kracke, Kentinental, and I walked to the bar. The rest of the club followed. After one round of pitchers, another pack came in; they were familiar looking, yet adversarial—the University of Central Florida's (UCF) surf club—and, by chance, they were on the same flight.

Daddy's gold card came out of select wallets, and a steady traffic of drinks passed over the bar to our tables where a game of "Quarters" morphed into

"Asshole," then to a game called "Pass the Pigs," where you toss two plastic pigs in the air and drink according to how they land. We bought pitchers for the UCF kids, and they bought pitchers for us.

Then El Capitán showed up, dressed to kill in a white silk suit, white tie, white captain's hat, and his new wife in tow. She cautiously looked at us as he pulled her by hand into the bar. He loudly and incongruously proclaimed, "My brother is a cop in Chicago. Drinks are on me."

She whispered, "This is *my* honeymoon, not theirs."

The bartender poured a round of thirty-some tequila shots. Kracke led the toast, shouting, "Here's to El Capitán." El Capitán slugged down three shots. His wife's face paled in disbelief—a prescient expression prefiguring dimensions of drama and pain that were to unfold. She turned toward the door, maintaining a firm hold on El Capitán's hand. You could see her character battling itself: her pathological clinginess deftly pummeling her desire to escape.

Finally Pollo made it to the bar. "Drink," said Kracke, handing him a beer. "You need this." Ever responsible, Pollo declined. He wanted to be driving to the beach just as soon as the plane landed, and in Costa Rica, driving is difficult enough sober. "Gordo, this is to the trip!" Kracke clanked mugs with me in a benediction of the surf to come. Gordo is what they call me, because of a little weight I put on after an operation I had in college. After a good six hours of dousing ourselves in suds, Aero Costa Rica made the boarding call, and we ran as a horde down the jetway tossing Frisbees and tackling each other.

Aero Costa Rica, March 4, 1994

An hour and a half into the flight: "This is your captain speaking," the voice boomed over the loudspeaker. It was not the soft tone typical of pilots. "You must calm down and return to your seats, or I will land the plane immediately." The free-for-all in the sky quieted to listen and then promptly resumed firing spitballs and rampaging up and down the cabin. Kracke fired off a wet spitball into the back of Pollo's head. Pollo slapped Kentinental in retaliation. A second later, I got one down the throat; I swallowed it, just as I would have to swallow the impetuous demands of the club. I was the club treasurer and felt obligated to straddle the line between having fun and keeping order.

Thirty-some college surfers, not drunk, but wasted, in flight to Costa Rica. Flight attendants were holed in their chambers. Paper airplanes with lewd messages criss-crossed the cabin. Golfing and business magazines flew forward and aft. Spitballs stuck to walls, windows, and the ceiling. Berating shouts for more free beverages preceded the theft of small bottles from an attendant's cart. The airlines don't put up with any sort of monkey business these days, but this was 1994.

We carried on for a while before the pilot warned again, "I will land this plane if you do not return to your seats!" Then he added, "I will not repeat this message again." A raiding party dispatched itself and produced two bottles of fine champagne, which went forward through the cabin from lips to lips. "Gordo, this is a fine life," said Kracke, champagne dripping down his chin.

"Yeah," I said, "drink it and enjoy it."

"The best plane ride of our life," he said, "and it's leading us to the best surf of our life."

The pilot gave another warning which didn't penetrate the volume of the party so well. And then the plane went into a rapid descent. But I knew—and Kracke knew—we weren't headed to tourist-friendly San José. Yet we still sang, and others joined in: "Show me the way to San José." Then El Capitán stumbled uphill to the rear, green in the face, hand to mouth. He rode out the landing in the stainless steel restroom. Outside, it was as dark as two nights at once. Who knew where we were? Guatemala? El Salvador? Belize?

The pilot forced the door open, and a cadre of camouflaged soldiers with AK-47s drawn charged down the aisle. Chaos broke out near the cockpit. Black-tied FAA officials yelled in Spanish at the pilot, co-pilot, and navigator. They in turn yelled back, pointing fingers at the flight attendants, who began crying and pointing at us. We were stone-cold quiet.

El Capitán, nearly ambulatory, stumbled out of the bathroom and looked wondrously at the soldiers. They sprang a wide-eyed ambush on him, knocking him backwards before even making contact. Then they refused to touch him with anything but the barrel of their guns, as he was covered in bodily fluids and spattered with puke chunks. Now local police were boarding the plane fingering their .357s. "It was him," yelled a flight attendant, pointing at the kid in our club who had stolen the champagne. A solider put a gun in the kid's face, and we heard "pfffffrrrppp" as he released his holdings into his boxers. We called him "Skid" from then on. In his first attempt to use Spanish, he cried out to the stewardesses and pleaded, "*Lo Siento! Lo Siento!*" as the soldiers tried to force him off the plane. Then someone shouted earnestly, "Dude, they're gonna kill him," and our faces went white, because we believed it so. Skid dropped to the ground and bellowed out cries. I could already see him in his cell notching the seven-hundred-and-thirtieth tick on the wall, as the guard pulled up his pants—Pollo had detailed this consequence and others in a pre-departure lecture about respecting the law and the others we encounter on our trip.

Now El Capitán was being forced off the plane, gun barrels at his back, and his new wife, crying, followed after him and the soldiers. The party was over. After a sobering hour, we were on our way with an air marshal guarding the two soiled suspects up in first class. For their champagne abuse, they would be served papers at touchdown.

Dude, Where's My Fin?

We rented vans, a big one ("White Trash") and a little one ("Red Rocket"), then heaped a mountain of boards precariously on the roof-rack—Kracke's board on the bottom, as it was ten feet long and four inches thick with extra glass to support his 265-plus pounds of buffalo elegance. Buffalo-butt Krackemoto's birth name is Chris Jardin, but when he makes a bottom turn his boardshorts drop and show his crack. He is also huge and hairy like a buffalo, thus his nickname.

We got lost, found the ferry terminal, waited for it, drove over the Nicoya Peninsula, and seven hours later found Nosara beach: four miles of sand and four miles of perfect, slightly overhead waves peeling in with multiple peaks. Who cared that the afternoon wind was chopping it up a little? We took the boards down and paddled out. Kracke went looking for his longboard fin, but it was in a cooler with our stoves, all of our food, and 100-plus bars of wax that had never left Orlando. He grabbed the bodyboard and met us in the lineup.

Pollo, the club president and best surfer among us, was carving huge cutbacks into what would be the only good swell of the trip. Pollo ripped for hours, unloading the anxieties of organizing the trip, the delay, the accident, and his fears that some of the kids might jeopardize the trip with drugs.

Kentinental paddled over to Kracke and said, "What's the hardest thing about riding a bodyboard?"

"What?"

"Telling your mom that you're gay."

"Fuck off," said Kracke, as Kentinental paddled into a pitching barrel.

If anyone in the club had a board that could float Kracke, they would not have lent it, because that's what you do—you abandon all concerns and goodwill in the face of bitchin' swell.

Buffalo-butt Krackemoto aka Chris Jardin dropping in at Playa Avellana ten years after his first visit, Guanacaste, Costa Rica. (Photo, John Lyman)

What Would Jesus Do?

A newlywed couple staying up the road decided to stash their clean, new longboards in our beach camp to avoid the long walk-and-carry that produces the majority of chafing and rashing in Costa Rica. Next morning, in the blue haze of the dawn, Kracke quietly picked up one of these longboards, and he and I walked into the warm water. The haze became clean light and turned the morning glass into a mirror of the sky. We were in knee-deep water on our way to perfect overhead, empty sets when the van horn started "honk, honk, honking!" Waking everyone up, the dude was yelling, "That's my new board, man!" Full of shame but not guilt, Kracke walked back, dropped the dude's board in the sand and picked up the bodyboard. There is no purity; in view of surf, we are all sinners.

We got two rides before the gang, now awakened, was in the lineup staring icily at their vice president, the thief. Kracke and I paddled some space between us and the pack. "I'm desperate," he pleaded, gripping the bodyboard. "I need it. Look at what we have here! Big waves, morning glass, miles of empty surf. This doesn't exist in Florida. That's why I'm here. It's not like I was stealing the board. It's not like that dude is using it now. Gordo, the board insisted that I take it. I would regret not trying to take it because that would be a failure to respond to *the call*. What would you have done?"

Tamarindo

We finished the session hungry, and drove into the little town of Tamarindo. Kracke promptly bought himself an $85 fin. Then we wandered through town, looking for a lunch spot. Construction crawled over a stretch of bay that would soon become the epicenter of Central American surfing. There were no waves and still the lineup was packed. Multiracial kids from all over the globe sat on boards in a clear blue sea, glistening with droplets of water, backed by green, fertile hills—a true Kodak moment.

Our lunch was satisfying. It had the substance food at home often lacks: The coffee had caffeine, the bread had carbs, the butter had fat, the beer had alcohol, and the mangos had flavor. At lunch we met a few travelers who were fond of using the verb *to do* as in "I *did* Nicaragua; next I'm *doing* Panama."

The word *do* leans toward an impulsive desire to love briefly that which you might abhor in larger measure. We, like them, were seeking less understanding than pleasure from Costa Rica's equally weighted scales of tedium and thrill. I could warn you, any of us could warn you: This "doing" is a path toward undoing.

Camping in the Jungle

Would we have chosen to part with five bucks each to hermetically seclude ourselves in an air-conditioned, bug-free hotel room, I would have happily starfished myself upon a saggy bed and stared at a hypnotic ceiling fan. A hotel room here is like a zone of seduction within the jungle, a place for down time, for drifting time, for cold beer and a game of Edward Forty-Hands with some wandering Aussies. (Can't piss or smoke or itch until you drink both of the forty-ounce beer bottles duct-taped to each of your hands.) But we were too cheap to stay in the hotel.

Instead of spending five dollars each, we pitched camp for two bucks apiece in a local's grazing field at the completely undeveloped inlet of Playa Langosta, two kilometers south of Tamarindo. Just after unloading both vans, a pack of horses herded through our camp. Boards splayed out, Kracke and Pollo ran to protect theirs, but Bob's got trampled and as the horse pushed off, it flung the board into a tree. No waves at this beach, either. Night came and, like eager entomologists, we beamed our flashlights into the outhouse hole to watch the dung-gobbling beetles make haste.

We stood under blazing, bright-burning stars, talking about going to the discotheque, when suddenly an owl swooped at Kracke. Instinctively, he kung-fu chopped it, missed, and the owl drew necessary blood from his arm. Your money is not enough; this country will always take back in other forms.

Kracke, searching for meaning, suggested the attack was payback for outhouse conversation in which we called *El Chupacabra* (the mythical bloodsucking, fanged, goat-munching monster of the lower Americas) "*El Poopacabra*." But I knew differently; providence had simply assigned him that owl along with a host of other frustrations to be administered in daily homeopathic doses.

Before heading to the disco, Pollo gave his second stern lecture about not buying, using, or possessing drugs. The talk was like water running off a duck's back. The club kids wasted no time in making a trade with a local, who got new boardshorts (with the tags still on them), a watch, pants, a hat, surf shirts, and money. They got a small spliff and an "I told you so" from me. But then, because I was the only one in the group who spoke Spanish, they sent me back to haggle with the local in the darkness. He offered a pinchy bit more.

Not My Vote

In the morning the Pacific wasn't producing, and the group, despite the officers' vote, decided the Atlantic might be giving, so the convoy, lusty for adventure, rolled out on the 150-mile, ten-hour cross-county drive. To pass the time, Kracke mooned the Red Rocket, and they lobbed bananas and coconuts at us. The Red Rocket broke down a few hours into the trip, outside of the town of Cañas. We renamed it the "Dead Sprocket." Pollo and I didn't give it a thought. We emptied everyone out of our van. Dickie, Bob, and I went to the capital to get a new one.

Many hours later, at 2 A.M., Dickie and I were barreling down the road, closing in on Cañas with Bob behind us. I warned Dickie of the huge bump and pothole ahead of us. He floored it and howled as I bounced to the ceiling and back down. "This is how you're supposed to treat a rental," said Dickie. When we got back, the group was huddled around the Dead Sprocket listening to a live broadcast by the band INXS. We loaded the wares into the new van, then Kracke directed the group to circle the broken van and piss all over it, not just the sides and the tires, but also the windows and the seats inside. We did it and we rolled.

Ten yards down the shoulder of the road, the big van seized up and shut down. As we ground to a halt, I could hear Kracke in the other van screaming, "Dude, no! No! Nooooooo!"

A quick check showed a large hole in the oil pan. Dickie had bounced it onto a rock. The convoy stopped and both vans emptied. The three hotels in town were filled. We surveyed the sleeping options and cursed Kracke for pissing out six good beds. But people found their sleeping niches in bench seats and on the van roof. Me? I went back to the pissed-on van. Exhausted from translating and from having to manage all transactions, I suffered the stink for the comfort.

For atonement, Kracke inflated his pool raft and set it down in a two-foot margin between the road and the fence of a lumberyard. All night, semis spawned dirt and debris tornadoes that pebbled Kracke through his dreams. Unshaven, with dust whitening his hair and beard, Kracke awoke to a posse of laborers telling him what they wanted for Christmas next year. Kracke stared blankly. He didn't understand a word. The group howled in laughter. Kracke hid under his sheet and snored for a while before a pack of kids began poking him with sticks, saying, "Santa Claus! Santa Claus! Are you dead?"

We're Rolling

"Hey dude, our van works fine," said Bob, the driver of the little van. "We're rolling."

"You're rolling?" said Kracke. "You've got to be fucking kidding me! We just sacrificed our day and night to get you a new van, and you're rolling?" Then, with less pleasantries than grace, he expressed his feelings on this matter to the same group who had iced him earlier for "borrowing" that newlywed's longboard. Kracke, with his fists tight, unloaded his verbiage in full Long Island accent. He lost favor with all, as the van, prioritizing on its driver's words, vanished in the distance.

"Dude, that's not cool," said Pollo breathing the road dust.

"None of this is fucking cool," said Kentinental.

Kracke paced back and forth sweating through his shirt.

"Let's take a walk," I said.

Pollo, Kentinental, Kracke, and I wandered desultorily through town, fingering postcards of world-class surf and topless women. Kracke found himself a beer. I'm not sure what the Spanish expression "My loaf is all dough" means, but maybe it applied to us here.

Here in this dusty town, I realized that Costa Rica had us under her buzzard wing, instructing us on this finer point: A surfing vacation will always be a parody of itself.

We found no waves in Puerto Viejo, our destination. Kracke, Pollo, Kentinental and I segregated ourselves as the others were not happy with Kracke. We tended our surplus of time with two-for-one Ronrico Cuba Libres at the beachside cantina as Black Uhuru's "Guess Who's Coming to Dinner" blared in the background. The other club members pooled their money and gave it to a shady dealer at the disco, who promised to be right back. The unfulfilled promise of drugs made them bitch and moan extra hard the following day. At least we had hangovers.

Our last day in town we surfed some mushy, waist-high waves that only groms would ride. Kracke didn't even paddle out—just stared and said he'd rather be shopping. The others accused him of having a bad attitude, and he told them to fuck off.

On our way out of town, windows down, stomachs empty, music blasting, we saw a familiar white outfit down the road. Kentinental slowed the van. It was El Capitán in his white suit, sporting his white captain's hat, arm-in-arm with his wife, giving her a kiss on the neck. We rolled by honking, waving, and screaming, "El Capitán! El Capitán!" like he was a movie star. Then his wife turned to look at us, and she was not his wife. She was a local. Kentinental stepped on the gas, blowing a dust storm into their union. Our final words were hard to devise, but to them, it was "Blow me" written large in the dust on our back window.

At the airport, Kracke said, "Gordo, let me summarize this trip: one real day of surf on a bodyboard; one rental van with $900 in damages on my credit card; one car crash; two breakdowns; owl and horse ambushes; and, of the sixteen people who began the trip, three will talk to me."

I didn't know what to say back.

"But here's the worst part," said Kracke. "I vowed to my parents that I would come back with the rest of you. Gordo, I want to stay. I've paid my dues. Our insufferable gang is leaving. But I'm here and my board has a fin! Why did I make that mindless promise? Why?"

Equatorial Lines

JENNY HEDLEY

A surf charter boat full of pros and photographers saw me take a towering set on the head. They could have counted slowly to fifteen before I came up bleeding badly. The next wave held me under again, while the charter sailed away from Bawa reef to the Mentawai Islands or beyond. A local fisherman in a pint-sized dinghy paddled into the impact zone and rescued me. He rowed me to the calm end of the island, a kilometer away, and charged 10,000 rupiah for the evacuation service. The owner of my rented bungalow ran to meet me. He hoisted me into a wheelbarrow and pushed me along the coral path back to the bungalow which was named New Mercy. It was over. I was done with surfing. The wound, wide and deep, would heal in a few weeks, but my nerve for big waves might never return. My shin throbbed in the hot sun as the wheelbarrow bounced along the path.

Stuck in bed, I revisited the origins of this year-long solo trip. As a child, the only thing that united my fractured family was surfing. My mom, brother, aunt, uncle, cousins, and I would throw seven boards on the car and push each other into waves beyond our ability. Hours later, shivering and wet, we'd grab dry towels, donuts, and hot cocoa.

Except for surfing, everything in my life was a perpetual internal battle between who I wanted to be and who my father wanted me to be. Though I only visited my father twice a month while growing up, he had considerable influence on who I would become. I saw myself wandering harmoniously

Bawa Reef's pure righthand power delivers a commensurate amount of joy and pain, Bawa Island, Indonesia. (Photo, Jenny Hedley)

toward self-discovery. My father expected me to be a Type A, straight-A overachiever. College was my chance to rebel against his vision, but after a few years of smoking, drinking, and one-night stands, I didn't "find myself" anything other than a dropout.

When I returned home for the holidays one Easter, my mom pulled out some reels of Super 8 film, and we watched a surf movie that I'd never seen. There was mom in short-shorts. A bandana held back her unruly auburn locks. Scruffy men carried longboards. Perfect empty Baja waves pitched. A beach bonfire followed some wild surf sequences. This was the raw footage of a surf film she had tried to make before the cast and crew dispersed into drugs, relationships, pregnancy, and jobs. My mom, well, she returned to California and started a family with a man who hated to travel. I was the result of that short-lived marriage.

Soon after seeing those reels, I sold my car, said goodbye to my boyfriend, and bought a one-way ticket to Indonesia. I was gone. My father was taking my dreams the same way he did my mom's, and what would be my ultimate reward for going back to school and getting good grades? A steady job? Confinement in a cubicle where quality of life is traded for a diverse portfolio and monthly SUV payments?

Just before my departure, I came across a surf movie in pre-production. The producer needed another *wahine* to add to the cast of Belinda Baggs, Pauline Menczer, Katie Coryell, Karina Petroni, and Daisy Shane. I drove up to Santa Barbara to meet with her. "*Hot Crush and Blue Liquid*," she said. "It's a reality surf movie." The title was no less retarded than her idea, but still I was psyched for the opportunity to meet her and her crew the next year on the Gold Coast of Australia.

The producer showed me her modeling portfolio before we parted. "Look at this image of me!" she pointed. The pictures showed her body alternately dressed up and disrobed. Her painted face seduced the camera. Her physical perfection embodied all that I despised about Southern California, where image holds precedence over being. I left all that bullshit behind when I got on the airplane. After takeoff, I reclined my seat and thought about it: enter reality TV and you enter the confusion of existence and its double.

First destination: A spot irresistibly shrouded in timeless mystique and malaria. Kevin Lovett's epic journey to Lagundri Bay, Nias, as chronicled in *The Surfer's Journal*, was my guiding light. I pushed off the plane and onto the first of two ferries that would get me there. I rested on the hot, tar-coated deck. Enjoying the breeze and the solitude, I unbuttoned my blouse to get some color on my pale stomach. I fell asleep thinking about the headhunting shamans and deadly mosquitoes that Lovett encountered on Nias. I dreamed of scorpions and snakes, the effects of anti-malarial pills coming on strong. As the sun began its descent into the Indian Ocean, I awoke and found my unprotected skin fiercely burnt. Water blisters formed and then erupted as I negotiated the grimy city streets of Medan. I shoved past leering men, their lips pursed suggestively on ABC cigarettes.

I hit an internet café in Medan, gateway to Sumatra, and found the producer online. We instant-messaged about my journey thus far, and then she had a surprise for me. My boyfriend was over at her place. They had just been surfing together. She sent a digital photo: her in nothing but a towel with wild, just-out-of-the-saltwater hair; him with a cat-got-mouse smile. I'd never introduced them. One of them must have sought out the other. Then they sent a photo of the producer topless. "Oops," she wrote.

"Isn't that funny?" wrote my boyfriend. I'd had enough. I wrote a curt goodbye, saying I would be out of touch for another two months. I left the café, my stomach a boiling, bubbling, red mess, and my temper its equal.

The ten-hour bus ride to Sibolga was typical of Southeast Asia. We made passes on blind corners and hit nonstop bumps, potholes, and flattened roadkill. Sweaty bodies were pressed two to a seat, shrill music threatened to blow out the speakers, and overturned buses littered the roadside. I felt I was drowning in a crush of bodies and fumes. I wanted to get to Nias immediately. When I got off the bus, I discovered that it was Sunday and no ferries were running.

I sought refuge at the first hotel I spotted on Jalan Horas. A strange man protested that I was checking into a prostitute's hotel and offered to help me find a safer place to sleep. My surf guidebook didn't cover Sibolga, the uncharted territory of "Hell on Earth," so I followed him next-door and upstairs to a stuffy, windowless room. It would do. I locked the door and set down my board bag, and the man called out that he would fetch me the next day. I didn't care either way. The dusty fan wouldn't work so I lay naked atop my sarong on the mildewed bed and fanned my blistered stomach, now the color of split-pea soup.

The next day the man lured me out with promises of good food and a waterfall. He drove me into the jungle. He sat on his *bemo* (a small pickup) with my backpack containing money, plane tickets, and my passport, while I leapt over the falls into a deep green pool. The cool water soothed my burn. Later he treated me to *nasi goreng* (fried rice, Indo style) in a *warung* (small restaurant). That night, he helped me safely board the ferry to Nias and escorted me to the top bunk in a small cabin. He then bent over my dirt-stained toes and closed his lips around them. I kicked my feet against the warm liquidity of his mouth. He swore that he loved me . . . that his wife was no good to him . . . that she had given him the scar that ran the length of his cheek . . . that he would pay me 200,000 rupiah if I would spend one night with him. Not to be made a twenty-dollar hooker, I forced him out of the cabin and turned the key.

I lay back down and exposed my tender stomach to the scanty breeze that flowed through the small cabin window. I drifted into nightmarish sleep, and then awoke to panicked voices crying and men shouting orders. It was midnight and the ferry was on fire. The flames danced just outside my cabin. I began to pray. I tried to squeeze my body out of my window to see if I could get out that way, in case we needed to jump ferry. I cursed myself for eating so much chocolate.

The epicenter of my panic was that I might never have the chance to realize my full potential. The men formed a brigade. Passing buckets of seawater, they put out the fire in an hour's time. Once it was out, I went to the bathroom—a hole with ocean beneath it. The key to my cabin fell through the toilet and into the sea. Maybe I had to earn the right to surf the legendary wave at Lagundri Bay.

Locked out of my cabin, I climbed onto the roof to sleep. A pair of doughy arms groped me awake. A sweat-soaked man pressed his erection against my ass. I wanted to vomit, and I wanted even more to throw him off the boat where he would drown and be forgotten. Instead, I elbowed him in the chest. He just laughed and rolled away. The close call with the fire had made me rethink my priorities in life. Maybe this dude's dying wish was to get his paws on some blonde chick. I felt ashamed of my body and wished I could disappear between the charred cracks of the boat.

We docked at Nias. The clean blue skies and lush green palms were full of promise. I surfed the epic right-hander with passion and love. I kissed Solo, a local surfer, with lust. His arresting brown eyes had me for days, until he began demanding money. He said it was to help his family, but he used it to pay gambling debts. Solo was a cold lover and reticent beau. He delivered on the promise of his sex appeal in measured doses.

When the waves at Lagundri reached double-overhead, the local boys told me I would break my board and die. Screw them. I felt invincible. With my eyes closed against the salty spray of the offshores, I took drop after drop into the ocean energy. Confident and at peace with myself, I laughed after getting pitched over the falls on a big set. This magnificent right-hander was impossibly perfect.

The bay soon turned into "Lake Lagundri," and I'd grown tired of Solo.

In a mood, the author prepares the Albatross for a windy surf at "Woogy," Central Coast, Australia. (Photo, Anne McAndrews)

I traveled to Bawa, one of the Hinako Islands, by boat and checked into the New Mercy bungalow. The swell came in at triple-overhead. I slapped on Chapstick and sunscreen and ignored the thunderous, sickening noise the wave made. I couldn't make it out through the shore break, so I paddled out at the keyhole. I made it outside, tense and shit-scared. The tea I had for breakfast came back up. I wasn't ready to take such big drops, so I paddled farther outside to wait and visualize myself riding one of these beasts.

A rogue set swung wide, and I scratched for the horizon. A thick lip crested way above me and hammered down two feet from the nose of my board. Instinctively, I duck-dived, as the Indian Ocean folded over itself. My surfboard flew from my hands, and I got driven into the spin cycle. My leash stretched out, then shot my board back at me and the glassed-in fin gouged my left shin. My shinbone destroyed the fin in equal measure. That's when the surf charter boat that came to check out "Bawa Power" spirited off and the fisherman rowed me to shore.

Where my mind was full of hope and promise for making and starring in a surf movie, it was suddenly emptied. I lay in bed with my leg elevated and listened to the waves pound the reef. The ocean had been good to me since my mom threw me on a board in Mexico when I was ten. But now I felt betrayed by the Bawa wipeout and haunted with the same feeling I used to get when my father would punish me for no good reason. Worst of all, I was afraid of the ocean.

My leg healed and I pushed on by boat, bus, and train to Kuala Lumpur in Malaysia, where I would catch a flight to Brisbane, Australia. I checked my email and found a message from the Supermodel producer of *Hot Crush and Blue Liquid*. She said all of the other surfers had dropped out or couldn't make it, and it would just be her and me in the film—with no "superficial hoopla."

To translate the email in more direct language, I was to be scripted into the margins of her vanity project. Enthusiasm drained out of me like an old birthday balloon. I considered going back home to America and imagined myself in Los Angeles traffic. Indifferent to my options, I boarded the plane to Australia. After takeoff, I reclined my seat and thought that my life was offering me second helpings. Here I was again, in the air, abandoned to my wants of self-fulfillment.

I had a few days on my own before meeting the crew at the Brisbane airport and was determined to overcome my ocean apprehension. I paddled into a Gold Coast lineup feeling out of place and paranoid. I fell and fell again.

A few days later, Skinny Seppo, a Santa Barbara surfer renowned for onboard surf cinematography, strolled though Customs and Immigration. I was fatuously attracted to him. Obeying a feeling that would never be mutual, I hugged him for one second too long. He was ignorant of my attention. We got on the road and he started bitching about our producer. She hadn't filled out the clearances for his camera equipment, and so Customs and Immigration had confiscated most of it.

I strapped his surfboards to the rack of the rental station wagon and drove south on the left side of the freeway to Burleigh Heads, where I'd surfed like a kook the day before. Uninterested in filming me, he grabbed his board and ran off into the lineup before I could stash the car key under the tire. I changed into a bikini and picked my way across the boulders. Unrelenting overhead sets swept over the algae-slick rocks. Waves that wouldn't have made me blink before my accident at Bawa had me paralyzed with dread.

I leapt into the gray-green water on my 7-foot Royal Albatross and paddled, mistiming things a bit. A double-overhead sneak set came right at me. I looked back to the boulders and then to the oncoming white wall. Weighing my options, I paddled back to the rocks, stood up, and started to run. I could hear the wave coming. I wedged my feet between two barnacle-covered rocks and held my breath until the waves passed over me. Then I paddled out past the breakers lickety-split.

A local burned me on my first wave. I stroked into the smallest wave of a set and kicked out down the line, experiencing for the first time in a long while the adrenaline rush of a snappy ride. A longhaired blonde from Mermaid Beach paddled up to me. "What happened to your leg?" she asked. I looked back at a palm-sized area bleeding profusely. The mermaid told me not to worry, pointing to an equally ugly cut the boulders had given her. An hour later, Skinny Seppo greeted me in the parking lot with his shortboard under his arm.

"Dude," he said, "I got, like, so barreled. Did you see me?"

I limped into the driver's seat of the Falcon, and we drove to the airport to pick up the second cameraman.

"Your leg looks *burly*," Skinny joked. "You get it? *Burleigh*."

Turtle, an assistant camera operator from Venice, California, swaggered through Customs with a small backpack and a DHD board. We waited for the Supermodel to arrive. After a fourteen-hour journey from Los Angeles, she strutted though Customs with an entourage of male baggage handlers. She was slim and gorgeous. I part envied her and part despised her. Whatever she'd done with my boyfriend, I was not going to ask. The men made a pile of luggage. Her bags were filled with bikinis; beauty kits; cases of wheat-free, yeast-free, sugar-free, dairy-free, supplemented meal replacements; an iBook; and a giant hard-plastic case containing her prized Canon XL1.

"Get the camera," the Supermodel ordered Turtle, "I'm driving."

I handed her the keys and squeezed into the back of the Falcon with Skinny. Turtle focused his deep-soul eyes on the Supermodel through the lens of the XL1. We screamed as she drove counter-clockwise at a round-about, swerving to avoid an oncoming vehicle. Not wanting to die in some lame car wreck with a Supermodel, I begged to take the wheel.

"Chill, you guys," she said. "It'll be good for the film. Stuff like this is great. You *were* filming, weren't you?"

Turtle and Skinny chuckled uncomfortably.

We checked into the Rainbow apartments overlooking Snapper Rocks on the Gold Coast. The Supermodel dictated the sleeping arrangements: "This is the boys' room," she said, pointing to a room with two twin beds, "and this will be the queens' room," she said, pointing to an airy room with a queen-sized bed. The next morning, she told me I fought her in my sleep. With a wave of her curling iron, she banished me to the corner of the living room. Even in Indonesia, I'd always had a bed to sleep on. Now I was paying $250 a week for the privilege of sleeping on a first-world floor. For breakfast I cooked pancakes, and she said, "If I ate that, I'd die."

She watched with morbid fascination as I dragged forkfuls of pancake through butter and syrup.

She said, "Watching you eat that makes me sick."

At dinner, I ordered pasta with shrimp, and she pulled the same routine. "If you actually eat that, I'll die." She seemed to suffer from a third-person eating disorder.

The next morning a roach scuttled off the wall and onto my stomach. "I'm going out," I announced to no one in particular.

"Wait for me," cried the Supermodel, as she lifted an aromatherapy mask from her eyes. "I just need to straighten my hair."

But I was already out the door and up the hill on a walk. No matter what I did, I couldn't please her. I wasn't skinny enough, and I wasn't vigilant enough over what entered my mouth. I walked for a while trying to clear my

Former ASP world champion and Byron Bay local Pauline Menczer tears up her home break.
(Photo, Jenny Hedley)

mind of all this. I ran into a board shaper selling pot, so I bought an eighth.

I came back to the apartment and entered the unnerving quiet. I looked at the others. Skinny Seppo called the Supermodel a bitch to her face, and she told him to, "Shut up and film." Why did she hire one person who despised her and another who made her sick?

She left the room and I shared my score with Turtle and Skinny. We chuckled about the birthday party we had attended the day before. The Supermodel showed up with her pubic hair hanging out of her teeny bikini, and no one could work up the courage to point out the obvious. Maybe I should have discreetly said something to her, but I was stung by her constant talk of my weight and diet.

For the time being, the four of us stuck together in an uneasy truce. Soon Pauline Menczer, former world champion and winner of twenty-eight Association of Surfing Professionals events, invited us to stay with her. We set up camp in the apartment below her house, just outside of Byron Bay. I was star-struck when I surfed with her for the first time. In the lineup, I told her how much I admired her powerful surfing.

"Yeah, well you stink, and you surf like a peacock. You squat like you're taking a poo," she said with a wink.

Meanwhile, on the beach, Skinny Seppo sparred with the Supermodel. "You can't even surf, you dumb bitch," he said, walking away from her and the project.

"You can't leave us," she said. "You signed a contract, and that's my foot-age in your camera." She wrestled his mini-DV camera from his grip and turned to run with it, but he grabbed and yanked her flowing hair. She hurled the camera at him, and he left with ten hours of underwater footage. Super-model strutted away and seemed strangely gratified by the exchange.

The next night, Turtle, the Supermodel, and I went out to a club in By-ron. I ordered an X-X-X-X.

"You mean a Four X?" quipped the bartender.

"Right."

"You shouldn't drink beer; you'll get a yeast infection," said the Super-model. I finished my beer and sparked a joint in passive-aggressive silence. A security guard approached me, and I stubbed out the joint and swallowed it whole.

"Get out, or we'll call the cops," he said.

Turtle gave me a faux-sorrowful look and said, "I'd go with you, but look at all the hot Brazilian mamas."

"You wanted this to happen," said the Supermodel shaking her head. "You're disgusting."

I pushed through the crowd until I could breathe the night air. The sting came to my eyes, but I refused to cry. Instead, I wandered past drunken lo-cals and hippies with their drum circles. I strolled the main street for hours. Pauline's house was at least ten miles away, and I couldn't remember the address or her phone number. At four in the morning, I heard Turtle shout-ing. I was so relieved that I hadn't been abandoned. I didn't mind that he asked me to wait while he walked off down an alleyway with his woman of the night, a full-figured Brazilian. They found a mattress, and I snoozed till dawn.

It rained as we loaded our boards onto the Falcon and waved goodbye to Pauline. We were chasing the swells up north. We didn't make it far along the road before the Supermodel said, "Stop! Let me get out. I can't see the other side."

"It's just rain," I told her. "It'll clear up."

"No, I just had a vision of death. Take me back to Pauline's house."

We dropped her off and then pushed on to Coolangatta where we re-laxed, ate dory fish with salted chips, and surfed Snapper Rocks till we had our fill. Life was good. Then the Supermodel showed up. Without saying hello, she ranted about some arbitrary amount of money that I owed her.

"Piss off," I said.

She shoved me with her scrawny arms.

I hoisted my board bag onto my head and walked to North Kirra to stay with my friend, a longboard champion named Louise Rosier. While Lou was at work, I was kept occupied by self-loathing, crying, writing in my journal, calling psychics, and eating chocolate. I looked in the mirror. I told the girl returning my stare that she was stupid, ugly, and useless. All the insults my father had once hurled now came from my own lips. Rather than criticize the situation I had created, Lou tactfully left a note on my board bag: "Let me out. I can't breathe." I pulled out my Albatross and surfed Rainbow Bay, Greenmount and Kirra while the WCT contenders tore up Snapper Rocks.

After surfing three days straight for eight hours a day, I came down with heatstroke. As time expanded and compressed, I slept for seventy-two hours. I awoke feeling that I had overstayed my welcome. It was time to move on. I bought a cheap car, and Pauline invited me to stay at her place. My mom bought me a video camera, and suddenly everything was in place for me to make my own surf film—to finish what my mom had started.

A couple of weeks later, I ran into Turtle on the beach, and he told me that the Supermodel had ditched the film project and run off with a twenty-year-old actor from Sydney.

She subsequently married him, divorced him two years later, then returned to Santa Barbara to live with her parents. Turtle married a Brazilian goddess and started work as a production assistant in Los Angeles. Last I saw of Skinny Seppo, he was living out of a VW van and making his surf videos in Santa Barbara. Solo reportedly works on charter boats in the Mentawai Islands—boats similar to the one that left me on the reef in Bawa. And on Boxing Day 2004, the residents at Lagundri Bay managed to survive the tsunami that destroyed all but two houses on the beachfront.

As for me, I've had a lump in the arch of my foot that has grown bigger and bigger since I returned from this trip. A couple of days ago, a doctor made an incision in my foot and removed a piece of coral reef that I'd stepped on in Nias. It had grown round and pearl-like from all of my missteps.

Bad Juju

JAMIE TIERNEY

A few weeks ago I went by the factory of my shaper, Todd Daniel Kayminski (TDK), in San Diego looking for a new small-wave board. He showed me a beautiful 6' 3" that was 19½" wide, a little under 2" thick, wide swallow tail—perfect for me. I asked him how much and he said two hundred dollars. I couldn't believe my ears. Two hundred dollars! "What's wrong with it? Why so cheap?" I asked.

"Bad juju," he said and then explained that he had shaped the board as a favor to a guy that he'd had a falling out with. The experience left a bad taste in his mouth, and now he just wanted to be rid of the board. Bad juju! Ha. Had he lost his mind? Who does he think he is, Miss Cleo? What's he going to tell me next, that I shouldn't surf Ala Moana wearing Greg Brady's necklace? I quickly wrote him a check before he came to his senses and upped the price.

The board was absolute magic. The best small-wave board I've ever had—fast, loose, responsive, one of those boards that feels like it has jets underneath it. I rode it up and down the coast at K-38, Bird Rock, Windansea, Oceanside, Trestles, Malibu; everywhere I went it wailed. I was headed for Indo in a month, and I could only imagine what this board would do at Bingin or Canggu or Macaroni's.

I called TDK and told him how much I loved the board. I laughed at his bad juju assessment. I mocked him. I told him I'd ripped him off. I ordered two more boards—a 6' 10" for my trip and a 6' 5" for my friend in L.A.

On my twenty-ninth birthday, August 20, I was in San Diego visiting some relatives. In the morning, I packed my cousins into my car. I had instructions to drop them off at Disneyland on my way to L.A. As we got into the car, I told them I had to stop at my shaper's factory to pick up some boards.

I arrived at the factory, peeled off seven hundred dollars in cash, and strapped the two new boards, along with the magical 6' 3", to my roof. TDK gave the stack of boards a shake. They were on tight.

I got on the I-5 and headed north. At the Sorrento Valley merge of the I-5 and 805, I started hearing a strange hum. I looked up at the nose of the boards above the windshield. They still seemed secure. Little did I know my eleven-year-old cousin in the back seat was pulling the rack strap that goes through the interior of the car. This was causing the hum. My cousin eventually pulled the strap loose.

Twack! All of the boards flew off the roof. I looked back in the rearview mirror and saw them fluttering in the breeze behind me. I swerved over five lanes of the crowded freeway and got to the shoulder. First thought: *There goes my trip.* I parked and sprinted back to the site of the catastrophe with a sliver of hope that the boards had survived.

The first board I saw was the 6' 10"—in two pieces. *Crunch!* Make that three pieces. The 6' 5" was still in one piece until an SUV plowed over it and smashed it into oblivion. I felt like I'd just witnessed a murder. But I was trying to stay positive—those could be replaced. Then I saw the 6' 3" in the middle of the car pool lane, as vulnerable as a baby seal on killing day in the Arctic. I steeled myself for its inevitable death when a miracle happened. A little gust of wind pushed the board ever so gently against the center divider. I could see it clearly; I knew there might be some damage, but it wasn't moving now. It looked like it was now stuck to that wall. I couldn't get to it because there was no way I could run across eight lanes in traffic, and I couldn't turn back around and pick it up because there was no left lane shoulder. It's okay, I thought, at least it's safe. I'll find a way to get to it. I'll ride it again.

I dialed 911 on my cell phone and asked for the California Highway Patrol. I told them I had lost three surfboards on the I-5 and was worried that a car might try to swerve around them and cause an accident. The dispatcher said someone would come right away.

I waited for an hour and a half, my eyes riveted to the 6' 3" on the center divider. Every so often, I'd actually see a cop driving down the freeway and I'd try to flag him down. They all passed me by. My cousins in the car were getting antsy. I saw them get out of my car, parked on the shoulder. They started walking toward me, perilously close to the freeway, to try and convince me to give up and get on with taking them to Disneyland. Yeah, right. I yelled at them to get back in the car. Mickey Mouse could kiss my ass. We weren't going anywhere until I had my board back.

I called 911 again and was put on hold for seven and a half minutes before I hung up. Finally, an orange Cal Trans truck pulled up next to me. Just as the driver rolled down the window to talk to me, a large blue American car, possibly a newer model Ford Taurus, slowed down in the car pool lane. The driver opened his door, and in one sickeningly fluid motion, reached down, picked up my board, stuck it in his car, and drove away.

I screamed like a five-year-old. I desperately tried to see the car's license plate, but there were too many lanes, too much traffic, and it was too far away; all I saw was a blur. A dizzying, paralyzing, impotent blur. I sprinted two hundred yards to my car and peeled out. It was hopeless to give chase, but I had to. The car and the thief were long gone. My board was long gone. But I pursued anyway.

I drove to Disneyland in silence. As calmly as I could, I told my cousin that his pulling on the strap had caused the boards to fly off my car, which had in turn cost me both a thousand dollars, and something priceless. He looked at me like a deer in headlights and said nothing.

It took me three hours to get to Disneyland because of the traffic. The congestion was even worse for the rest of the ride back to L.A., and I didn't get home until after 5 P.M.—eight hours after leaving San Diego. What a birthday. I popped open a beer, sat down on my couch, and cried.

My First Day in Bali

JOHN BRASEN

It was a long time ago. It was the *Morning of the Earth*. Well, the Alby Falzon movie had just come out anyway. The footage of Rusty Miller and Steven Cooney surfing the long, walling lefts of Uluwatu for the first time was pretty inspiring stuff, so I took a break from my job behind the bar at the Woolgoolga Pub in northern New South Wales and headed for Bali.

Arriving early morning, my girlfriend and I settled into a cheap room in a *losman* in Kuta and then caught a *bemo* out to the temple, taking in the sights, sounds, and smells, fairly buzzing from our first look at Asia. Perched on the towering cliffs that surround the Bukit Peninsula on the bottom tip of the island, the thousand-year-old Uluwatu temple is a colossal stone structure guarded by gargoyles of exotic Hindu gods and inhabited by bands of belligerent monkeys. During the thirty-minute journey down from Kuta, our *bemo* driver told us that during World War II more than a hundred local villagers committed mass suicide by jumping from the cliffs at the temple rather than surrender to the invading Japanese. A disconcerting place, let me tell you.

Looking south, the Indian Ocean stretches all the way to Antarctica—an unobstructed swell-fetch from the roaring forties of the Great Southern Ocean all the way to the tropics. Arriving on Christmas Eve, it was the height of the wet season, and I had no idea it was the wrong time of year for the offshores.

Back then the lineup at Ulu was a mile or more walk from the temple through jungle and scrub to the cliff-tops above the break. We trekked there through squally rain to find a couple of flimsy thatch shelters and a solitary old massage lady. The surf looked pretty solid, sideshorey and untidy, but it looked manageable and there were two guys out, way around on the outside corner, and they seemed a long way out to sea.

I should have stopped and taken a decent look, but over-amped, I grabbed my brand-new 7' 6" single-fin pinny and scaled down a bamboo ladder that dropped through a cave to a chamber at sea level. The girlfriend, meanwhile, settled down for a massage.

"Have a nice surf, dear."

The tide looked to be coming in and as I paddled across the lagoon the current was really racing. It suddenly occurred to me that it was more serious out here than I'd thought. By the time I got to the white water I was heading flat-chat down toward Padang. I didn't know the name at the time, I just saw really big cliffs. I rolled under a dozen or so waves, copping a flogging. Finally, I saw a bit of a break and figured I was nearly out the back.

There seemed to be two swells, one wrapping down the reef and one coming in square, and there were some ugly looking double-ups. Then this thing started barreling down the reef toward me. It looked easily double-overhead, and I realized that what I'd seen so far was between sets. It turned square and then converged on my head, drove me into the reef, and held me there.

I absolutely shit myself. It wasn't just that it was big, it was nasty. And there'd be more. It was gray and drizzly, and I was getting tired and a little lonely. I was rattled and ready to go in, but against the current there was no way I could get back to the cave without making it out the back then paddling all the way around. After a harrowing half-hour hammering down in front of the cliffs, I eventually made it outside, way outside, and began the long haul back.

There was no sign of the other guys (who were those other guys?) when I finally got far enough south to line up with the cave. I knew I had to catch one wave, which wasn't too thrilling. The wind had picked up and had switched straight onshore. I stayed wide and watched a couple of sets—they were bumpy, twisted, and unpredictable.

A big one with a short wall loomed, and I paddled onto it and shoulder-hopped for a while, looking for a place to straighten out. Proning a la Greg Noll, I death-gripped the rails and the wave exploded up my arse. But somehow I bounced out the front and then held it all the way across the lagoon. I surfed it straight up into the cave, ricocheted off the wall, and nearly slammed into the roof. After staggering up the ladder, I collapsed on the grass and heard: "Hey there you are. Did you catch many? I dozed off . . . was it fun?"

"I fuckin' near died! You mean you didn't see any of that?"

I've never really liked Uluwatu since.

On the way back to town I began to feel all elated. I'd gotten out of there with only some reef rash and torn boardshorts. I was thinking I could really go for a Bintang beer or seven and a nice meal.

The first couple didn't even touch the sides. I was Happy Christmasing all the Euros in the bar, and I knocked over some chicken satays before ordering the special shrimp omelet. I demolished that and got halfway into the next beer, and it began to taste pretty ordinary. I just couldn't swallow it. I tried a vodka but wasn't into it. I realized I was exhausted; maybe that experience at Ulu worked me over more than I'd thought. I told the girlfriend, who was merrily ensconced at the bar, that I thought I'd go and put my feet up for awhile.

Laying on the bed, I felt very queasy. Those bloody prawns! I was getting that sweet, sickly saliva taste you get when you know there is no way you can avoid a spew. The toilet was outside in a tiled courtyard, and I jumped up and ran for it. I got as far as the door and projectile vomited all over the tiles. I hung onto the door jam heaving for a while, then figured, great, I've gotten rid of that. I turned out the lights and went back to bed.

Some time later I thought, here we go again. I jumped up in the dark, flew out into the courtyard, slipped in my previous spew, and did a full head slam into the tiles . . . then I started spewing again. I lay there thinking, Jesus, Bali is hardcore! Then I felt these things crawling on my legs.

Rats! They'd come into the courtyard and were eating my first spew. My screams could have woken the gods and the ghosts way down on the cliffs of the Bukit.

Christmas Day 1972 was very quiet, couldn't drink a beer, didn't want a surf.

Paybacks

MARK "FINGER" TAYLOR

Five minutes late, I was five minutes late. It was 4:35 A.M., and I was supposed to meet Rob at his apartment, "the Roach Motel," at 4:30 A.M. But neither Rob nor his car were there. Either he never made it home from the previous night's partying, or worse, he left without me. Never mind the reasons I was late—like making a thermos of coffee and packing food for us, or driving thirty miles to his place at this ungodly hour. But, I was late. It was 4:35 in the morning, and I told him I'd be there at 4:30. I had snuck out of the house without waking the wife or kids, packed the Blazer with my board, wetsuit, and supplies, and drove like a madman to Rob's.

I made the rest of the ninety-minute drive to the beach alone. The sun had almost risen when I pulled into this Northern Oregon point break. There was only one other car in the parking lot—it was Rob's, and the hood was still warm. That meant he had just arrived. Rob had waited until exactly 4:30, and because I hadn't shown up yet, he left. Not cutting me any slack, the bastard. I walked down the cobblestone path toward the break until I saw Rob in his wetsuit, standing on the rocks waiting for a lull to get out. I yelled his name, and when he turned, I did what any friend would do to a friend who left without them—I flipped him off. Because I was carrying the board in my right hand, I flipped him off with my left hand, full finger extended. He shouted up, "Didn't think you would make it that early. Thought your wife wouldn't let you go. She's been giving me the stink-eye lately."

"You're full of shit," I hollered. He was squirming and I was enjoying it. That's what friends are for.

The dawning sky showed the conditions: six- to eight-foot drops, head-high walls breaking left. The waves looked really tasty—peaky nuggets, clean, fast, peeling, and expansive, with no one else out. Just the way I like it. It was a minus tide, and there was a lot of green slime on the rocks.

I suited up in record time, gloves and booties and all. As I stood on the slimy rocks waiting for my lull, I lost my footing and slipped. With my board held tight in my right hand, I put out my left to break the fall. I broke it with my middle finger first. I got back to my feet, and the pain in my left hand was immense. My middle finger was cocked sideways and bent at a forty-five-degree angle from the knuckle. This was the same finger I had flipped Rob off with five minutes earlier. I figured that I had broken my finger, but it didn't look so bad covered in a thick wetsuit glove.

A lull in the waves came, and I decided to go out and see what would happen. I waded out deep enough, where I could jump on my board and paddle outside to where Rob was sitting. It hurt like hell to paddle. I told Rob that I wasn't going to last long because of my broken finger. I showed him, flipping him off again, this time with a crooked finger. He didn't believe it until he came over right next to me and looked closely. He tried to pull it back in place, but it was impossible in the water. He just pulled me toward him.

While we were playing tug the finger, a set showed up. The first wave came right at me and instinct took over. Forget the pain, I was going to ride this wave. I paddled into position, turned, and went. It hurt to paddle, and it hurt pushing off my board to stand up. I forgot about the pain when I was up and riding. When I kicked out, I was committed to a full session. I wasn't going to stop surfing that day for a finger. For two hours we had it all to ourselves—wave after wave.

Negotiating the white water and rocks on the way in was less painful than the fifteen minutes Rob spent pulling on my wetsuit glove trying to remove it. That hurt. The cold water must have kept my finger from swelling. It wasn't broken, but it was dislocated. We tried to set it again with no luck. I discovered that as long as I kept my finger elevated, the pain was tolerable. Rob loaded my board on top of my Blazer. Now, I had to drive back to town by myself.

It was still cold out, about forty-five degrees, so I started the car, turned on the heater, and poured myself a cup of coffee from my thermos. I'd be

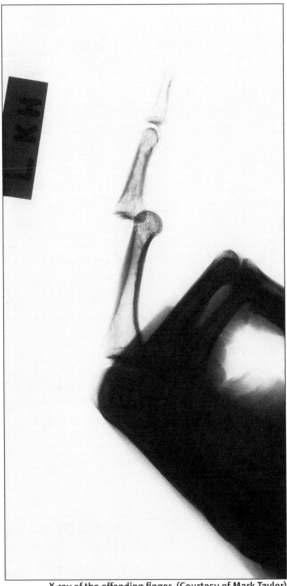

X-ray of the offending finger. (Courtesy of Mark Taylor)

damned if I gave Rob any. As I warmed up, my finger began to throb, swell, and hurt. I didn't pack any ice and there were no stores around to buy any. By the time I finished my coffee, my finger was killing me, so I rolled my window down and stuck my hand out of it, thinking the wind chill would work as good as ice. My whole hand got cold, fast. To keep my hand warm, but to still keep my finger in contact with the wind, I tucked my remaining fingers together in a fist, back into the flip-off position.

So here I am driving home, board strapped to my roof, flipping off everyone who was going toward the ocean. A lot of people gave me the finger back, especially other surfers. We are an easily aggravated bunch, and I make friends wherever I go.

I was almost home, and my finger had swollen to three times its normal size. It hurt like hell. I went to the emergency room at the hospital near Rob's place. They X-rayed it, injected it, set it, and wrapped it. So now my finger was splinted and white, bandaged in the permanent fuck-you position.

Because I was so close, I went back over to Rob's to show him what he had done to me. After all, it was his fault, right? He didn't seem to think so. He figured it was a payback for flipping him off in the first place. Maybe he was right, but I was still pretty pissed off at him.

Though I did gain a new nickname, I'll never regain all of the mobility in my finger. The doctor told me that had I tended to my finger right after the injury, instead of surfing with it, it would have fully healed. I let his absurd hypothesis pass without comment—obviously, he was not a surfer.

'Fraidy Cat

MATT GEORGE

Hoopa Valley, California — Noon.

I've never told this one to anyone before.

I was up in Klamath County, up on the Oregon border doing a story on Greg Noll, and on my way home I saw what I thought was a promising little cove for a river mouth setup down at the bottom of this big steep valley. I pulled over, grabbed my board, and hiked down to check it out. Took about an hour.

I was wrong about the surf. The bay was too deep; the white water I saw was caused by a submerged rock. But the place was picturesque. A perfect little protected cove, just a dimple on a map, with a white sand beach on the edge of a blue deep-water drop-off. You could feel it against your face, the deep and the cold, out there where the ocean turned to cobalt. Like standing at the door of a open refrigerator.

There were otters and gulls and a couple of giant sea lions bobbing among the rocks. Rafts of seaweed undulated and roiled silently, like oil slicks. I stood on the beach, taking it in, perspiration trickling down my forehead. I wiped it away with the back of my wrist. And that's when I noticed something odd. Something perfectly odd. All the animals were looking at me.

Not just keeping an eye on me but looking right at me. Not surprised, not alarmed, not even curious. They just were all . . . looking at me. And then, a few seconds later, they all started to swim towards me. Every one of them.

They swam slowly, deliberately, quietly, but all the time keeping their eyes on me. Even the gulls, pumping their little webbed feet, moved toward me. The otters were side by side. The sea lions brought up the rear. I could hear them chuffing.

Growing up on the central coast, I'd observed a lot of marine animal behavior close up but nothing like this. These things just kept coming on, getting closer, not menacing at all, real calm like, but with intent. I found myself taking a few steps back towards the woods. Then a few more. They kept coming on. I looked around real quick; there were no signs of any human beings around here. No footprints in the sand, nothing.

I felt fearful. The eerie kind of fear, and I left that place without ado. I walked into the woods backwards, turned, found the game trail that I took down to this place, and jogged a little recklessly. Damned if I didn't look over my shoulder once or twice as well. I even stopped to listen once. I had to force myself not to run.

By the time I calmed down, I found myself lost. I took a bearing off a bald ridge and a copse of giant redwoods in the distance and started walking. I found what looked like a small footpath. After a bit I stopped. Six barefooted prints were impressed in a spot where there must have been a patch of mud. I kneeled down and touched them. The dried edges flaked in my fingers. I took my foot and tried to fit it into one of the small splayed craters. Too small. A child's print.

I kept on for a bit; I had no idea where I was. This was a northern Californian redwood forest, mind you. A lot like a desert in that everything starts to look the same after a while. About ten minutes later, the trail finally petered out as it reached what looked like an impenetrable wall of dried brush, like piled up tumbleweeds.

I took a few breaths as goose bumps shivered down my spine. I looked at the wall of brush again. There was something about it that was just too orderly. I stepped closer to it and saw evidence that it was definitely man-made. I walked around the periphery of it and found a small tunnel in it. Room enough for a child.

I put down my board and crawled into it, figuring that if I could get through this way, then I'd come back for the board. The tunnel twisted twice to the right and once to the left; after about twenty yards, I popped out into a clearing. I half expected to see someone there. But there was no one. I don't think there had been anyone there for quite some time.

I found myself dwarfed by a semicircle of trees that faced a small running creek. In the middle of this clearing there was a pit about the size of a small car. I stepped over to it and saw that it was terraced inside, like a mini-amphitheater, and worn smooth. A pile of leaves had formed in the bottom of it. The ground was foot-smooth all around it as well, but I could see no prints, only a few tattered feathers at the bottom. I recognized that the feathers came from a seagull and perhaps a spotted owl. There was also hair, like a dog's or a cat's, stuck to the edges of the terrace steps here and there.

I looked around. Shafts of light danced down through the trees and onto the scene, making things seem almost heavenly. I felt like I was underwater. That's when I heard a crackling in the underbrush.

I froze. I could tell whoever it was, was cautious. And coming my way. Then I heard some more crackling off to my right. Two people now. Another twig snapped. I just stayed stock-still. More stealthy crackling.

Hello? I said out loud.

And as suddenly as the noises had begun, they stopped. I waited for a full five minutes . . . nothing. Just the creek babbling away. The hair on the back of my neck was standing straight out, and my heart was beating like a rabbit's.

I ran for it. On hands and knees I crawled through the tunnel, grabbed my board, and scrambled up an embankment towards what I thought might be the highway.

By the time I got back to the main path, I'd calmed down a bit. Obviously just some deer walking around, I told myself, trying to get to the water. But I still hadn't worked out the animals in the cove, and I could still feel their eyes on me, especially the otter.

I kept my pace quick and eventually found the highway.

Ten days later, I came across a fishing guide on the region. In this guide I read that the Tolowa Indians, particularly small in stature, used to live in the area. They were basket weavers, coastal fishermen, good with spears and may have practiced ritual cannibalism. They were believed to have practiced transformations, such as shapeshifting. Apparently they sought immortality through the act of melding one's spirit with that of certain animals.

My mouth went dry.

Crossing the Line

BY JEFF PHILLIPS

Reef Campground, Sonoma County, CA

"We hereby christen thee . . . Blue Devil!" I yelled and threw the bottle with all my might down on the center of the hood. The cold Budweiser bounced off, sailed thirty feet up, and landed unbroken in the dirt next to my dog, Idaho. I traced my fingers over the new dent in the hood of the used truck that we had just bought for a six-week trip to Baja. I tried again with another name "El Nemo!" and this time the bottle broke with a beautiful sound. Dan and I clanked beers, toasting to a perfect surf vacation.

San Diego/Tijuana Border Crossing

"You know," Dan said, "you get into Baja and you can just feel control slipping away." He pushed his hands outward and wiggled his fingers. I looked behind us to make sure the boat, a 13-foot Boston Whaler, was still attached to the hitch. Dan didn't know how true this was. If I'd had a map that cartographed the future of our trip, there would have been an "X" marked two weeks from the moment of Dan's prophesy, with the caption: "unrecoverable situation."

Ensenada, Baja Norte, Mexico

Three Mexican mechanics worked in the concrete bay under the truck while Dan and I made the first good use of the forty-dollar patio chairs I'd bought

All the gear they needed to get so deep they might not return, Punta Eugenia, Baja Norte. (Photo, Dan Murray)

at Home Depot, sleeping in the sun with our feet up on the tailgate. We napped, played backgammon, scratched Idaho, and consumed Pacificos for six hours while they rebuilt the transmission and installed a new clutch.

Santo Tomás, Baja Norte, Mexico

According to our last call to Surfline, the swell was due to hit in twenty-four hours, and we still had seven hundred miles to cover, the last hundred on dirt roads. I was hurried and anxious to get to the reeling lineup at Isla Natividad to meet the swell. And that's all I could think about for the thirty minutes that we were stuck behind a semi as it slowly wound its way up a mountainous section of road. After cresting the mountain, I came to a place where I could see most of the road ahead, except for a short stretch around a bend. It was the best shot I'd seen, so I went for the pass, accelerating quickly with the steep downhill grade. An oncoming pickup truck appeared from nowhere with startling immediacy. I locked up the brakes in a screeching attempt to drop back behind the semi. Too late! I let off and corrected out of the slide. Tucking into the gap between the front and rear tires of the semi, I said, "Come on, baby!" as we shot it three abreast. The semi gave me a few more inches to the right and the oncoming truck drifted a few feet into the dirt on the left. We rocketed through, cheating some serious Baja road mojo that has wrecked the cars and lives of many surfers. I took a few deep breaths, dropped back behind the semi, and he immediately signaled, with his blinker, for a safe pass. I pulled around and we were on our way.

Dan should have given me a hard time—we were both pretty shaken-up—but he just busied himself with guide books. A few hours after night fell, we pulled off the road to roll out the bags. The stars burned brightly in Baja.

Way Down Mex 1, Baja Norte, Mexico

In the morning, miles from nowhere, El Nemo lurched and choked and complained with all manner of noises, until he finally gave up the ghost on a long downgrade. We coasted a mile or so before I bounced the truck and boat ungracefully on to a roadside berm at the bottom of the hill. Silence set in, and the possibility of surf at Natividad receded with a finality that almost left a sucking sound. Our trip was suddenly and grossly devoid of the Baja magic. Now we were just two losers and a dog with a dead truck and a useless boat stuck in the dusty, dry, hot sun. *Fuck.*

An hour of fiddling and our best, uneducated guess was that the fuel pump was broken. A semi stopped and offered us a ride. I shoved Dan a wad of bills as he climbed in and told him to get food as well as the fuel pump. "What if it's not the pump?" he asked. "That's what the food's for." The heat waves rose from the road and slowly swallowed the semi. What were the chances he would find a store with the part, I wondered, and what were the chances that was the problem?

All the anticipation of getting to Baja, the scrambles and excuses and lies to leave two days earlier than planned just to catch this swell, and all of El Nemo's problems just piled up and collapsed like a house of cards. I gave up all hope of making the swell. It was easier to stop worrying about it.

No sooner than he left, Dan came back with a smiling Mexican man in a rusty pickup. I was frustrated that he'd brought this chubby character he'd found just down the road instead of following through with the mission, but I tried not to show it. With greasy hands, the desert mechanic went straight to the fuel filter, like we had, but instead of blowing through it to test if it was clogged, he sucked, then spit a huge mouthful of gas onto the dirt like mouthwash. Nope, fuel filter was clear. He then unattached line after line and repeated the process. After a couple of minutes of sucking and spitting enough toxic fluids to drop an elephant, he looked up at me, pointed to the fuel pump and said, "*Es malo.*" I could have strangled Dan then; instead I shot him a look behind our gas-guzzling friend.

But not to be beaten, the mechanic rummaged around and found a long piece of fuel line in the boat. He placed a five-gallon gasoline can on Nemo's roof. He stuck the fuel line in the can and sucked some fuel through to start a siphon. Then he plugged the flowing line straight into the carburetor and, as gas spilled over the sides, he gestured wildly for us to start the engine. Nemo started immediately! We thanked our rescuer, paid him a few bills, and bounced back onto Mex 1. Every fifteen minutes, I climbed out the window to look on the roof and check our fuel level.

Guerrero Negro, Baja Norte, Mexico

We found a new fuel pump in Guerrero Negro and installed it while a rat pack of ten-year-olds tried to pilfer gear from the truck and boat. I've always felt uncomfortable in this Mad Max town; maybe it was the tourists who were stabbed down the road a couple of years before. Dan couldn't understand why I was so testy when he said he wanted to get groceries before leaving Guerrero Negro. We left without incident, fully stocked with supplies, and shortly turned onto a perfectly straight, eighty-mile stretch of washboarded dirt road. Better for everything involved to just slow the hell down on these loud, nerve-jangling roads, let some air out of the tires, and putter slowly along enjoying cold beers. Accordingly, our spirits were high when we met Don Gato.

Punta Eugenia, Baja Norte, Mexico

Francisco Patron, aka Don Gato, gave us a camping spot in his backyard on the very tip of Punta Eugenia—the westernmost point of Baja. We had met him in the nearby town of Bahia Tortugas, where he extended the gracious invitation.

It was night when we arrived. The surf was roaring and pitching phosphorescent green off the point. There wasn't a breath of wind. A crew of local fishermen came to check us out. We proffered Samuel Adams and Sierra Nevada beers, and they returned the favor with advice on launching the boat and crossing safely to the island. We were relieved that they didn't think us foolhardy for taking a 13-footer in open seas. Of course, we hadn't yet seen the dubious conditions they unquestioningly tackled in their open-keeled *pangas*.

We slept fitfully as the surf grew louder. At dawn, we backed the boat down to the beach, launched it, and immediately got stuck trying to drive back up. I could've left Nemo there for all I cared, but the fishermen came down and helped us push him back up the beach. We hopped in the boat, idled halfway through the natural harbor toward the entrance and the open ocean. Then the engine died. I looked down at the prop and discovered that it was a twisted mess of rope and kelp. Jackasses. We'd run over mooring

Idaho, the dog, prior to her terrifying abandonment. (Photo, Aubrey Mescher)

lines. There was nothing to do but put on our wetsuits, get out our diving knives, and cut it free. We jumped into the water and Idaho followed us, swimming around in circles as we took turns diving and cutting. The fishermen on the beach watched with bemused smiles. We were worried they'd be pissed about the mooring, but they didn't seem too upset.

We got the prop free and started the engine, but every time Dan tried to put it into gear it sputtered and died. Well, we'd bought a backup 7.5-horsepower engine before we left in case of emergencies, and this was an emergency. I pulled on the backup's starter rope—nothing. I pulled it again. Nothing. I pulled maniacally again and again and again. Nothing. I yelled profanities at it as I fell back in the seat, and then the morning quiet enveloped us.

The soft light of the Baja sunrise graced us. A perfect south swell pounding just outside the natural harbor walls taunted us. Isla Natividad visible in the distance called to us. We paddled the boat back toward shore. Halfway there Dan said, "Let's give it one more shot." He started the main engine. It started fine, but again died when he put it into gear. "Do it again," I suggested, "but slam it faster to full throttle." The boat roared to life, accelerating full-speed through the harbor. Dan deftly wound around the boats and mooring lines, and into the open water near the harbor mouth where he pulled into a slow circle and stared at me.

In preparation for this trip, Dan and I had agreed to a number of safety rules regarding the boat: test it out in calm conditions before blindly heading into oceanic swell; have local forecasts of wind and weather; keep an operating backup engine on board; and carry a weather radio, GPS, and emergency broadcast radio.

Now, we had one marginally operating main engine, a busted backup engine, no idea about weather or wind, no inkling of the size of the seas in the channel (except that they were big), and no electronics.

"What should we do now?" Dan asked.

"Go for it!" I said. What other choice was there, really?

The seas got progressively bigger over the first mile but maxed out at a size the boat could handle, and Natividad grew prominent on the horizon. We found perfect overhead lines reeling hollow barrels at Open Doors, with a bridal veil of offshore spray. There was one guy out. The Baja dream. We high-fived, set anchor, and jumped in.

Small eddies swirled behind my hands as I stroked toward the wave, the trials and stress of the past five days settled. The edges softened and the dust was carried off me; I felt reborn. We surfed our hearts out that day and the next.

Punta Eugenia, Baja Norte, Mexico

An eternity of flatness—exactly twelve days—followed our first two days of amazing surf. Over this time, our camp, our smelly selves, our useless gear, and our boredom all became a dusted-over part of the landscape. We developed a daily routine. We drank coffee at first light while watching the pelicans dive. Then we checked the surf on both sides of the point—always ankle-slappers. Next we engaged hope and decided to boat over to Isla Natividad. Maybe, just maybe, the waves were breaking there, we told ourselves each day, though we knew the waves would not be breaking. Dan would be-

Jeff Phillips riding Open Doors, empty and perfect, Isla Natividad, Baja Norte.
(Photo, Dan Murray)

gin lugging all of our boat stuff down the bluff to the harbor, making a pile of dry bags, wetsuits, four surfboards, extra leashes, fishing poles, tackle boxes, gasoline cans, lunch, and sleeping bags. (Just in case we found amazing surf at the island, we could sleep there.) Meanwhile, Idaho and I would swim out in the cold water and row in the boat. Day upon flat day we motored around in the boat exploring the tiny island, fishing for elusive tuna and soaking in the sun. Not the surf trip we had imagined, but not bad either.

Isla Natividad, Baja Norte, Mexico

On the thirteenth day of the flat spell, we idled out of the natural harbor. I floored the boat, and we leaned back into our seats to enjoy a mellow ride over seven miles of glassy waters. When we got to the island, Open Doors was too small to surf again, but down the way, at Old Man's, a slow-rolling, longboard-style wave was working. We sped over and checked it out. It was bigger than it had looked. The sets were head-high and building. Dan suggested we try to tow into them—a ridiculous proposition given the measly 35-horsepower outboard on the 13-foot Whaler. But after two weeks of flat surf, Dan and I were bored and ready for something new, such as learning how to whip ourselves into waves. If we were ever going to practice, this was the place—these non-threatening waves that walled up and rolled for a hundred yards before crumbling were perfect.

　　Worried about getting pressure dings on my new 6' 4", I told Dan to go first, and then I'd check his board when he was done and make my decision. Dan suited up and jumped into the water with his 6' 4". He cried, "Hit it!"

and I went full throttle and looked back as he worked his way to his feet. I circled into the break from the outside and looked for a likely swell. I picked a little one starting to form and turned sharply to line it up. But I'd turned too sharply and Dan sank before the rope became taught again. Towing is more complex than it seems.

As I circled around to get him, a significant set rolled in, so I motored outside to let it pass. Then I swung back in and Dan snagged the rope. "Hit it!" he called again.

I saw the locals gather on the beach inside, watching, waiting for the payoffs or consequences of our folly. We had endlessly amused this same gang with our fancy lures, rod holders, overflowing tackle boxes, surf rods, and complete inability to land any fish over the past week.

A promising set showed outside. I raced to it, picked what looked like the biggest section, then turned gradually, and came over the backside. I gained a lot of speed as I went down the front slope of the swell. With that momentum, it felt like I'd pull Dan into it perfectly. However, when I got to the bottom and out on the flats, the drag of him going up the backside slowed me down so much that Dan didn't get over the wave. The wave caught up to me and slowly passed beneath the boat.

The next swell was the biggest of the day thus far, and it was already wall-

Jeff Phillips (L) and Dan Murray display the one and only catch of the trip, Isla Smith, Baja Norte. (Photo, Dan Murray)

ing up. I angled in at full throttle, more or less parallel to the incoming swell. This time I could get Dan into the wave. Idaho, sensing trouble, or maybe just uncomfortable like she usually is in boats, was trying to climb into my lap. I pushed her back and looked behind me as Dan whipped himself into the forming wave. The boat accelerated with his release. I thought I could jet back out onto the shoulder and into the channel, but the peak kept shifting out to the right—the place where I was trying to beat it. Even though I was going twenty-five mph, the peak stayed even with me, approximately twenty feet out from the starboard side (my side) of the boat.

The wave on my right just got closer and closer to breaking. The wave reached me and, still running parallel to it, I began to tilt to port. This made the boat grab water at the front left corner of the square-shaped whaler hull. To correct, I turned left directly down the face of the forming wave. With the downhill slope, I quickly accelerated out onto the flats and immediately carved back to the right to head for the shoulder again. All the while Idaho clawed at my lap.

I steered straight back up the wave, hoping to shoot over the shoulder to safety. But then the lip started to pitch up at the top, so I took another turn down and into the flats, and then swung sharply back up and onto the wave. It was going to start peeling fast down the line now and the only thing I could do was to try and hold an edge on the face and surf it. I glanced toward shore; it was close enough that straightening out was no longer an option. The locals' eyes were fixed on me.

I tucked up onto the steepening face and set my line. Though the throttle was maxed, I pushed harder on it. With one hand I got a death-grip on the railing to my right; with the other I resolutely held the steering wheel. The boat caught the energy of the wave and accelerated dramatically while the engine red-lined with a high-pitched scream.

Even at this speed—the fastest the boat has ever gone—I couldn't out-run this shifting overhead wave. A section formed up in front of me. On a surfboard, I'd relish this view as an oncoming barrel. I'd stall a bit to slow down, dig a hand in the face, and watch as the lip threw out and over my head, enclosing me in a wicked tube. But in the boat, I just held a straight line right into the section, midway up the face, on a line that should never be taken in a Boston Whaler. The acceleration hit and the boat was canting at sixty degrees. I was hanging off the uphill railing on the right side of the boat looking down toward the left side, and the front left corner started to pearl. The corner buried deeper and deeper until all I could see was water running over and through the boat. Somehow the boat powered through as the wave face flattened slightly and the corner rose back up out of the water. Thankfully, the boat shot out of the section.

With hands clenched, I faced the final peak that separated me from the shoulder. This section was dredging even steeper than the last, and I was even deeper behind it. It didn't look good. "Come on, baby." The acceleration when I hit the steep of the curl was appalling, and the boat tilted quickly to port. The front left corner pearled again and the boat tilted fast into a flip. Before it reached a ninety-degree angle, I let go and let the momentum of the flipping boat shoot me out and over the flats. The boat was going over and I didn't want to be under it. I penetrated the water headfirst and well clear of the disaster that was about to explode behind me. I had done the unthinkable—a five-thousand-dollar boat, my dog, most of our surfing gear, and our ride back to the mainland, tossed to the surf.

Before I even broke the surface, I heard the dull whine of the engine reverberating in the water. I surfaced dumbfounded. Idaho was standing on the seat that I had just vacated, and the boat was headed full-throttle into the deep-water channel.

Idaho looked balefully at me as the boat sped away. *Oh, shit,* is all I can remember thinking. The tow rope was whizzing through the water about five feet to my right; I could see the handle racing toward me some feet back. I took two fast strokes and grabbed the speeding line. After some rope burn, my grip locked down on the handle, and I was instantaneously jerked to twenty mph. I submerged like a torpedo, and then arched my back to angle my head toward the surface. I got a breath of half air and half seawater. The friction of the water pulling on me was unbearable, like hanging from a pull-up bar with someone else hanging off your clothes. I couldn't let go of the handle or I'd lose the boat once and for all, but I couldn't keep holding on. I rolled over on my back and was immediately more comfortable. The water washed over my head, but left a nice air pocket where I could breathe. My body was on a better plane and it wasn't quite as hard to hold on.

The boat was either headed out into open ocean or headed for the rocks. I couldn't tell which, but neither was good. Would I be able to swim back once I couldn't hold on any more? Could I hold on until the boat ran out of gas? Would Idaho survive if she got pitched onto the rocks?

I was powerless over the situation and losing strength. I had time to contemplate the unthinkable. I couldn't send my dog into the open seas. I desperately worked my way up the rope hand over hand. I made about six grabs before my wet and rope-burned hands couldn't hold on any longer. What would I have done when I got up to the engine, anyway? I let go of the rope with a gasp and watched as the handle jumped and skipped away from me. I was alone, floating in a soul-shattering doom; my heart sank like a stone.

The boat was headed away from shore and into the open seas. But it did have a slight arc in its trajectory that might bring it back around. Dan paddled toward me on his surfboard. The boat kept to its long arc, and soon it had come clear around. I was looking at the front of it approaching me. As it came nearer, I couldn't tell which way I needed to swim to avoid getting run over. If I chose the wrong way I wouldn't have time to swim down four feet to clear the prop. I swam to the right, and the boat flew by so close it made my skin tingle. On its next trip around I looked at the railing to gauge the possibility of grabbing it. It'd rip my shoulder out of the socket.

Dan had reached the circle now. I thought maybe he would grab the rope on his board and work his way up to the boat. Instead he undid his leash and swam into the circular path of the boat, eyeing the boat railing. In the time it took him to realize it couldn't be done, the boat might hit some chop, straighten out, and that would be that. I needed to get to his board.

I swam to the surfboard as fast as I could and paddled to intercept the boat's path. When the boat circled around, I stroked hard toward the rope snaking through the water. I got it with another monumental jerk, recovered, and started working hand over hand again. It was much easier this time, being on top of the surfboard. My weight on the line dragged the boat into a tighter arc, slowing it down considerably. I pulled frantically, taking advantage of the slowing boat. I passed Dan once, and he shouted something unintelligible while I flagged fifteen feet back from the motor. My hands were too tired and rope-burned to hang on much longer, and the engine was going to be problematic to climb over. I could see that this method, too, was going to fail. Then I saw Dan swimming right into the boat's path. It looked like the boat ran him over, but then I saw his hand reach up and grab the rail. Dan was flapping along the side, and then swinging his foot up toward the rail. He missed, and his legs got sucked under the boat. He pulled them out and swung a foot again. Finally making a connection, his whole body rolled up and over the railing and into the boat.

Dan jumped to the driver's seat and killed the engine. The boat drifted to a stop and the line became slack in my hands. Silence enveloped us. Dan and I stared at each other. "Yeah!" I yelled, then climbed into the boat and held Idaho. "Oh, my God," I repeated over and over in an idiot's mantra while holding Idaho, who seemed no less scared than she normally was in a boat.

Dan and I felt sick. There was no need to talk about it. After a time, I asked Dan to drive us back over to a short peak breaking off an outside rock. We anchored there, dove in, and paddled to the wave. I calmed down as I felt the push of the swell. Under the deep Mexican sky, we surfed all afternoon even though the peak was just a steep drop and a turn. We spoke only occasionally about a wave we'd just caught or a set that was drifting in.

It had been a team effort, and we'd got the boat back because neither of us gave up. But Dan's had been a special act of courage. I wanted to thank him for saving my dog, the boat, the trip, and the day. But the event was so improbable, so dauntingly imbecilic, and so gratifyingly lucky that the best thing to do was to quietly contemplate it between sets as the swell rolled beneath us.

Homeless Surf Challenge

MICHAEL MIGDOL

Encinitas, California—July 1999

The beach-dwelling homeless characters who inhabit our local spots in South-ern California are an inseparable part of the surf scene. They spend their days at the beach downing malt liquor, bumming smokes, and enjoying the sun. One afternoon, as I was suiting up for a surf, a homeless dude heckled me, saying, "Yeah, better get out there. Wind's gonna pick up!" Wow, I thought, this guy actually possesses some surf-forecasting ability. It occurred to me that we might have a few homeless rippers on our local beach. At our next editorial meeting at *Automatic* magazine, we decided that we should, once and for all, find out which of these vagrants rips the hardest and who has the right to heckle. And so the first "Homeless Surf Challenge" was organized.

From the dusty alleys behind liquor stores, the trash-strewn boardwalks, and the sides of freeway off-ramps, they came to compete. These transient competitors put down their cardboard signs to battle each other in two- to three-foot, sloppy conditions.

Two days before the contest, we learned that the top contender and local favorite would be unable to make his heats because he was in jail after assault-ing a police officer. This unforeseen incident left the contest wide open and totally unpredictable.

It took the better part of the morning on contest day to get the contes-tants from their stairwells and parking lots to the competition area. We opted for a four-vagrant heat format at seven minutes each. Half of the competitors were almost too drunk to paddle out. Longer heats would have had devastating effects on their endurance and would have given the waiting contestants too much drinking time. Yet the magazine did have a liberal supply of malt liquor on hand for the event.

The final format of the contest was three seven-minute heats. Heat one's contestants were Gunnery Sergeant, Unmedicated Jeffrey, Transmitter Joe, and George. The four men stripped to their underwear and paddled out. Sergeant didn't make it out past the white water and came in without even standing up. George made it out, but decided the water was too cold and paddled in. This left Unmedicated Jeffrey and Transmitter Joe to battle out the remainder of the heat. Unmedicated got halfway to his feet and fell. Transmitter Joe paddled into the wave of the day, a solid three-footer. He proned down the face and incredibly made it to his feet in the soup. That wave won the heat for Transmitter Joe. Unmedicated Jeffrey took second. They both advanced to the final.

In the next heat it was Alabama Pete, Carl, Will the Messiah, and a guy who we'll simply call Stinks of Urine. The judges eliminated the Messiah because he never left the shorebreak. Instead of surfing his heat, he stood on the inside and tried to baptize the other contestants as they paddled out. Alabama Pete made it outside but threw up and decided to come in. Carl and Stinks of Urine picked off a wave each, and although neither of them could get to their feet, they made it out past the shorebreak. This was enough to advance them to the final.

Shortly after that heat ended, a little scuffle erupted between Carl and Transmitter Joe over a cigarette butt. After rolling around in the sand a while, Carl got up and walked off screaming obscenities.

The final got under way without Carl. Unmedicated Jeffrey had the eye of the tiger, reaching the outside first. But it was Transmitter Joe who drew first blood. He paddled into a solid two-foot wave and proned it to the beach. Then he walked up to the sand and sat down with Stinks of Urine who was spent from his earlier heat and unable to get past the shorebreak. Unmedicated answered with a little left. He tried to stand but fell to his knees. The judges scored him in the high 8s for his drop-knee approach. Unmedicated picked off another left and made it to his feet for a split second before floundering. This last wave sealed his victory.

In the awards ceremony, the forty-ouncers were cracked and Unmedicated Jeffrey was given his prize: a shopping cart full of Mickey's malt liquor. His only words were, "Chey, chey. Oh man, I win, I win."

The Idiot Savant

SUSAN CHAPLIN

Obviously odd, Roger leaned against a wall and convulsed with laughter. The wall was stained with dust from the cane fields and looked like the backdrop for a mass execution. It was an ugly scene—and one I wasn't ready for. A taxi had dropped me at Lagane's Bungalows, a low-key accommodation I'd found by reading a guidebook over my neighbor's shoulder on the plane. Tamarin Bay was my sixth stop on a worldwide surfing trip. Having just arrived on Mauritius from South Africa, I wasn't in the mood for catastrophe.

Yet it happened. Jacques Lagane, proprietor of Lagane's Bungalows, had a puppy—a shin-high, bat-eared thing with a voice like a female jackhammer. Trying to bite me, the dog got its teeth stuck in my sandal. When I bent over under the weight of my sixty-pound backpack to dislodge the animal, my nose hit a piece of rebar. Then a huge, torpid young man I'd seen drifting around Lagane's when I first arrived stared at me and laughed.

Jacques felt bad about it, brought me a bottle of The Phoenix beer and a towel with ice for my nose. After my third beer, things didn't look so bad. Seated on my backpack behind Jacques' rebar fence—the one I'd banged my nose on—head tilted back to stanch the bleeding, I looked around at the exotic surroundings. I was on a tropical island in the Indian Ocean, east of Mozambique and Madagascar, south of Seychelles. Clouds grew up above my head like the ghosts of giant trees, sliced through by a silver rotary of full moon.

But the ocean sounded bad to a surfer: a slapping somewhere, like tired hands clapping. It was March, the cyclone season. The waves would come.

My focus came back to Roger who looked as wide as he was tall—about six feet. He had stopped laughing; his body was seized with strange voltage. His arms and legs twitched. He babbled, then made come-to-earth sounds, like hailstones landing in mud. Something wasn't right in Roger's brain. But I sensed a power, a potential for focused motion in this boy. He reminded me of a giant bowling ball—just temporarily sidelined.

Strong from surfing, slightly round from The Phoenix beer, Jacques, a Franco-Mauritian in his mid-twenties, toted my board and backpack upstairs. Towel still clamped to my nose, I followed. After the travels and trauma, my basic room seemed palatial.

From my little window, Jacques and I studied the Mauritian cane fields— a greenness dense and solid as armor. Sticking out from the emerald sheen was the island's landmark mountain, Montagne du Rempart; it looked primeval and sharp as the tooth of a monster that devoured the world.

An affable man, Jacques invited me to a party—a forty-third birthday party. "Tonight," he said, "for an expat Aussie surfer named Harry, a popular boy in Tamarin." The party soon exploded below in raucous shouts and music. Guests walked right up to Roger, talked to him with great animation, and asked him questions. Roger alone understood his incoherent, mumbled answers.

Harry, the birthday boy, arrived last. The sun had burned the sandy hair from the top of his head, and I saw, since he grinned a lot, that he had few teeth. A blond leprechaun, he darted amid the dark pillars that were Tamarin's local surfers. I went to meet him.

Harry led Roger to a peaceful corner of Lagane's yard. "C'mon, Roger . . . yeah, c'mon, mate. Surf's up t'morra. Yer gotta get some rest."

Harry came up to me and said, "Don't mind Roger, mate. He surfs. That's what matters. Surfs like a pro. Outta the water, we take care of him. He does have another talent. Eatin'. Loves bread and butter. Pretty soon he'll be so big he won't be able to surf. Then his life'll be over . . . There's a name fer people like 'im isn't there?"

"Idiot savant?" I said. A poet's light had come on in Harry's eyes, so I continued. "They're a special kind of genius. Most of 'em are retarded—half dead upstairs, really. But they've got a tiny talent so sharp and fierce that the rest of what makes them up—maybe the rest of the world—kinda hides from it in fear of getting burned."

"Fair dinkum," Harry said. When he grinned, his pink tongue filled the gap where his front teeth should be. His eyes sparkled like blue stars. "Describes Roger to a T. Goodonya, mate. But doesn't that apply to everythin'? Like we live in the tiny spark of ourselves. With darkness all around. An' waves, mate." Harry squinted, intense. "Especially waves are . . . whaddya call it . . . idiot savant. Waves are born to break, they can't do nothin' else."

Men pounded Harry's back, wished him happy birthday, gave him fried fish and rice.

Lagane's barbecue blew gusts of incinerating meat and fish over the crowded yard.

Perching beside me on a crate in Lagane's yard, Harry said, "Gotta understand this place, mate. Yer old aren'tcha?"

"Fifty," I said.

"Don't wantcha t'get hurt. Mauritius is an island city. Everythin' and everybody here. Franco-Mauritians, Sino-Mauritians, Creoles, Indians. Catholic, Muslim, Hindu, Christian. Everyone gets along. Nobody fights. But Indians, the politicians, marry Indians. Creoles marry Creoles. The Chinese run the food store. By the way, need groceries? Noel an' Shirley's Chinese store's right up the street." He pointed, rambled on, "The Franco-Mauritians, they own the cane fields an' the land. They're the rich blokes. Creoles are the dancers, the athletes, the surfers. Dedune is a Creole."

We watched a dense knot of dark, fast-talking—or intently listening—young Creole men surround something as an oyster shields its pearl. "Dedune is in there, mate," Harry said. "Dedune is king of Tamarin. Nobody catches waves without him. C'mon, mate." Harry took my hand. "Take ya t'meet 'im." Harry peeled back the dark shell of disciples around Dedune. For sure, he was a specimen, a black pearl of a man. Tall as Roger, but slim, sculpted in every muscle.

Harry had said he was a local soccer star and, along with Roger, one of the best local surfers in Tamarin. "The sheilas, mate," Harry whispered. "He loves the sheilas."

Pearl-shiny, Dedune's eyes met mine for an instant. "You punch her, Harry?" Dedune asked in English. He looked at my nose and laughed. Then he was eaten again by his crowd.

Harry led me away. "No worries," he said. "Least he knows who ya are. Don't step on 'is toes."

Harry counseled me on surfing Tamarin Bay. "First day, don't paddle to the peak. We won't give ya waves. Sit out the back an' watch. Only one place to take off . . . two maybe. One on the shoulder's shallow as hell. But you can wait till one of us misses a wave. There's a Frenchman from Reunion comes over to surf Tamarin. He owns that spot. Good luck.

"Oh, an' if you see Roger, try an' keep 'im out there. Else 'e'll go in an' eat bread."

Roger's metamorphosis was riveting. I witnessed it while sitting on the beach the next morning, nursing my nose, my board over my knee. A swell had come in the night.

Slipstreaming Dedune's crowd, which glinted with sharp surfboards and advanced on the waves like a war party, Roger threw his bare feet out in front of him like black cinderblocks. He carried his board under one arm, a lump of bread pureed to doughy butter in his sledgehammer fist.

Harry spiked him along from behind. "Gimme the bread, Roge." Harry speared the damp dough with his finger, lobbed it away.

Wading unsteadily into the sea, Roger left his idiot self like a snakeskin on the beach. In the water, he was savant. Paddling his big wide board he moved like a ripple over the sea. Timing the sets, he probably arrived at the lineup with his hair dry. He was lost in the crowd.

There must have been a hundred surfers out there—and the swell was growing.

Tamarin Bay doesn't so much break in a large swell as transform itself into a true Atlantis. The great city's emerald turrets and ramparts are built of the fierce, fluid structure of the sea. I watched many would-be conquerors of this citadel-swell fall short of glory. A strong circular current pulled paddlers to the peak over the reef, recycled them again through the white water—after which many of them limped ashore.

I was sure the vanquished soldiers looked with empathy at my nose.

Smooth as the zip on a Ziploc® bag, I saw a surfer join the green surfaces of an overhead wave. Roger, Dedune, Harry? The glare was too bright for me to see.

I lost track of time as I watched them from the beach. The swell was dropping. I timed twenty minutes between big sets, then I paddled out a channel forming between the main break and a smaller beach break. Going right to the shoulder Harry told me about, I saw a lone rider.

Thin and dour, my age, with a surf hat on, the Frenchman from Reunion didn't return my *bonjour*. Beneath our feet, the water struggled with its shallowness. Big, convoluted coral heads floated like hard brains in the silty wa-

Susan Chaplin, the author, surfing less crowded waves in Pescadero, Baja California, 1998.
(Photo courtesy of Susan Chaplin)

ter. Tamarin Bay is full of silt brought by the Riviere Noire from the cane fields inland.

The Frenchman and I waited for a wipeout. Now, I recognized Roger. Up and riding, he melted into any sweet spot like butter into something hot. Harry was a thief. When a wave was up for grabs, Harry stole it and hid in the tube. Dedune was flanked by so many surfers good at imitating him, I couldn't pick him out.

Waiting until a surfer wiped out up the line, the Frenchman craftily seized an empty shoulder. But every time I went to paddle, he was there. Finally, the Frenchman didn't paddle back out. Then I got my chance. I hopped enough shoulders to know that wherever a wave is caught in Tamarin Bay, it's special.

The swell lived only two days—after which I sought more peaceful residence than Lagane's: a pure-white cottage with red shutters hidden on a Tamarin back street.

Harry, who had stayed in this rental cottage himself, introduced me to my new landlady, Tiano. She was fifty-two, solid as a bag of salt. She worked at the Tamarin salt factory, a simple structure that dried seawater in shallow terraces. The salt was raked, stored in gleaming mounds, then put into bags which were sewn shut—mostly by Tiano.

She wore high, rubber boots, a pointed Chinese hat, and a salt-white smile. She lived in a tin shack behind my cottage. Her creative garden—a collection of cans, old toilet bowls, bisected plastic jugs from which burst an astonishing variety of flowers and plants—separated my place from hers.

My first night as a tenant, she invited me to dine in her hut. She owned a bed, four chairs, a glass-doored cabinet full of Oriental china, and a table. Above the table was a tiny, candle-lit china statue of Pere Laval, the man Mauritians credit with bringing Christianity to the island.

Tiano set the simple Creole meal—rice, meat, hot sauce, pitcher of water—on the table. She bowed her head and prayed to God and Pere Laval. According to her, he was Tamarin's patron saint of suffering. Tasting Tiano's hot sauce, I felt Pere Laval would approve of my suffering.

Tiano, too, suffered. Pulling an envelope from a drawer in her cabinet, she said, "*Je souffre, je souffre, Suzanne.*" She pointed at her stomach, her back. The envelope contained film from a C.A.T. scan. Doctors, she said, couldn't find the problem.

I made the mistake, later, of doling out pain pills from my first-aid kit. She came to my house every day after that for more pills, and for stories about my, thus far, two-year solo surf trip.

Tiano loved the idea of my surf trip. "*C'est un voyage pour cherchez les vagues* (a journey for finding waves)." Culturally, from what I saw, Mauritians could never understand why an older woman would shoulder a surfboard and travel the world.

From Tiano, I learned Tamarin's gossip and taboos. When I told her I'd climb the hill behind the salt factory she said, "*Mais non . . . c'est interdit.*" She couldn't say why or who had forbidden it. Just climbing the salt factory hill had always been taboo.

One day she said, "A bad man lives next door. Whenever you pass him, just say *bonjour*. Look down and keep going. *Tu as compris* (Understand)? He robs people and always wants money. He rents that house and never pays his landlord a rupee. *Tu as compris?*"

I said, "Wa-a-ay" a lot to Tiano. She instructed me continuously, ended each rule with, "*Tu a compris?*" Don't leave cushions on the front porch. Cats will sleep on them. Don't put the key in the flowers. The man next door is always looking. "*Tu as compris?*"

She caught me hemming cut-off pants, "Obviously you can't do that," she said and seized the pants. Her hands slid like shadows over the fraying cloth,

which healed beneath them in a perfect seam. "You can't do everything, Suzanne," she said. "People who sew can do this better than you."

A simple statement about simple genius.

Roger was often at *petanque* contests. When the surf was flat, locals played
petanque in the street that led to the waves. A metal, baseball-size ball was
hurled at a target ball placed in a ring drawn in the dirt. Putting as many
balls as close as possible to the target ball seemed the aim of the game. The
target ball was often struck by other balls, which produced a *crack!* heard
throughout the town.

Roger couldn't play *petanque*, but was the mascot for the Tamarin team.
He stood on the sidelines, babbling, cheering, eating fistfuls of bread. When-
ever the players made an important move, they looked to Roger for support.
If he saw me at a game, Roger touched his nose and laughed.

Monthly tournaments drew competitors from Seychelles and Reunion.
Dedune was a *petanque* champion. Harry didn't play the game much.

Harry paid me a visit after I'd been a few weeks at Tiano's. He'd injured
his elbow in a wipeout and sought solace. I gave him "The Treatment," something I'd learned in the Caribbean: scrub the infected wound in hot salt water, cauterize with pure salt and lime. Bandage and hope for the best.

Daily, Harry appeared for his treatment.

"Ah, mate," Harry said, while I scoured his elbow. His time in Tiano's cottage had coincided with the loss of a girlfriend. "Wasn't even surfin' then . . .
ya know, enlightenment's a fuckin' lightning flash. Fuckin' universe is lit up
for a moment. Then it goes dark. You see the big picture in a flash. Then
it's fuckin' gone. All or nothin'. Idiot savant, if you know what I mean." He
grinned.

After his elbow healed, I didn't see much of Harry.

When Tamarin Bay stirred again, I thought to check other surf spots. A
peninsula to the south, Le Morne, had a reef break. But I didn't have a car
and travel with a board on a bus was difficult.

Harry had whispered, "Go to Souillac."

Souillac is on the southern tip of Mauritius.

One morning—with my camera, not my board—I caught the bus to
Souillac. I usually took the bus to Port Louis, Mauritius' capital, once a week
to buy groceries.

As usual, the Tamarin bus stop was a pageant. Crowds of Hindu women
dressed in vermilion, bright-yellow, and purple saris, with gold and ochre

spots on their foreheads, were waiting, gossiping, their saris swaying as if they were butterflies drying their wings.

Pronounced "*le buish*"—sort of like stepping in something soft and sticky—in Creole, the Mauritian public bus connects all parts of the island and carries passengers from all walks of life, except the rich Franco-Mauritians.

The buses are painted in a bright, solid color, like pink or purple, and filigreed with design of another color. My bus was crowded, three to a seat. Held up by the crowd, I stood in the aisle. To reach Souillac, I changed buses in Baie du Cap, a town on the way south, and waited for another bus in the shade of a dense, needle-swept grove of casuarina pines. In the shade of the casuarinas, which the wind played like a violin, I ate *roti*, a Mauritian sandwich of flour-wrapped vegetables and fish. Shade is cultivated here in beach-facing groves, around doorsteps, benches, and other points of congregation.

Once I got there, Souillac didn't seem like much of a town. It was a monument to the power of the Indian Ocean, which besieged a ragged cut in the reef in fifteen-foot walls. A sign said, "*Bains Dangereux*" (dangerous to swim). I was glad my board remained at Tiano's. Looking for a place to take pictures, I was attracted to a small cemetery near the cataclysmic sea. Under towering clouds, bathed in mist from the surf, the scene had an apocalyptic menace that looked photogenic.

Climbing an iron gate to reach the graveyard, I stood on what may be the least populated coastline on Mauritius. Focusing on a peeling blue wooden cross, with green breaking waves and black cloud in the background, I prepared to snap the shutter.

Three teenage boys gamboled like puppies in the aisles between gravestones. "*Bonjour*," I said. All groups have a leader, guided either by conscience or its antithesis. Which and who of the boys was it in this group?

Two of the boys were very dark, probably Creole. The third had fine features and the ash-black skin of India. With glazed, red eyes, this boy wobbled on his feet. "Give us the camera," he said in bad French. On a whim, I seized the tallest Creole by the arm, enticed him down to the ground by my camera.

"See?" I pushed his eye to the viewfinder. "*Magnifique*." I invited the boys to view my picture and lectured to them about photography.

But the Indian boy said again, "Give us the camera." I put away my gear, slowly.

"How do you like Mauritius?" the tall Creole asked.

"Love it!" I looked from one young face to the other as if they suddenly belonged to angels. Then I made a mistake: "Do you go to school?"

"We don't go to school," said the smallest Creole.

"Work?"

"We don't work," the Indian said. "We want the camera."

Everything packed but the tripod, which swung beside me like a truncheon, I stood up. I was taller than the boys, but against three—not a chance. "I can't give you the camera." I took out my wallet, which contained only money needed for the day. "I can give you money."

The boys stared at my wallet. The tall Creole said, "Put that away!" He turned on the other two boys, disciplined them like an alpha wolf, and they fled into the graveyard corridors.

"I like you," the tall boy said to me. "My name is Jean Luis. I will accompany you. You realize," he said, "I saved you. The others . . . *ils sont des méchants*. They take from others. I am different."

In payment of his kindness, we settled on a T-shirt from my hometown, San Diego. The T-shirt said "Padres" and fit my new friend perfectly.

The surf was head-high in the bay when I got back to Tamarin. I'd been three months at Tiano's. It was my last day on Mauritius. Made bold by my impending departure, I paddled to the peak. Harry, Dedune—even a few pale Franco-Mauritians in flashy Lycra—seemed happy to see me.

When he was surfing, Roger never laughed at my nose.

"Catch one wave in Tamarin Bay," Harry advised, "you got all the waves in the world,"

The boys gave me a wave, the best of the bay. Skating across and down, I drew a connecting line on the giant triangle that completes the universe— my universe, at least.

I fought for a few more rides. Hoping the Frenchman from Reunion was absent, I moved down to my shoulder. No one there, so I got my fill.

On my last one, however—as if the sea itself created the Frenchman from Reunion—I had company.

The Frenchman took off behind me, bottom turned around me, ended up with me behind. I caught a rail in his backwash. The coral tapped my elbow painlessly. I was initially grateful to be uninjured. Then I checked the spot of impact, and saw a deep bullet hole at the bottom of which was the sinister white gleam of bone.

What to do? Seeking Harry, I paddled to the peak. Only Dedune was there. Looking down from where he perched aloof in the branches of his tall being, his strong black eyes met mine. He said, *"Allez au dispensaire.* (Go to the medical clinic.) But go early."

The Indian nurse in Tamarin's public clinic always fixed his surfing wounds, Dedune said, then took off on a wave.

When I bolted to Tiano with my injury, she was aghast. Something in her seemed subdued, even crushed. "What will you do now?" she asked. "Go home?" When I reassured her that my *voyage pour cherchez les vagues* would continue as soon as I was healed, she was ecstatic.

"*Allez au dispensaire,*" she said, with her salt-white smile.

Mid-afternoon was not the time to arrive at the Tamarin clinic. The male Indian nurse was drunk. Smelling of gin and fish, truculent, with gray hair and yellow eyeballs he greeted me.

The cover on the examining table was sprayed with blood. Stained latex gloves dangled from an unlined garbage pail.

Hurling me on the table, the nurse brought out a harpoon-sized needle and clumsily injected anesthetic. When he sewed me up, I was far from numb, but I kept my face calm. He said, "Are all women cowards? Or is it just Americans?"

Because Mauritian medicine is socialized, I didn't tip him.

Outside the clinic, Harry waited for me. He looked proudly at my new stitches and announced, "Dedune has invited you to his birthday party."

Like many Mauritian houses, Dedune's place was a cooling grotto masquerading as an overheated tin shell. Inside, the house was dark and smelled of sweat, booze, and frying food. From somewhere, Roger babbled and cooed. When he saw me, he touched his nose and laughed.

Grinning at me with the hole between his teeth and flashing his sapphire eyes, Harry patted the empty seat next to his. Car headlights twinkled the tinsel on the walls. Red and white balloons bumped the ceiling.

When Dedune strode in with his surfboard, the house lit up, burst into song: "Happy Birthday" in Creole. Dark women drifted in, wearing long skirts and short blouses that left their midriffs bare. They kissed Dedune on both cheeks. I kissed him too.

Sitting back down, I noticed that all the women but me had left the room. Harry said stay. Barefoot females passed plates of food and beer from behind a curtain. I drank The Phoenix beer and listened to surf stories with the men.

Soon, I felt compelled to join the women behind the curtain. I was hugged and given a beaker of bourbon. With the dark women, I giggled and stole food from plates passed through the curtain to the men. Soon I was drunk enough to dance the *sega*, a graphic fertility dance passed down from Indian and African slaves. Usually danced in deep sand, tradition forbids lifting the feet from the ground.

I walked back to Tiano's while I still could. Someone followed me. It was Roger rolling along behind—a huge black bowling ball hurtling toward anonymity in the gutter of the oblivious night.

Harry was right, I thought. Roger had grown bigger during my short stay in Tamarin. Soon, he wouldn't be able to surf.

What could be sadder, I wondered, than an idiot savant without his gift? But, as I knew Harry might say, "He's like the rest of us, mate. We all lose it all in the end."

Roger took another turn in the road from mine. I called after him, "Roger! Roger! Roger!" He turned toward me, tapped his nose and laughed.

Because it was his way of embracing me, I laughed with him.

"*C'est un voyage pour cherchez les vagues,*" I whispered to the both of us.

On Life and Death in the Ocean

FERNANDO AGUERRE

San Diego, California — December, 2003

It was busy at Reef that morning in December. I was planning a sales meeting when I received a call from the Argentinean consul. He spoke urgently, saying that he had just been called by the mayor of Mar del Plata. The mayor had asked him for help on behalf of the parents of José María Castro, a bodyboarder from Mar del Plata—my hometown in Argentina. José María had drowned the day before while riding huge waves with his friends in Hawaii at Rockpile, on Oahu's North Shore. His corpse was in Oahu but his parents did not have the funds to fly themselves to Hawaii, nor to fly their son's body back to Argentina for a proper burial. I didn't know José María or his family. The consul asked if I could take care of the return of his remains to Argentina. I agreed to make all the necessary arrangements.

After hanging up, I thought I couldn't begin to imagine the pain and heartbreak of having a son killed far away and not being able to give him a proper burial. All at once, I was in a state of total devastation, feeling his parents' loss. I immediately thought about my triplets and the infinite pain I would feel if one of them died, even if it happened while they were doing what they loved most. I imagined José María fighting for his breath while his friends watched helplessly from the beach.

I later found out that José María and his friends were having the last surf session of their trip. The next day they were scheduled to fly back to Argentina to spend Christmas with their families. They had gone out at Rockpile and were surfing in modest waves when suddenly the surf turned big. Everybody went in but José, who waited for a set wave. It came, he took off, and bottom turned to set up for a huge tube ride. But then the thick lip hit him in the middle of his back as he lay flat on his bodyboard. He disappeared for some minutes, and when he resurfaced down the beach, he was dead, his lungs filled with a half gallon of water.

Over the next three days, I coordinated the many necessary details such as releasing his body from the Hawaiian authorities, repatriating it via an airline flight, and hiring a funeral company ten thousand miles away to take delivery of his corpse. I wanted all this to happen quickly for the sake of his parents. A week later José María's remains arrived in Argentina where his family held a funeral and buried him properly.

I asked the mayor to keep my name out of the news and not identify me to the family. I requested he simply let the family know that I did what any parent would and should do for another parent given the circumstances. The mayor kept his promise, but somebody told somebody else and the parents found out my name.

A month later, I was in Mar del Plata for the Reef Classic, the main surfing contest in Argentina's surfing tour. From the privacy of the upper level of the scaffold, just behind the announcer, I watched the whole scene—a sunny day, a packed beach with hundreds of beautiful girls, and surfers enjoying their lives. Suddenly, I felt a need to turn around and look back. I saw an older lady coming toward me who I did not recognize, but I instantly realized who she was. She came to me with tears in her eyes, gave me a big, long hug, a hug that will stay with me for the rest of my life. I held her in my arms, while we both cried, not saying a word. Finally, she told me how thankful she and her family were.

I was speechless for a moment, then I told her, "I'm sure you would have done the same for any other parent in that situation." My wife, who was next to me, also realized who she was, and hugged her. The three of us spent a couple minutes in silence, holding hands, with tears running down our faces. When she left, my wife and I turned around and looked at each other, then we looked at the ocean. We decided to go home. We walked to our car in silence and drove away.

Maps

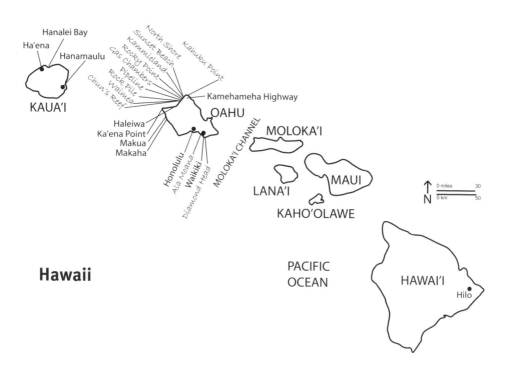

Hanalei Bay
Ha'ena
Hanamaulu
KAUA'I

North Shore
Sunset Beach
Kammieland
Rocky Point
Gas Chambers
Pipeline
Rock Pile
Waimea
Chun's Reef

Kahuku Point

Kamehameha Highway

OAHU

Haleiwa
Ka'ena Point
Makua
Makaha

Honolulu
Ala Moana
Waikiki
Diamond Head

MOLOKA'I CHANNEL

MOLOKA'I

MAUI

LANA'I

KAHO'OLAWE

0 miles   30
N   0 km   50

PACIFIC
OCEAN

HAWAI'I
Hilo

Hawaii

These maps show the approximate location of places and surf spots referred
to in the text.

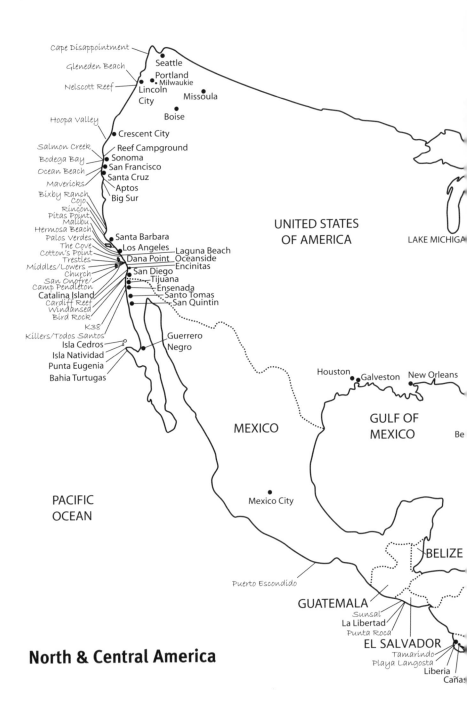

Cape Disappointment

Gleneden Beach

Nelscott Reef

Seattle
Portland
Milwaukie
Lincoln City
Missoula
Boise

Hoopa Valley

Crescent City

Salmon Creek
Bodega Bay
Ocean Beach
Mavericks
Bixby Ranch
Cojo
Rincon
Pitas Point
Malibu
Hermosa Beach
Palos Verdes
The Cove
Cotton's Point
Trestles
Middles/Lowers
Church
San Onofre/
Camp Pendleton
Catalina Island
Cardiff Reef
Windansea
Bird Rock
K38
Killers/Todos Santos
Isla Cedros
Isla Natividad
Punta Eugenia
Bahia Turtugas

Reef Campground
Sonoma
San Francisco
Santa Cruz
Aptos
Big Sur

Santa Barbara
Los Angeles
Dana Point
San Diego
Tijuana
Ensenada
Santo Tomas
San Quintin

Laguna Beach
Oceanside
Encinitas

Guerrero
Negro

UNITED STATES
OF AMERICA

LAKE MICHIGA

Houston
Galveston
New Orleans

GULF OF
MEXICO

Be

MEXICO

Mexico City

PACIFIC
OCEAN

BELIZE

Puerto Escondido

GUATEMALA

Sunsal
La Libertad
Punta Roca

EL SALVADOR

Tamarindo
Playa Langosta
Liberia
Cañas

North & Central America

CHINA

Tianamen Square

Kathmandu   BHUTAN

NEPAL

BANGLADESH

INDIA

BURMA

LAOS

THAILAND

VIETNAM

SRI LANKA

CAMBODIA

MALAYSIA

MALDIVES

Ahangama

Weligama

Medan

Sibolga

Asu

HINAKO ISLANDS

Bawa

Sirombu

Lagundri

Nias

SUMATRA

Padang

Kuala Lumpur

INDIAN
OCEAN

MENTAWAIS ISLANDS

Lance's Rights

Macaronis

Sikakap

G-Land

Asia & Indonesia

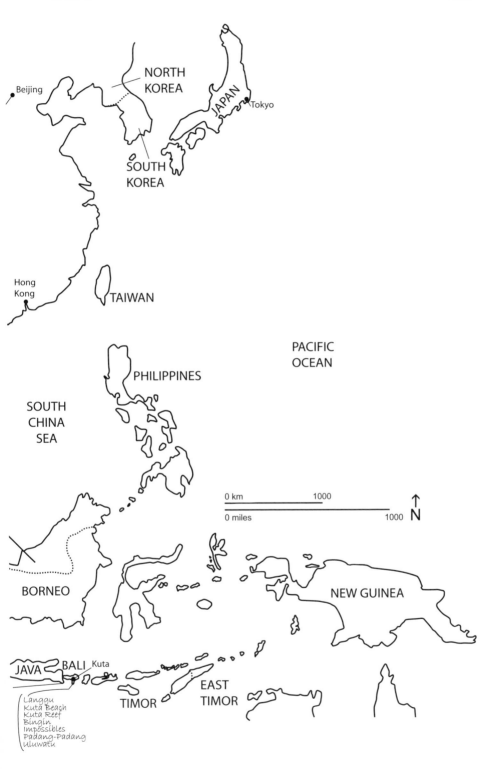

Beijing

NORTH
KOREA

JAPAN

Tokyo

SOUTH
KOREA

Hong
Kong

TAIWAN

PACIFIC
OCEAN

PHILIPPINES

SOUTH
CHINA
SEA

0 km   1000

0 miles   1000

N

BORNEO

NEW GUINEA

JAVA   BALI   Kuta

Langgu
Kuta Beach
Kuta Reef
Bingin
Impossibles
Padang-Padang
Uluwatu

TIMOR

EAST
TIMOR

Southern Africa

NAMIBIA

BOTSWANA

ZIMBABWE

MOZAMBIQUE

AGULHAS CURRENT

Johannesburg

SWAZILAND

SOUTH
AFRICA

LESOTHO

Umtata

Durban
Port Edward
Pottsville
Transkei
(Wild Coast)
Dwesa-Cwebe Forest Reserve
Breezy Point
Queensburg Bay
Yellows Point
Gonubie Point
Nahoon Reef

Drakensberg Mountains

EASTERN
CAPE

ATLANTIC
OCEAN

WESTERN
CAPE

Port Elizabeth

Port Alfred

Hout Bay

Cape Town

Mosselbaai

Dungeons

The Sentinal

Outer Pool

J-Bay/Supers

Igoda Mouth
East London

ROARING FORTIES

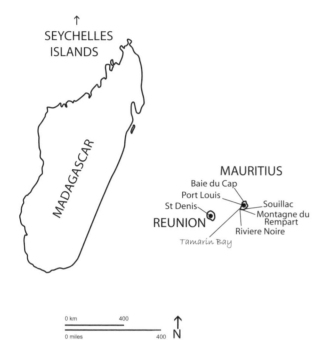

SEYCHELLES
ISLANDS

MADAGASCAR

MAURITIUS

Baie du Cap
Port Louis
St Denis
REUNION
Souillac
Montagne du
Rempart
Riviere Noire
Tamarin Bay

0 km 400
0 miles 400

N

INDIAN
OCEAN

Australia

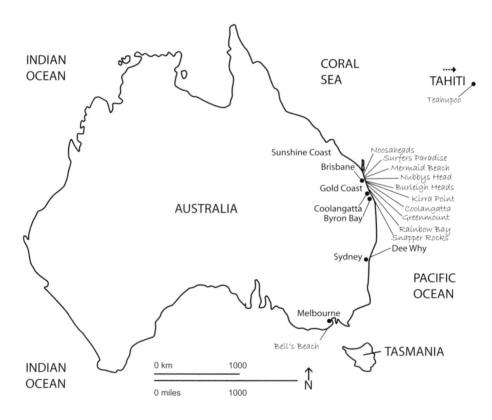

South America

VENEZUELA GUYANA FRENCH GUIANA

COLUMBIA

SURINAME

Mancora

Cabo Blanco

PERU ECUADOR

BRAZIL

Pernambuco

Machu Picchu

URUBAMBA RIVER

Lima

Cusco

Pico Alto Punta Hermosa

BOLIVIA

Backless Wonder Iquique

PARAGUAY

Rio de Janeiro

CHILE

← EASTER ISLAND

PACIFIC OCEAN

ARGENTINA

ATLANTIC OCEAN

Buenos Aires URUGUAY

Mar Del Plata Monte Video

ROARING FORTIES

0 km   500
0 miles   500

↑ N

Europe

ATLANTIC
OCEAN

SCOTLAND
NORWAY
UK
DENMARK
SWEDEN
IRELAND
NETHERLANDS
ENGLAND
Calais
Dover
GERMANY
ENGLISH CHANNEL
BELGIUM
Paris
AUSTRIA
FRANCE
Biarritz
SWITZERLAND
PORTUGAL
Nice
SPAIN
CORSICA
Livorno
ITALY
BALEARIC ISLANDS
ELBA
CANARY ISLANDS
MEDITERRANEAN SEA
SARDINIA
MOROCCO
AFRICA
SICILY

0 km   500
0 miles   500

N

Contributors

FERNANDO AGUERRE was born and raised in the coastal city of Mar del Plata, Argentina. In high school, he organized and disc-jockeyed parties of 2,000 people or more on weekend nights. The local military mayor of the city banned his parties. So he turned his attention back to his favorite sport, surfing. A year later, in 1977, the military banned surfing in Argentina. In response, Fernando founded the Argentinean Surfing Association, which eventually lifted the military ban. In 1979, Fernando, along with his brother and mother, opened the Ala Moana Surfshop in Mar del Plata. While Fernando attended law school, the surf shop evolved into one of the leading beach clothing manufacturers in Argentina. In 1984, with a law degree in hand, Fernando turned down job offers and left Argentina to visit his brother, Santiago, in San Diego, California. Soon thereafter, Fernando and Santiago were leading 500 visitors a year on guided surf tours to Isla Natividad in Baja California, Mexico. In 1985, Fernando and Santiago used their $4,000 in savings to start Reef. The two-man, one-desk operation sold 3,000 pairs of flip-flops in its first year. Reef quickly became the largest beach sandal company in the world. In early 2005, the Aguerre brothers sold their remaining shares of Reef. Currently, Fernando is the president of the International Surfing Association (ISA). He surfs as much as he can at Windansea, his home break in La Jolla, California.

SHAWN ALLADIO is the founder of K38 Water Safety and K38 Maritime Security Training. She is the mother of two and one of the few women to venture into the men's world of extreme big-wave surfing. There are many brave men who aren't asleep in the deep because of Shawn Alladio. She is one of the world's most experienced personal watercraft (PWC) drivers in heavy water conditions. She has a thriving business teaching PWC driving and rescue techniques. She educates law enforcement, lifeguards, tow surfers, and the military. She is the only female instructor in the entire Navy SEALS program. She also provides water safety management to big-wave contests around the world. As a professional PWC racer, she holds national and world titles for endurance racing. In 2005, Shawn was awarded the National Award of the National Water Safety Congress for superior efforts in education. And, since 1993, she has represented 200,000 registered PWC owners through the California Department of Boating and Waterways.

STEVE BARILOTTI, *Surfer* magazine's editor-at-large, began surfing in Santa Barbara as a teenager. During his tenure as staff editor for *Surfer,* from 1989-91, Barilotti covered the gamut of the surf scene and co-launched the award-winning *Beach Culture* magazine. A veteran photojournalist with more than 500 articles and photos published worldwide, the ever-nomadic "Barlo" has ventured to the most remote fringes of the surfing frontier over the last decade. Steve's essays were recently featured in the anthology *The Perfect Day* and *The Surfer's Journal's* book of portfolios of renowned surf photographers Art Brewer and Ted Grambeau. A Southern California native, Barilotti is currently working on an anthology of his own work, as well as several documentaries.

JOHN BRASEN is the editor of *Pacific Longboarder* magazine (since 2001), and before that was co-publisher of the *Australian Surfer's Journal* (1998-2000). A sporadic contributor to *Tracks* and *Surfing World* since the 1970s, his former guises include extended stints as a musician, darkroom operator, photographer, advertising copy writer, scaffolder, steel fixer, bartender, banana farmer, brick layer, truck driver, and commercial fisherman. A lifetime surfer, he is fifty-three years old, lives at Noosa Heads in Queensland, Australia, and surfs every day possible . . . a longboard at the points and a mid-length at the beachbreaks.

CARLOS BURLE was born in Pernambuco, Brazil, and now lives in Rio. His father, a chicken farmer and a race car driver, helped him save money to buy his first surfboard at age thirteen. He surfed his way in ASP competitions but left the pro surfing circuit in 1986 to pursue big-wave surfing on

Oahu's North Shore and on Easter Island. He remained largely unknown until February 1998, when he beat out the world's best big-wave surfers to take first place at the inaugural Reef Big-Wave World Championships at Todos Santos. (Shawn Alladio, another contributor to this book, rescued him twice during this competition). The contest earned him national hero status in Brazil. In November 2001, he towed into a 68-foot face at Maverick's (on a Waverunner® borrowed from Shawn Alladio). You can see him in such movies as *100-Foot Wednesday* and *Billabong Odyssey*. He surfs regularly in the Red Bull Big Wave Africa contest, the Mavericks Surf Contest, and at contests held at Jaws and Todos Santos.

SUSAN CHAPLIN is a writer and a photographer. Her work appears in *The Surfer's Journal, The Surfer's Path, SWIM* magazine, and the *Caribbean Compass*. Chaplin is an avid surfer and athlete. She twice completed the Ironman triathlon in Hawaii. In 1993, she set off solo on a worldwide surf trip that would take three years and touch twenty countries. Chaplin now focuses on paddleboarding. In August 2004, she became the first person to paddle the five big channels between Guadeloupe and Grenada. Chaplin lives full-time on Tortola in the British Virgin Islands, where she writes, surfs, and paddles.

BUTCH CONNOR was born in Los Angeles in 1960. He lived in Southern California until after high school, when he joined the Navy (in Florida) for a four-year tour. On returning to California, he moved away from the crowds of Southern California to the wine country of Northern California. There he divides his time between raising three children and his other passions: surfing and photography. Butch is a technician for the telephone company and has worked in this trade for the past fourteen years.

CHRIS COTÉ was a former half-assed pro surfer. Sponsored by companies like Ezekiel, Billabong, Hurley, Reef, Arnette, and others throughout his career, he used his wit, humor, and good looks to acquire money and free clothes—rather than his mediocre surfing ability. After the pro surfing sham ended, Chris worked as a marketing guy for most of the same companies he rode for—another well-executed scam to do little and still get paid. After writing a few articles for *Surfer*, Chris was seated at the round table of hand-picked experts to start *TransWorld SURF* magazine in May of 1999.

Chris wormed his way from the simple title of writer to the illustrious title of editor. Along the way, Chris was published in *Playboy* magazine, various international magazines, hosted a variety of surf events, got married, toured nationally with his band Kut U Up, and even got barreled for his first time ever in Indonesia. As of now Chris is in his cubicle in Oceanside, California, plotting and planning how to somehow buy his wife one of those really cool Louis Vuitton purses she's had her eye on—she'll have to keep waiting. He's also in development of a new talk show called *Meet the Pro*. Look for it on channel 2,789 very soon. He loves you all, by the way.

JOE DOGGETT is an award-winning outdoor writer and photographer with the *Houston Chronicle*. He has held that position since 1972. He lives in Houston, Texas, and writes three columns a week, primarily covering the traditional outdoor sports of fishing and hunting. He is also a contributing editor for *Field & Stream* magazine.

Doggett started surfing in 1964 in Galveston, Texas and remains an active surfer. He sold his first published article, a fictional piece on storm surf in Texas, to *International Surfing* magazine in 1965. He is a goofyfoot and rides a single-fin longboard.

RICK DOYLE was born in Los Angeles, California, in 1954, and started surfing at Windansea at age eighteen. Facing a low lottery draft number, he enlisted in the U.S. Navy and spent four years repairing missile guidance systems on F4 Phantom Jets during the Vietnam War. Honorably discharged in 1976, he settled in San Diego to surf competitively and to work as a carpenter and as a foam-injection molder at Jim Mizell's "Aquatic Energy" surfboard factory, in Huntington Beach, CA. He attended San Diego State University (1976-1980). While in college, he held an internship with *Surfer* magazine under the mentorship of Tom Servais, Art Brewer and Jeff Divine. He worked for a decade as an NFL team photographer for the San Diego Chargers. He continued to shoot for surf magazines while holding a position as staff photographer for *Windsurf* magazine under editor Drew Kampion and photo editor Craig Peterson.

For the past twenty-five years, he has worked as a traveling surf and sports photographer. His images have appeared in *Sports Illustrated, NFL Game Day, ESPN, Surfer, Surfing, Windsurf, Wakeboard, Waterski, Vogue* and various other magazines and newspapers. He has produced three films *Red Water* (with Dana Brown), *Silence* (with John Dulich), and *Native State*. Currently, Rick lives in Waialua on Oahu's North Shore.

RAN ELFASSY can't shake the feeling that he's the luckiest guy in the world. Currently living in Hong Kong and working as the senior editor for various medical publications, Ran nurtures his love for science, the sea, mountains, and life with his adventurous wife. Beyond chasing waves, Ran has been using his art to raise awareness of environmental conservation. As of February 2004, he has made and sold a different weekly self-portrait on eBay. With an end goal of making and selling 350 different images, Ran hopes to document his adventures and make this world a slightly better place. The photos and tales of his adventures can be found on his website: www.ranhasa.com.

JOHN FORSE, 57, began surfing in 1962 and quickly became obsessed with it. Now he is a heavy equipment operator and a producer of surf videos. He has produced such videos as *The Endless Winter, Another Endless Winter,* and *Nelscott Reef, First Assault,* a movie about pioneering tow-in surfing at the reefbreak out in front of his house in central Oregon. He has been featured on numerous local and regional TV shows on surfing. He is also a part-time commercial actor. His articles have appeared in *Surfing* and *Surfer* magazines. He operates the website Nelscottreef.com.

Former professional surfer **MATT GEORGE** has been a senior contributing editor/photographer for *Surfer* magazine since 1985. Of note was his 1998 feature film *In God's Hands* and his 1999 NBC series *Wind On Water.* Both opened to mixed reviews. Matt also directed and hosted the TV show *Surfer Magazine* which aired on ESPN from 1987 to 1998. He is currently at large in Indonesia doing tsunami aid work with Surfzone Relief Operations, his non-profit foundation based in Newport Beach and San Francisco, California.

JENNY HEDLEY, 25, is the writer/producer/director of *Surfabout: Down Under*, an experiential memoir filmed in Australia and New Zealand (Official Selection of the 2006 International Festival of Cinema Technology). Her essays, including "Indo: One Woman's Adventure" and "Australia," have appeared in *Surf Life for Women* magazine, and her photography is featured in *Golf Living.* A recent participant at USC's Summer Production Workshop, Jenny worked as a production assistant on *Walk the Line*, a Fox 2000 film, and is working on her feature screenplay, *xyy.*

GLENN HENING is well-known for his accomplishments as a surfer both in and out of the water. In 1984, he founded the Surfrider Foundation, a leading environmental protection organization. In 1995, he started the Groundswell Society, which has been called the "voice of conscience for modern surfing." An experienced writer, traveler, and public speaker, Glenn is observant, incisive, and often outspoken. He has been profiled or interviewed in many publications, including *Reader's Digest* and the *Los Angeles Times*. He surfs every chance he gets, usually across the street from his home in Oxnard Shores, California. Recently he self-published surfing's first "epic" novel, *Waves of Warning*.

BUZZY KERBOX started surfing at age ten in Hawaii. He turned pro at eighteen and surfed the pro circuit from 1977 to 1983, landing in the top 10 six years straight. In the '80s, he split his time between professional windsurfing, modeling, and surfing. In 1992, he innovated tow surfing with Laird Hamilton using a Zodiac in the outer reefs of Oahu's North Shore. In 1994, he began towing in at Jaws in Maui. At age forty-nine, he is still a waterman, and still towing in to the largest waves on the planet. He won third place, twice, in the 32-mile Catalina paddleboard race, and he completes annually in the Molokai Channel race and in professional longboard events. He lives in Maui with his wife and three boys and works for the Honolua Surf Co. as a team rider and spokesman.

NATE LAWRENCE is staff photographer for *Surfing* magazine. He divides his time between Santa Cruz, California and Kuta, Bali.

BEN MARCUS was an editor at *Surfer* magazine for ten years. He now writes freelance for a variety of publications and has a couple of books to his name: *The Surf, Skate and Rock and Roll Art of Jim Phillips* (Schiffer Books), *Surfing USA!: An Illustrated History of the Coolest Sport of All Time* (Voyageur Press), and *The History of Surf Wax* (forthcoming from Schiffer Books). Currently he is writing two illustrated books: *The History of the Surfboard* for Voyageur Press, and a book of action sport stickers and patches for Schiffer Books. Ben writes articles for *The Surfer's Journal, Surfer, Surfing, L.A. Weekly*, the *Los Angeles Times*, and anyone else who is willing to put up with him. He lives in Malibu and surfs occasionally.

MICHAEL MIGDOL is a stay-at-home wife who loves to cook, read, write, garden, and craft. He is publisher and editor of *Automatic* magazine, which he has taken from relative obscurity to national prominence.

NATHAN MYERS is managing editor of *Surfing* magazine. A graduate of UC Berkeley, he was the primary researcher for *The Encyclopedia of Surfing* and has written for the *Los Angeles Times, The Surfer's Journal, Australia's Surfing Life,* and *Surf Europe*. He lives in Encinitas, California.

STEVE PEZMAN was born in Los Angeles, California, in 1941 and began surfing in 1957 in Orange County. He spent the summer/winter of 1962 and 1963 in Hawaii riding the North Shore before the crowds developed, when there was still a pioneer vibe to the experience. Returning to California, Steve attended Long Beach City and State colleges, lifeguarded, and served in the merchant marines (delivering stale beer to Vietnam in 1965). In the late '60s, he began shaping custom surfboards with short stints at Hobie and Dewey Weber before settling in at Haley, Vardeman, and finally his own company, Creative Design Surfboards (with partner Stu Herz), which began as a contract shaping business that introduced private label manufacturing to the surfboard industry. The business became a Huntington Beach surf shop on Coast Highway during that town's golden era. In 1968, he began freelance writing about surfboard design and travel pieces for *Petersen's International Surfing* magazine. He became associate editor in 1969, but five months later the magazine folded, and he moved to *Surfer* magazine as associate editor (taking over editor Drew Kampion's position) in 1970. Later that year, Pezman became publisher of *Surfer* and served in that capacity through 1991. Currently, he is the co-founder and publisher of *The Surfer's Journal* with his wife and business partner, Debbee. He writes and speaks out about surfing when the chance presents itself. He has three sons and lives in San Clemente, California.

JEFF PHILLIPS started surfing while studying abroad in Australia. Since then, he has traveled the world in search of epic waves, often accompanied by his Border Collie, Idaho. A Bay Area native, he returned to surf Ocean Beach for years before moving to Santa Barbara to pursue his master's degree in environmental science. He now works as a Fish and Wildlife biologist. Through the years, he has chronicled his adventures in short stories, essays, and a newsletter he writes for friends and family to document monthly conditions and new surf stories. When he's not surfing, Jeff satisfies his taste for adventure by mountain biking, rock climbing, fly-fishing, and white water rafting.

BRUCE SAVAGE, who also goes by Tubesteak, Sabrina Wentworth, Terry-Michael Tracy, The Great Kahuna, and The Pit Commander, was the point man in the complex social structure of Malibu during the '50s and '60s. Tubesteak has written numerous articles on surfing which have appeared in such magazines as *Life, The Surfer's Journal, Longboard, Surfer, H20*, and *Sports Illustrated*, and many books, including *World Without Violence* by Arun Ghandi, *Men who Ride Mountains* by Peter Dixon, *Stoked* (new edition) by Drew Kampion, and *Above the Roar* by Matt Warshaw. He also appeared in the movies *Damn Yankees!, Gidget*, and *Riding Giants*. These days he goes to the beach on weekends to brush up on Legendhood. He has seven children, all grown up: Pamela, Patrick, Michael, Jonathan, Jennifer, Moe, and Jocelyn. The story "Miki Goes to the Movies" falls somewhere between the lines of creative non-fiction and historical fiction.

MAGILLA SCHAUS is a Great Lakes surfer, Buffalo firefighter, activist, and actor. He has swum across Lake Erie four times, twice handcuffed. He is the co-director of the Eastern Surfing Association's Great Lakes District and the president of the Wyldewood Surf Club. He has contributed photography to *Longboard* and *Eastern Surf Magazine*. He is a contributing editor and photographer to the book *Surfing the Great Lakes* by Peter L. Strazzabosco (Big Lauter Tun Books, 2001). His film credits include the surf movie *Unsalted* and the B-grade Hollywood productions of *Shadow Creature* and *Tainted*. Magilla is married to a Canadian Great Lakes scuba instructor, with a fourteen-year-old stepdaughter who surfs. He resides in Buffalo, New York and St. Catharines, Ontario.

JAMIE TIERNEY is a freelance journalist and screenwriter living in Los Angeles. He's written extensively for *Surfing, Surfer, The Surfer's Journal* and the *Los Angeles Times*, among others. He currently works as the editor of Quiksilver.com. Since his "Bad Juju" experience, he has never again driven a car with his surfboards strapped to the roof.

MARK "FINGER" TAYLOR has been surfing in the Northwest since the mid-1970s. He has homes both in Washington state and on the northern Oregon coast. He learned to surf in the mid '60s, growing up on Oahu, and then living on Kauai in the early '70s. His work in the marine industry for a propeller manufacturer takes him up and down both coasts of the U.S. He travels with a board, and you can usually find him in the water when he's not working, giving him many opportunities to injure himself again and write more stories.

REX WITKAMP was born in 1975 in Florida. He is half Dutch and half Nicaraguan. He learned to swim before he learned to walk. Rex's surf travels have taken him to Central America, the Caribbean, and Mexico. Rex's wife, Sabrah, is the vice-president of Sisters of the Sea, a non-profit which organizes the largest women's amateur surf contest on the East Coast. They live in St. Augustine, Florida. Rex was medically discharged from the Army only months after volunteering to serve.

Editors

PAUL DIAMOND grew up in Washington, D.C. He worked as a photojournalist for United Press International in Pittsburgh and later taught writing at Ohio University and Tulane University. He now lives in Seattle and works as a writer and editor most of the year. He spends his summers with a pack of kids at surf camps in Oahu, Costa Rica, and Baja California.

TYLER McMAHON grew up in Virginia. For three years he worked as a Peace Corps Volunteer building rural aqueducts in El Salvador. Now he teaches writing in Idaho and surfing in Southern California.

Bibliography

Barilotti, Steve. "Laughing to Disaster." A small part of this story originally appeared under the title "Rat Stick," *Surfer*, October 2000: Vol. 41 no. 10.

Brasen, John. "My First Day in Bali." *Australian Surfer's Journal*, January 2001: Vol. 2 no. 4. (This story has been edited and revised since its original appearance.)

Chaplin, Susan. "The Idiot Savant." Originally published as "The Idiot Savant: A Metaphor for Surfing Mauritius," *The Surfer's Journal*, Summer 2003: Vol. 12 no. 3. (This story has been edited and revised since its original appearance.)

Doggett, Joe. "Baptism with Bradshaw." *H20*, 2002: Vol. 6 no. 3. (This story has been edited and revised since its original appearance.)

George, Matt. "Red Water: Bethany Hamilton and the Teeth of the Tiger." *Stab*, March 2004: No.10.

George, Matt. "Four Wipeouts That Changed the Way We Surf." *Waves*, March 2003.

George, Matt. "Three Portraits of Sumatra." *Waves*, July 2003. (This story has been edited and revised since its original appearance.)

Hening, Glenn. "Lost Cause in El Salvador: The Filming of *Big Wednesday*." Originally published as "*Big Wednesday*: Then and Now," *Pacific Longboarder*, December 1998: Vol. 1 No. 4. (This story has been edited and revised since its original appearance.)

Migdol, Michael. "Homeless Surf Challenge." Originally published as "First Annual Automatic Homeless Surf Challenge," *Automatic,* October 2000: Vol. 2 no. 8. (This story has been edited and revised since its original appearance.)

Noll, Greg. "Greg Noll's acceptance speech at the 2004 Waterman's Ball on behalf of Miki Dora for the SIMA Lifetime Achievement Award." St. Regis Monarch Beach Resort & Spa in Dana Point, California, 28 August 2004.

Pezman, Steve. "Capers in the Key of 'T': Trestles Memories." *The Surfer's Journal,* Fall 1998: Vol. 7 no. 3. (This story has been edited since its original appearance.)

Savage, Bruce. "Miki Goes to the Movies." *The Surfer's Journal,* Fall 1992: Vol. 1 no. 3. (This story has been edited and revised since its original appearance.)

Taylor, Mark. "Paybacks." *Surfer,* 1994: Vol. 35 no. 6. (This story has been edited and revised since its original appearance.)

Vandersee, Charles. "American Parapedagogy for 2000 and Beyond: Intertextual, International, Industrial Strength." *American Literary History*, Fall 1994: Vol. 6. (A portion of this essay inspired a portion of this book's introduction.)

Rights

Acknowledgments

Thanks to all the contributors in this book for your hours of writing, editing and revising, to the photographers who are working when they could be surfing, and to those contributors whose work didn't make the final cut.

Thanks: Matt Warshaw for remote access to your surf library; Ben Marcus for your inimitable genius and hyper-attentiveness; Ingrid Emerick for project support; Ian MacKaye, Guy Picciotto, et al. for music to work by; Barlo; John Forse; the brothers George; Eric Akiskalian of Towsurfer. com; Malcolm Gault-Williams of legendarysurfers.com for writing a piece on the Palos Verde Surf Club which we didn't wind up using; Glenn Hening for saying it like it is; Shawn Alladio just for being herself; Jono and the Surf Club crew at University of Melbourne, circa 1992, who taught me to surf and brought me out for more; Pablo, Daril, and Darrell for taking me into Melbourne's underworld; Joshua Graae for lending me an Al Merrick board that Tom Curren had once surfed, and for not being upset when I returned it in two pieces; Dan Chaon for your parting words; Marshall and Mariel for being survivors and their parents for good guidance; Mr. and Mrs. P, Dave and the Dayspring gang for three summers of Nags Head surf and a lot more; Whig and Mary Jo of Trails Wilderness School for running a fine surf camp, and all my campers, Sam and Jess included, but not Commander Spaz; the San Diego crew: Jennifer, Dude-Yo of the Tilted Stick, Fogeltronic, Dusty Baker, Nigel, Kevin, Lisa, Laura Dane and Shana Sharfi for offering up their couches and for watching Junior (the French Bed Warming dog) each time I left for Mexico; Mike and Zoe, Bill and Rosanna for distant closeness; Neem Karoli Baba; my mother; and for Julia, whom I adore.

—*Paul Diamond*

Special thanks to Terry Senate for keeping me in the water and for all the magic surfboards. Thanks to Mimi Rock, Security Dave, Dusty, Lauren, Jessica, Brian, and the rest of the Groundswell crew.

Thanks to everybody at Camp Pacific, especially to James Mears for making me look good out there for once. Thanks also to Al Greenberg for teaching me about italics, and to Mitch Wieland for showing me how to hyphenate.

Thanks most of all to the La Libertad crew for teaching me to surf and for dodging my flying board with smiles and encouragement, especially Chuck Norris, Fogeltronic, Palo de Coco, Mike Osland, El Pelon, Dawn Card, the Chino, and all the other pagans who provided ground-based support.

—*Tyler McMahon*

GIVE BACK

First, a wave of devastation

"I am so happy SurfAid is here helping us because it means we are getting important vaccinations and treatments. We need to be healthy to rebuild our village. We are so much in shock here and we are weaker than before. We are worried about our children and we ask for more help in their names." - Pak Arif, Aceh fisherman, lost boat and house in tsunami

SurfAid has always approached health care by attacking the root of the problem. We solve health issues through long-term disease prevention and health education. A band-aid solution has never been good enough for us. SurfAid is committed for the long haul. We need your help.

Next, a wave of compassion

Get on it. Join SurfAid today!
Donate at www.surfaidinternational.org
& Buy Our BANDTOGETHER Wristbands
and Help SurfAid Save Lives!

SURFAID
INTERNATIONAL

GIVE BACK

SURFZONE
★ RELIEF ★
OPERATIONS

Surfzone Relief Operations is a no-nonsense, direct aid operation
which mobilizes rapidly to bring disaster response and humanitarian aid to any
remote coastline in the world. We are concerned surfers
dedicated to helping others in need. Join us at www.surfzonerelief.org

GIVE BACK

I started surfing at the age of nine, and over the years I've hogged more than my share of waves. Now I'm just an old fart going on 67, who's been lucky enough to spend my life doing the things I've loved - surfing, diving and fishing. I don't really think I have much to offer in the way of advice, but I do know one thing.

At this stage of my life nothing gives me more pleasure than seeing my kids following in my footsteps and developing that same sort of life long love affair with the ocean that I have had.

I also realize that my generation, myself included, should have done a better job in taking care and protecting our oceans and beaches. We could have left it in a little better shape for the next generation to enjoy.

It pains me to think that these kids coming up may not have the same opportunities that I have had to make the ocean such a huge part of their lives. And that's probably as good a reason as any to have the Surfrider Foundation around to kick us in the ass once in a while, and remind us how important it is to keep our oceans, waves and beaches healthy.

That's why I'm joining the Surfrider Foundation. Because it's never too late to get involved.

Greg Noll
Surfer, Diver, Fisherman
Surfrider Foundation
member #90888

Surfrider Foundation
AFTER ALL, IT'S YOUR BEACH
http://www.surfrider.org
1-800-743-SURF

GIVE BACK

GIVE BACK

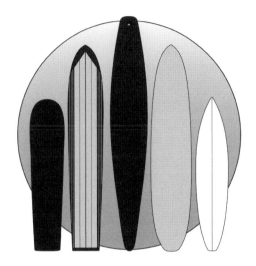

Surfing Heritage Foundation

Preserving surfing's roots for future generations

Come visit the world's largest collection of historically significant surfboards:

110 Calle Iglesia
San Clemente, CA 92672

Public viewing hours:

11 A.M. – 3 P.M.
Tues., Wed., & Thur.

For more information call 949-388-0313 or visit www.surfingheritage.org

The Ocean Conservancy

Advocates for Wild, Healthy Oceans

www.OceanConservancy.org

For information on submitting a story to the next volume of this book
visit www.thesurfbook.com